I,
CITIZEN

A BLUEPRINT FOR RECLAIMING
AMERICAN SELF-GOVERNANCE

TONY WOODLIEF

Encounter
BOOKS

New York • London

First American edition published in 2021 by Encounter Books,
an activity of Encounter for Culture and Education, Inc.,
a nonprofit, tax-exempt corporation.
Encounter Books website address: www.encounterbooks.com

Manufactured in the United States and printed on
acid-free paper. The paper used in this publication meets
the minimum requirements of ANSI/NISO Z39.48⎕1992
(R 1997) (*Permanence of Paper*).

FIRST AMERICAN EDITION

LIBRARY OF CONGRESS CATALOGING-IN-PUBLICATION DATA IS AVAILABLE

LC record available at https://lccn.loc.gov/2021004437
LC ebook record available at https://lccn.loc.gov/2021004438

1 2 3 4 5 6 7 8 9 20 21

DEDICATION

For my mother, a lifelong nurse. And for the others in my family who work with their hands and heads and backs as pipefitters, mechanics, welders, waiters, carpenters, drywallers, technicians, and painters. For my grandfather who drove a bread truck, and my other grandfather who cleaned banks. For my grandmothers who fed us from their gardens. For my aunt who took us in when we had no home. For the men before and after me who served in the United States Navy, the Army Rangers, and the Marine Corps. Together you—and millions like you—make this country work; you protect it, you still salute its flag. To the people ruling from Washington, DC, you are the forgotten, the expendables, an abstraction. But you will always be my people. Lacking your skills and fortitude, I had to resort to writing, but I hope I do you proud.

CONTENTS

FOREWORD

If you peruse the references at the end of this book, you will find that many of them are academic. I want to give readers confidence that what's contained herein is more than a pocketful of breezy impressions from political blogs and news magazines. I leave that sort of impressionism to cable TV political commentators and your unmarried aunt who went to Wellesley and has many firm opinions which she inflicts on her end of the table at Thanksgiving.

The endnotes, meanwhile, are headed by page numbers so you can find whether some source I cite, or some peculiar claim I make, has a corresponding anchor in the world of verifiable fact. I apologize if the endnotes are cumbersome, but being neither a postmodernist nor a journalist for the *New Yorker*, I have no recourse but to try and substantiate my claims. Endnotes referencing a specific book or article don't contain all that source's information, just the author's last name, the title, and the year it was published. That way, readers who want to confirm that the title is related to what I say the source is about, or that the publication date doesn't render it obsolete, can do so without having to flip back and forth between the main text, the endnotes, and the references section.

Books are complicated, aren't they?

INTRODUCTION

THE RIGHT TO REMAIN SILENT, BUT NOT THE ABILITY

Port St. Lucie, FL, 1977

The first time I read the US Constitution, I was nine years old. I did not read it by choice. This particular copy was a worn little booklet that my mother had angrily thrust into my hands. Mama was an oncology nurse, not a legal scholar, but she always had a heart for the downtrodden and a concomitant fury at bullies. The occasion for her anger that day was my compliance with what she viewed to be unconstitutional questioning by an agent of the state.

That's how she characterized it, but in fairness I should note that this "agent of the state" was an animal control officer. I had narrowly beaten him in a race to snatch hold of my dog Chrissy (I got her on Christmas Day) who had once again released herself on her own recognizance from our back yard. When I knelt with my arms wrapped around Chrissy's chest to keep the animal control officer from dragging her away, he whipped out a clipboard and started firing questions at me. What was my name? Where did I live? What were my parents' names?

I dutifully answered, because he was a uniformed adult holding what appeared to be an official clipboard. His interrogation was cut short, however, by my redheaded mother, who advanced on him with a barrage of righteous speechifying that made Clarence Darrow look like a mime. Chrissy and I stood behind Mama as her invective drove the agent of the state back into his truck and out of our subdivision. I never saw him on our streets again. I have never been sprung from wrongful imprisonment by an attorney, but I imagine it feels something like that.

I was pretty well satisfied with how things were sorting themselves out until my mother whirled around and laid into me. "You had no business answering that man's questions! Don't you *ever* tell someone whatever he wants to know just because he works for the government!"

Most of Mama's lecture, which lasted across the street, through our back yard, and into our kitchen, is lost to memory. I can faintly remember phrases that struck me as peculiar at the time, but which became familiar as I grew up around that woman, like "agent of the state," and "fascists," and a host of more colorful phraseology that respect for her memory precludes me from sharing here.

At the conclusion of her jeremiad, Mama yanked open a kitchen drawer, pulled out that booklet, and shoved it into my hands. "Here!" she said. "Go to your room and don't come out until you've read the whole thing."

Most kids I knew got punished for cussing or skipping school, and their punishments were grounding, or getting whipped with a belt. My mother locked me in the room with the US Constitution because I'd sung like a canary to an agent of the state. This, I've come to realize, explains a great many subsequent happenings in my life, up to and including the book you now hold in your hands.

"Whenever you find yourself on the side of the majority," Mark Twain wrote in his own booklet, "it is time to reform." Twain moderated that view a bit, adding parenthetically: "or pause and reflect." Mama was not always one to pause and reflect, but she did teach me a healthy skepticism of officials, experts, and people who otherwise consider themselves to be Big Deals. Such a posture is practically a hate crime these days, but there once was a time when conservative-libertarian-socialist anti-Establishment Constitution-wielding mothers were recognized as legitimate heirs of American pragmatism.

Mama also taught me to be, like her patron saint Mark Twain, skeptical of any belief that people demand I embrace—especially when the people doing the demanding occupied positions of authority. It's a mindset that served me well in school, certainly not in terms of grades and the adoration of teachers, but by making the tedium tolerable. I acquired the habit of reflexively challenging claims that smelled more like dogma than fact, and faithfully emulated my mother by resisting directions to do, say, or believe anything just because someone in authority said so.

I was insufferable—just ask the teachers who had to read my novella-length screeds against Abraham Lincoln and Franklin Roosevelt, penned solely because our textbooks went a little too far, to my prematurely jaundiced eye, in praising famous men. I had to learn the hard way that history is replete with people far smarter and wiser than me, and so the findings of scholars and the traditions of communities are often rooted deep and well. Just because a majority says it's going to rain, in other words, doesn't mean you ought to leave your umbrella at home. Some things are true even if the *Washington Post* says they are.

But if enough of the right (or wrong) people agree with each other, it ought to make us curious. Something that sparked my curiosity enough to set me on the path to writing this book was the chumminess of Republican writer David French and progressive writer Ezra Klein during an episode of the latter's podcast. Their topic was American political polarization, about which they had each written books. What struck me was that while both have made a living cheerleading for opposing teams in the perennial American game of politics, neither evidenced the slightest remorse for his part in stoking polarization. Indeed, both seemed to think the problem lay not with political pot-stirrers like themselves, but with everyday Americans. What was especially ironic is that both writers have a history of attributing the basest of motives to their political opponents. Their lack of charity epitomizes—if not drives, given their positions of influence—present-day American political animosity. And yet there they sat, French sycophantically signaling to Klein's listeners that he's not one of those *evil* right-wingers, and Klein coolly suggesting that, present company excluded, all of America's problems are rooted in the implacable racism of conservatives.

It occurred to me, listening to these elitists weigh America in the balance and find everyone but themselves wanting, that they hadn't the slightest idea what everyday Americans believe. This was immediately followed by the disconcerting epiphany that neither do I. Thus began the inquiry chronicled in this book.

I soon realized that this was more than an inquiry into the source of American political animosities. I was questioning the future of the American experiment itself. Our nation's founders erected a system that depends on the ability of citizens to hear one another out, move slowly when passing laws, and compromise with people they dislike. Extreme political polarization, characterized by hatred of the Other Party and unthinking loyalty to one's own, corrodes these essential virtues. If our present state of disunion really is driven by deep divisions among everyday Americans, there is no saving us. Klein's solution, which amounts to giving the Democratic Party maximum power to reshape America and permanently suppress conservative dissenters, is a recipe for civil war. French's solution, on the surface a very reasonable call for return to "healthy federalism," amounts to—given his negative view of his fellow Americans—an admonition for the unruly kids in the back seat to sit still and stop antagonizing each other. Anyone who's been on a long car ride with bickering children knows how realistic *that* solution is.

The question this book sets out to answer, therefore, is whether We the People are capable of governing ourselves as the Founders intended. Are Americans really just overgrown, closed-minded, belligerent children on an unending car ride? Or do we share values, convictions, and a greater charitableness toward our opponents than, well, David French and Ezra Klein?

What I found as I delved into American public opinion was heartening. Despite what you've heard from pundits across the political spectrum, it's not ordinary Americans who are bitterly divided into diehard blue and red camps. Our political class certainly is, and it directs roughly 20 percent of American voters who constitute its reliable foot soldiers. Most Americans, in contrast, remain tolerant and trusting of one another, and share a great many values. The fact that majorities have elected increasingly extreme candidates is a reflection of the political class that offers those miserable choices, not of the voters who hold their noses and select one over the other. This truth points to the other theme in this book, which is that our political class has values and interests at great odds with regular Americans, which is why it prevents us from exercising the authority granted to us in the Constitution. I'll touch on this point in the next chapter, and return to it in subsequent chapters, illustrating exactly *how* political elites have undermined American self-governance.

Next, I'll turn to the essential question that, depending on the answer, will determine whether to press forward or fold up shop: Are Americans capable of self-government? Many smart people point to data that indicate we are not. One of the disadvantages of cleverness is that sometimes you can talk yourself into believing foolishness your grandmother could have spotted a mile off. The field of political science is filled with people who should have run some of their ideas past their grandmothers.

Along the way, this book will consider what regular Americans believe. My purpose in doing so isn't to argue that we should align all our public policies to the latest public-opinion survey—in fact, on many issues I find myself outside the mainstream of American opinion, and perhaps you do as well. I simply want to illustrate just how starkly members of the political class on the Left and Right are out of step with everyday Americans. Therefore, the beliefs of a substantially loud and growing portion of our fellow citizens, who are so enthralled by politics that they're willing to believe whatever party leaders tell them, need to be considered, too.

The gap between what ideological elites running DC believe about the common good, and what everyday Americans believe, explains why the political class has worked so hard to undermine American democracy. The political elites don't want We the People to rule, because they don't trust our judgment and they despise our beliefs. I don't think they're very fond of us as people, either.

For readers who are no more excited about democracy than are members of the political class, I'll encourage you to consider that justice demands we not behave as they have done, circumventing the will of Americans to get the outcomes they want. Rather, we should roll up our sleeves and do the harder work of persuading our neighbors of the merits of our beliefs. These are the rights and obligations enshrined in our Constitution—that Americans reason with one another in pursuit of the common good.

The good news is that our neighbors tend to hold values that make them amenable, I believe, to solutions my well-meaning friends on the Left *and* Right favor. Not all of them, but some. What's more, the Constitutional blueprint of governance that begins with the self, then the family, then the community, then the state—with the federal government a distant and very limited safeguard—offers far more opportunity to establish policies and norms under which we want to live than does our present political dysfunction. Rather than try to seize power in DC and force our countrymen from coast to coast to live under our ideal regime, we can have a diversity of governance, based on what people in different communities and states conclude is best. Ideologues hate letting people make those kinds of choices. But doing so is not only just, it's the only way to ward off rising acrimony that threatens to destroy our national union.

After contrasting the beliefs of partisans with those of regular Americans, the book will examine some of the destructive ways the political class has worked to set American citizens—in particular their own partisan foot soldiers—at one another's throats. It will also expose two phenomena that are corroding self-governance and liberty: the unchecked and metastasizing agencies of the executive branch, and the shameful abdication of responsibility by our elected representatives.

Following on from that, the book will consider the only alternative to imperial rule from DC: self-governance within a federalist system. Just as American freedom began in the states, we've reached a point where they're our only hope of reestablishing that freedom. That, in turn, will illuminate a remedy to partisan toxins proliferating outward from DC. The roles the political class wants us all to play are corrosive to citizenship, but they're also thin. Maybe we can puncture them.

The final chapter poses the most important question: What can you and I do about all this? Unlike other well-meaning authors, I'm not going to offer nostrums that amount to "change human nature," "push the federalism button," or "hunker down in the hills." I'm going to suggest practical steps you can take right away, just as I have. I'll also offer steps you can take alongside your neighbors, and, if you're feeling inspired and ambitious enough, causes you can take up in your community and state.

I, Citizen is the title of this book because retaking our country isn't something some distant organization or movement will do, it's a commitment each of us as individuals must make. You may not have sworn an oath, but that doesn't absolve you of responsibility, nor does it absolve me. We can reclaim our freedoms as citizens when each of us stops waiting for someone else to go first. When each of us steps out in faith. This is why, I realize all these years later, my mother got mad at *me* for what the dog catcher did. Because every one of us as citizens is responsible for keeping our government in check.

A final note before I get started: in the remainder of this book, I'm going to say some unpleasant things about people in what I call the political class—politicians and their backers, operatives, agents, lackeys, flunkies, pollsters, apologists, spokesmen, and various hangers-on. I want to be clear that just because I believe the political class behaves reprehensibly as a whole, this doesn't mean that I think every single person in it is therefore reprehensible. There are some fine people in public service, caught in a system they want to change just as much as we want to see it changed. But there's also a flock of shitbirds. If you're reading this and you're a member of the political class, I trust you'll know, deep down, which of the two you are. I invite you to take as much offense as you deserve.

As I said at the outset, this is a story about hope. The truth is, no matter what ideologues and talking heads claim about America, we are still bound by shared values. We all want good schools for our children, safe neighborhoods, steady work, and many other blessings of liberty. We share commitments to fairness, justice, and self-determination. Despite our political divisions, a majority of us want similar outcomes, but those desires diverge from the wishes of the political class. This hidden reality is where we'll turn next because it explains why, for all their talk about democracy and the people, elites in both parties recoil from the idea of letting We the People govern ourselves.

1

THE GREAT AMERICAN CON

Gabriel: "Do you know the difference between a hustler and a good con man?"

Fitz: "No."

Gabriel: "A hustler has to get out of town as quick as he can, but a good con man—he doesn't have to leave until he wants to."

—Steven McKay, *Diggstown*

THE KANSAS CITY SHUFFLE

Winston-Salem, NC, 1985

I was a sixteen-year-old kid out with my girlfriend on a Friday night. We were at the county fair, where we wandered a lane crowded by brightly lit booths advertising competitions of chance and skill. Carnies invited us to toss baseballs into milk jugs, shoot basketballs through hoops, and pop balloons with darts. They made the games seem easy, but I'd never had much luck at them. I couldn't throw a ball fast enough at the pitching booth, or swing a mallet hard enough to ring the bell at the strongman game. Still, I really wanted to win a prize for my girlfriend.

I'd resigned myself to the indignity of leaving empty-handed, when I noticed the weight-guessing booth. I figured that it, like everything else there, was rigged in some way. The carny working it was probably trained in weight calculations based on a person's visible dimensions. Maybe he even had secret markers to judge my size, like those strips in convenience-store doorframes.

The thing was, it was bitterly cold that night. I was wearing a thick sweater underneath a heavy coat. There was no way, I reasoned, the carny would be able to discern my true weight beneath all that padding. His training, his secret height and width estimators, and whatever else he had up his sleeve were going to be worthless tonight. A sly smile crept over my face.

I plunked down the three-dollar price and winked at my gal. Sure enough, the carny looked me up and down, then barked a weight that was thirty pounds too high. I chuckled, stepped onto the scale, and let gravity reveal the magnitude of his failure. My girlfriend clapped her hands. I stepped off the scale, held out my hands, and received in my palm a tiny stuffed animal that had been stitched together in a Chinese sweatshop. I'd just paid three dollars for a trinket worth twenty-five cents.

I'd assumed the game was about weight, but really it was about economics. I didn't know it at the time, but this ruse was an example of what con men call the Kansas City Shuffle. In the KC Shuffle, the swindler doesn't trick you into trusting him; he tricks you into imagining you understand the nature of his con. You put yourself on guard against the trick you *think* is coming, and as a consequence you overlook the real trick. The deviousness of the Kansas City Shuffle is that you do the con man's work for him. You distract yourself.

This is where our punch-drunk American democracy now finds itself. We *know* cadres of political elites aim to direct our lives, run up the country's debt, and stick us with the bill. And thanks to the nonstop attack machinery arrayed by both major parties, most of us have some sort of theory about how the bad guys aim to stick it to us. We've been fed story after story (fine-tuned by whatever your Internet browser and Gmail messages indicate you're willing to believe) explaining how Russian oligarchs, the Kochs, George Soros, the Chinese Communist

Party, Catholic legal scholars—whoever serve as the scariest boogeymen given one's particular psychological triggers—are working behind the scenes to steal our votes, poison our minds, and radicalize our kids. We understand, better than any general or military strategist in history, the movements and intentions of our enemies. All we have to do is click on cable news, talk radio, or social media and it's all laid out for us.

We know the score; or, at least, we *think* we do. And given what we think we know about the schemes of people we believe to be our enemies, we can deduce whom we should vote for, what to thumbs-up on Facebook, where to send a check, and which thoughtcrimes must be reported to Twitter's mind-control police. Like the dupes of the Kansas City Shuffle, we imagine that we're too attuned to the facts to let the wool be pulled over our eyes.

The distressing reality, however, is that—just as in the Kansas City Shuffle—we're distracting ourselves from the real con, and losing something vital in the process. Anything a carny or confidence man might cheat us out of can be replaced. However, what's being jeopardized in the Great American Con is irreplaceable. The stakes are higher than we realize, and we're running out of time.

THE DARK BEFORE THE DAWN

I want to make clear that this story has a happy ending. Or, at least, it *can* have a happy ending, depending on what you do after you read it. At the very least, it's a hopeful story, and in a way it's a love story, too.

Yet, every true love faces trials, doesn't it? And as for hope, well, that's only necessary where there's peril. So, while I'd like to just skip ahead to the hopeful part, I have to talk first about the danger facing the American republic. The darkness that's settled over our land. The present trial of the American soul. We need to understand *why* hope is needed, before considering where it might be found.

So, into the darkness we go.

WELCOME TO THE MACHINE

Nashville, TN, 2020

The staging of the final 2020 US presidential debate revealed the Great American Con in a microcosm. Each contender stood on a stage and declared what laws he would create, what foreign nations he would punish, and how he was going to make a pandemic disappear. We Americans sat before our digital screens and listened to the Great Men contend for a kingship.

The backdrop for this spectacle? A large, blown-up image of the Declaration of Independence. As we learned in school, that document contains both promise and aspiration: *we are all of us equal, we are all of us free.* In a matter of days, each of us would equally be free to choose who would rule over us for the next four years; who would send our sons and daughters into harm's way overseas; issue proclamations that would reorder vast swaths of our economy; and mandate which people and products would be allowed past our borders.

Rather than recoiling at the candidates' naked aspirations to unchecked power, We the People sat there sizing each of them up in hopes of guessing which one would be best able to make good on all the things he had said he was going to give us. It's how we've been taught to evaluate them by the talking heads who have weaseled their way into orchestrating these events. It's an alien notion these days to ask not whether a politician's promise is a good one, but instead whether he ought to have the power to promise it in the first place. *The land of the free,* goes the penultimate lyric in our national anthem. You know the words; we play them before ball games (though not before presidential debates). Do we still mean them? Do we still *want* to live in the land of the free?

If so, how did we come to this?

Most of us understand that what we hear from the stage of a presidential debate is often just big talk. Candidates know they don't have the power to create jobs and amend the Constitution. But politicians, because they're humans like the rest of us, (that's our working hypothesis, anyway) certainly crave dictatorial powers, often with good intentions. That human reality is why the American Founders created a host of checks and balances to restrain both would-be tyrants and emotional mobs. We were taught in high school that our freedom is enshrined in the Declaration of Independence, as our charter, and backed up by the Bill of Rights. The latter contains those sacred promises we read in our textbooks: that courts of law will protect our speech, our religious practices, our guns, even our right not to have our beds commandeered by Hessian mercenaries.

Almost from the outset, a struggle emerged between political parties whose leaders have competing convictions about the purpose and practice of government. Viewed in the best possible light, political parties have served to check one another's ambitions, just as James Madison expected of factions in American society. They have done this in large part by drawing us citizens to one banner or the other. Because we are Americans, many of us think of political parties like sports franchises. We root, root, root for our home team, overlooking its players' transgressions as we recite the worst behaviors on the other side. Our political talk shows have the feel of ESPN programs, breaking down who won or lost yesterday, who might win or lose today, and what juicy new player scandals have come to light.

The danger with political teams is that, like sports teams, their hunger for victory increases as the stakes get higher. They look for any edge, no matter how unscrupulous. Advances in technology since the 1990s have afforded both sports and political teams more powerful methods of gaining that edge. For athletes, this has meant advances in training, opposition analysis, and legal (and illegal) enhancements to physical performance. For politicians, these technological edges have taken the form of insights into voter psychology, investigations into the pasts of their opponents, and tools for raising money from coast to coast. Both political and athletic teams face tremendous temptation to win at all costs, even by cheating and breaking the law, thereby driving away all but the most rabid, unprincipled players and fans.

This intersection of greater stakes and more powerful technology in the political realm is where things have begun to go awry. Even in George Washington's day, politicians and their operatives showed a willingness to lie, cheat, and manipulate. The Founders, knowing full well their own natures, worked to restrain these impulses through what, to outsiders, could seem like an unnecessarily complicated and slow governmental structure. Given that men will never be angels, James Madison wrote, we must erect barriers to their baser instincts.

Mostly it worked, somewhat imperfectly, as institutions constructed by imperfect men can only ever work. The machinery of American government certainly suffered at least one catastrophic failure, in the decades leading up to and culminating in a civil war over the most enduring shame of the American Founding—its uneasy acceptance of human slavery. Our government has endured other bouts of dysfunction and abuse since then. It is, like all people, imperfect. It has failed in the past, with deadly consequences. It might fail again.

It helps to think of our government as a machine because otherwise it's tempting to blame our problems on the bad people within it. Make no mistake; there are plenty of bad people in government—just as there are bad people in business, academia, the media, charitable foundations, and even religious organizations. But the interconnected and counterbalanced nature of the US government, combined with its massive growth since the early 1900s, means that the worst of individuals can only accomplish so much mischief. Even a dedicated cabal of evil people would find it all but impossible to bend the entirety of the US government to its ends. The machine was built to resist the self-interest of its agents by deploying—in a brilliant governmental innovation—the self-interest of other agents within its machinery.

When that machinery starts to rumble and quake, therefore—as it did in the years preceding the Civil War, for example—it's easy to find villains to blame because there are *always* villains maneuvering their selfish ways through the halls of power. And yet, most of the time the system works, in spite of them. In some respects, it works *because* of the selfishness that animates them.

I say the system has *mostly* worked because Americans have largely enjoyed peace, rising prosperity, and justice for generations. Not always, and not for everyone all the time, but certainly in comparison with the only real standard we can apply, which is the results realized by other countries throughout history. For all its faults, America has been a good place to live, a fact proven by the millions who have come to our shores, and the reality that our harshest domestic critics rarely choose to pack up and leave. The point is that when the machinery of government begins to break, it's too simplistic to single out one wicked person, or a bad political party. There's something deeper at work.

It's important to reflect on this because the machinery of our government is now malfunctioning. Whereas the major parties and their leaders had for a century offset one another's power, mostly keeping their animosities from spilling over into the lives of everyday Americans, it feels more and more like we are on the verge of open warfare with our fellow citizens. A quick trip through the comments section of any news article reveals a depressing level of hatred expressed between people who know nothing about one another except their party allegiance. Surveys show a collapse in tolerance for members of the opposing political party. Other surveys reveal that a shocking number of Americans say they'd consider violence to settle political disputes. A panoply of historians and other academics have gone on record saying we are closer than we've been in decades to another civil war.

Are they right? Hopefully not. But are things the way they're supposed to be? No. Not at all.

A CONFEDERACY OF DUNCES

There's an unconscious conspiracy afoot. Political elites, long held in check by our Constitution and one another, have overrun the guardrails. Pursuing the self-interest that has always driven powerful people, but aided now with new technologies, egged on by the prize of unprecedented power in Washington, DC, and unchecked by many of the old, boring rules that once kept politicians in line, members of the political class on both the Left and Right now function as if they're in cahoots. Locked in a battle for power, and deploying a host of persuasion mechanisms to seduce everyday Americans into joining them, they've unwittingly triggered the biggest game of Kansas City Shuffle in human history: the Great American Con.

Every KC Shuffle has two components: the outer game; and the steal. The outer game in our Great American Con is political theater. National politicians and the media companies that subsist off them crave dollars and eyeballs, and these accrue to the loudest, the brashest, the most combative drama producers. These dramas offer, like every good story, heroes and villains. Opposing elites within the political class work feverishly to persuade us who is which. Good-versus-evil struggles are what get clicks, fill coffers, and win battles of public opinion.

Our nation's political theater is the outer game, the distraction. It's me as a sixteen-year-old kid again, thinking the carny's gambit is to guess my weight. The steal, meanwhile, has been effected by the political class's relentless centralization of authority in Washington, DC, much of it in the hands of unelected judges and executive agency officials. Whereas America's Constitution assigns most of the work of governing—and, therefore, citizenship—to communities and states, our nation's capital has become an imperial city. When real authority resides in communities, citizens are more likely to engage, to express their values and views, to hold government officials accountable, and even to become elected representatives themselves. When authority sits in DC, it belongs to the political class. The rest of us are relegated to the roles of bystanders and sometimes cheerleaders. We come to believe that *citizen* is synonymous with *voter*, which is an utter corruption of that concept.

In other words, what the political class is stealing from us is our right to self-governance, which is essential to American citizenship. Citizens governing themselves is the ethos of our Constitution. It's rooted in the faith that we can hold our elected representatives accountable, and practice virtues that make invasive government unnecessary. A decades-long ideological war waged by political elites in our name, however, has punctured the reservoir of goodwill that characterized American civil life for generations. Simultaneously, centralization of power in DC has eroded the authority of our elected legislatures, which has reduced our control over our own government. As a consequence, we are losing both the ability and the freedom to govern ourselves. How, then, will we continue to define and pursue that "more perfect Union" described in our Constitution's Preamble?

We won't. Our overseers will define it for us, and claim to pursue it on our behalf, primarily through rules and dictates crafted inside their imperial city. American self-governance will be displaced by the selfish rule of our bipolar political class. Since neither faction within their ranks has yet realized its dream of utterly destroying the other, power will continue to shift back and forth from Left to Right, while everyday Americans try to avoid whiplash.

If this dynamic continues, we may well keep a semblance of individual rights, albeit in truncated form, and even deceive ourselves into believing that we still reside in the land of the free. We'll still well up when we listen to our National Anthem at ballgames. But our unique American freedom as citizens to govern ourselves will be lost.

2

THE AMERICAN SPHINX

"Were the pictures which have been drawn by the political jealousy of some among us faithful likenesses of the human character, the inference would be, that there is not sufficient virtue among men for self-government; and that nothing less than the chains of despotism can restrain them from destroying and devouring one another."
—James Madison, *Federalist No. 55*

MAMA, GET YOUR GUN

Oak Ridge, NC, 2020

It's a Saturday evening and we have friends over. They're far to the left of us politically, but we all like each other very much. We attend the same church, and while we hold strongly to our respective political beliefs, we stow those opinions when we're together because friendship and community matter more to us than proving a point. I've warned my older children not to violate this truce, but this doesn't stop one of them from prancing through the living room in a goofy-looking MAGA beach hat that he scrounged from God knows where. Our friends either ignore him or don't notice, but I make a mental note to exact punishment at a later date.

Soon after, my oldest son, home on leave from the US Marines, walks quickly past the dinner table holding his AR-15, atop which is a new laser scope that he needs to sight in. His best friend from high school follows close behind, clutching *his* AR-15 with fancy new laser scope. Our friends, of course, have grave reservations about whether the Second Amendment extends to scary-looking, large caliber weaponry. One of them surprises me, however, by asking where we go target shooting. She tells us that she intends to buy a gun. This is weeks after the eruption of violence following George Floyd's death at the hands of police in Minneapolis, and now right-wing elements have begun to demonstrate in some cities, which in turn has sparked more violence. Our friend worries for her safety, and she worries specifically about what right-wingers might do. She doesn't perceive *us* as threats, even though we're far to her right on many political issues. She also holds our son, the Marine, in high regard. In fact, more than once she's mused about how nice it would be if he and her oldest daughter could hit it off as a couple and eventually get married. She adores our family. It's the unhinged right-wingers *out there* who worry her.

We talk about what kinds of guns are best-suited for personal and home defense. I offer to show them how to handle their weapons if they decide to acquire them. They trust us to show them these things, just as we're happy to see them become armed. To make the point even clearer, we enjoy having them watch our small children, and trust them completely to do so. Likewise, they trust their beautiful daughter to be in the company of our armed and decidedly-to-the-political-right sons. Yet, to the extent that our families harbor unease about people who are armed and angry somewhere *out there*, we envision people whose political beliefs align closely to those that we overlook in one another.

We each, their family and ours, believe people animated by our respective beliefs are capable of great violence as a consequence of those beliefs, and yet we have no fear of such violence from one another. Why? Because we share more in common than that which separates us. What we share—love for family, faith in God, enjoyment of good beer and food and complicated board games—matters more to us than our conflicting opinions about the Second Amendment.

Many weeks later, my wife and I have people of a very different political composition over. It's Thanksgiving, and we're hosting my side of the family. They're all blue-collar, many of them to *our* political right. My brother and I sit on the back deck with our dear old Aunt D. She squints at us through her cigarette smoke and asks if we have guns.

"What do I need a gun for?" my brother asks with a scowl.

"For when they come after you," Aunt D says.

"Who's going to come after me?"

"Watch the news," she says. "There's a lot of bad people out there. The world has gone crazy."

"Nobody's going to mess with us," says my brother.

Aunt D shakes her head. "Well, when they come after me, I'm gonna be ready."

Nationwide, background checks for gun permits spiked in the summer of 2020, topping 3.9 million in June alone—the highest monthly total since the FBI began tracking it. The National Shooting Sports Foundation, relying on surveys of gun-store owners, estimated that 40 percent of sales were to first-time gun owners. What's more, 40 percent of these first-time gun buyers were women, while 58 percent of total gun sales, which were nearly double the annual figures from the year before, went to African-Americans. Americans of all types seem more scared, and the people they fear are fellow citizens on the other side of what many perceive to be a widening political chasm.

Many Americans have become inclined to despise and distrust someone more because of his political party than any other factor assessed by pollsters. For perspective, this means that on average, Americans are now more likely to hold prejudiced views of a person based on how he votes than because of his religion, gender, or even his race. While perhaps this represents some kind of backhanded progress in the history of American discrimination, it's a deeply troubling harbinger—especially given that a rising number of Americans express violent feelings toward their political opponents. In the weeks before the 2020 elections, survey analysts reported in *Politico* that since 2017, more Americans on the Left and Right say violence against fellow citizens is justified in order to advance their political aims. This sentiment is strongest among the most ideologically partisan respondents, who are also more likely to feel satisfaction when their political opponents are injured or die. Americans appear to be increasingly divided by political party, and the stronger their partisanship, the more vicious they become.

Our internecine animosity has certainly been worse; a century-and-a-half ago, more than 600,000 Americans were killed by their countrymen during four years of internal bloodshed. Surely we can do better than the Civil War era, can't we? Americans in those dreadful years had powerful reasons to resort to violence over politics and debate. I hope we aren't as close to the brink as we were in 1860, but I think it's clear we're closer to it than reasonable people want to be.

Why is that? Have our divisions sunk deep enough to justify this level of hostility? Political party tribalism aside, just what is it that we disagree about? One need only listen to the talking heads and political influencers on cable news to get some answers to this question, but what happens when we stop listening for a moment to the people who profit from our strife? What do we know—really—about what Americans believe, and why those beliefs matter? The answer to that question can't be discovered by watching political talk shows or logging on to Twitter. The answer is also likely to displease a good many people, perhaps including you. That answer, however—despite superficial evidence to the contrary—is a source of deep hope for America's future. In fact, it's our only hope.

Before we get to the hopeful part, let's consider the bad news. In this chapter and the next, I'm going to draw on public-opinion research to paint a grim picture of the present state of American common sense and civic virtue. I'm going to lay out the best case against American self-governance the experts can offer. In the chapter after that, I'm going to show you how they're dead wrong.

A clue to their error can be found in a description the adult son of President John Quincy Adams, in his studied reflection on the life of Thomas Jefferson, applied to America's third president: "He did not always speak exactly as he felt, either towards his friends or his enemies. As a consequence, he has left hanging over a part of his public life a vapor of duplicity [...] the presence of which is generally felt more than it is seen." It's fitting that Jefferson was one of the first thinkers to ruminate on the nature of "the American mind," because the foregoing description befits not only our third president, but America itself. As political scientist Stanley Feldman has observed, "we know more about how people do not think about politics than about how they do."

What research reveals about all the ways Americans *don't* think about politics could fill a book, and has. Several, in fact. Repeated surveys indicate, for example, that most Americans have a tenuous grasp of basic economic and political facts. We get confused about whether inflation is getting better or worse, and forget that an incumbent president presided over hard economic times if employment picks up a few months before his reelection bid. Perhaps even more unjust is the fact that we blame politicians for things they can't control, like droughts, floods, even shark attacks. Accountability at the voting booth is a key tenet of democracy, but it's hard to imagine how voters can hold politicians accountable when they're so shortsighted and unaware.

This doesn't necessarily mean, by the way, that the majority of Americans are too stupid or disinterested to be good citizens. Economists have explained for decades that ignoring politics may be a rational decision for the average person. After all, the odds that one person's vote will decide a presidential election range from a trillion-to-one if you live in Wyoming, to a million-to-one for Virginians. Viewed in this light, one could argue that the people who pay close attention to politics are the ones lacking common sense. This reality does call into question, however, whether we citizens can collectively exercise the judgment necessary to elect decent public officials and boot out bad ones. Whether rational or not, widespread ignorance appears to threaten the proper working of the American republic.

But wait, there's more bad news. Most Americans not only possess scarce knowledge of political and economic facts, they harbor conflicting, seemingly incoherent opinions about public policies. If you asked average Americans about welfare a decade ago, for example, you would have gotten mostly negative responses, even though nearly three-quarters of them simultaneously believed that "government should guarantee every citizen enough to eat and a place to sleep." Milton Friedman and John Maynard Keynes would be equally appalled.

More recently, consider the mystification of Nobel Prize-winner Paul Krugman, expressed in a series of Twitter posts soon after the 2020 elections, upon learning that Republican-leaning voters in Florida gave Donald Trump 350,000 more votes than Joe Biden while simultaneously approving a $15 state minimum wage. On the opposite coast, he noted with equal exasperation, California voted nearly 2-1 for Biden while exempting Uber and Lyft from the state's law curtailing the ability of companies to avoid paying worker benefits. It appears—to scholars, at least—that Americans are schizophrenic regarding public policy.

Meanwhile, in panel surveys that ask the same individuals over multiple years their preferences regarding everything from government regulation of housing to federal aid for minorities, researchers repeatedly find inconsistency. The very same citizens, in other words, who believe government should provide health insurance one year believe it is best left to private industry two years later. People who once supported foreign aid subsequently oppose it. And so on.

Compounding obstacles to Americans' ability to hold politicians accountable is the fact that many of them see through partisan lenses. People's evaluations of facts flip-flop based on their political allegiances. In President George W. Bush's second term, for example, more than 70 percent of Democrats with high levels of political knowledge said the size of the federal budget deficit was very important. Four years later, with Barack Obama in the White House and the deficit 800 percent higher, less than 30 percent of this group felt the same. Republicans certainly aren't immune. As inflation soared in 1971, only 37 percent of them expressed support for price controls—until, that is, Richard Nixon announced on national television that he was implementing them. After that, 82 percent of Republicans said price controls were a good idea.

It appears that many of our fellow citizens have low political knowledge and inconsistent opinions, and vote for politicians primarily out of blind partisan loyalty. Little wonder that political philosopher Jason Brennan concludes we should replace democracy with rule by educated, competent technocrats. All of those thoughtless voters haphazardly filling out their ballots in election after election are, he says, like air pollution. So long as tens of millions of citizens are allowed to get away with it, the relatively small contingent of non-polluters will be ineffectual at cleaning up the body politic.

I suppose he has a point. If ignorance and inconsistency are the defining features of American democracy, then we may as well shut down this quarter-millennial experiment in liberty right now, because partisanship that's impervious to facts, combined with rising hatred for supporters of the Other Party, are a deadly combination. Maybe the political class is right after all, and we're better off leaving power in its hands. This was the conviction of progressive writer Herbert Croly, founder of *The New Republic*, who argued in 1909 that a powerful central government overseen by experts was essential, because "the average American individual is morally and intellectually inadequate to a serious and consistent conception of his responsibilities as a democrat."

Most public-opinion research does indeed yield a pessimistic impression of the American mind, but much of this research only scratches the surface of core American beliefs. What are we really measuring when we ask Americans their opinions about a president, or immigration, or the size of the welfare state? Let's pretend, for a moment, that you're one of those survey respondents. Consider this question from a nationwide survey administered for decades by researchers at the University of Michigan:

> Some people think the government should provide fewer services, even in areas such as health and education, in order to reduce spending. Other people feel that it is important for the government to provide many more services even if it means an increase in spending. Where would you place yourself on this scale, or haven't you thought much about this?

You're supposed to pick a spot on the scale, with the number *one* at the "fewer services" end, and *seven* at the "spend more" end. So, are you a *one*? A *seven*? Maybe a *four*? Perhaps you want some clarifications before you answer. Like, what does the pollster mean by "government?" Just the federal government, or also states, even cities? How should you answer if you believe government-provided health insurance would be a great idea, but you also believe the Department of Veterans Affairs serves our nation's veterans so poorly that its hospitals should be turned over to private management? And, what else is covered by the phrase "many more services?" You just read an article about police departments installing hidden cameras everywhere. Is that what you're asking for if you circle *seven*—a blank check for every "service" that government bureaucrats can conjure? On the other hand, if you move your answer closer to *one*, does that mean you want your grandmother to get only one meal a day in her nursing home?

Now that you've pondered this question, you don't know *what* you think about it. The pollsters might as well have asked how much you like to eat things, or whether you believe Americans should have more or fewer blankets on their beds. Any number on the 1-7 scale could make sense, depending on the context.

Suppose, irritated by how nebulous this question is, you elect to join the 15 percent of Americans who report that they haven't thought about it. Uh-oh. Now you've done it. Declining to seat yourself on the pollsters' scale gets you tossed into a statistical bucket with the fools and the disinterested. It means, as public-opinion scholars Christopher Achen and Larry Bartels claim in their 2016 book, *Democracy for Realists*, that you haven't thought about "the central domestic policy issue of the past three decades."

The truth, of course, is that professors Achen and Bartels haven't really thought about that question either. Nobody, beyond a few crusty socialists and their sworn libertarian enemies, sits around thinking about whether the abstraction known as "government" should be bigger or smaller. We think about whether our town should build more parks, whether our state is wasting the money it spends on public schools, and whether the federal government should offer a basic income to the very poor. We think about these and other specificities because we live in actual and specific communities, not a disembodied country overseen by an abstraction called "government."

Why, then, do opinion researchers collapse such context-dependent questions into singular queries? Are they simpletons, or sadists? The answer is regrettably less dramatic, though perhaps just as damning: they think the rest of us should think about politics in the stark terms that characterize their own thinking. *Grow government or shrink it. Be for capitalists, or be for workers. Institute racial preferences in hiring, or let minorities fend for themselves.* Ideology provides a structure, explain political scientists Donald Kinder and Nathan Kalmoe, in which "ideas are arranged in orderly, predictable patterns," so that "change in one idea requires change in others." Ideology imposes a rigid order on a person's political opinions.

The either/or questions out of which political scientists build surveys make sense to them, because the *real* questions in their minds are dominated by ideological principles, not practical context. Whether we're going to have an interventionist government, say, or let the free market reign. Whether we're going to maximize personal liberty, or mandate morality. Political scientists believe what should guide your answers to survey questions is the logic stemming from ideological principles.

There's nothing inherently bad with an individual embracing this kind of philosophical purity. I admire people who become strict vegans because they don't want animals harmed, or who ride bicycles to reduce their carbon footprint. I may not agree with their premises, but I respect their ethical consistency. No matter how much you or I might respect a philosophical purist, however, we certainly wouldn't want him crafting surveys for regular people. The vegan will ask us to indicate on a seven-point scale whether we think people should eat as much meat as they like, or protect animals at all costs. It's a perfectly sensible formulation to an animal-lover, but people who prefer to eat *some* meat while treating animals as humanely as possible won't fit. The bicyclist, likewise, will ask us to choose whether we prefer to avoid using fossil fuels whenever possible, or to drive the biggest trucks we can afford. Most people don't fit on scales anchored by these kinds of conflicting principles. We'll tend to clump toward the middle, which is exactly what Americans do when confronted with survey questions crafted by ideology-besotted academics.

Now, imagine that the vegan and the bicyclist put their heads together and construct a spectrum. At one end is selflessness, at the other, selfishness. To be consistently selfless is to protect animals at all costs, bike wherever you can, and embrace several other such practices. To be selfish is to eat as much meat as you can, own several cars, and so on. They use our answers to those individual questions to assess how coherent our beliefs are. A survey respondent who reports trying to conserve energy while frequently eating steak demonstrates inconsistency on the selfless/selfish spectrum. Likewise for vegans driving Ford F-150s.

Most Americans, if the vegan bicyclists were in charge of surveys, would therefore be judged to have incoherent beliefs. We'd irritate them by blending meat-eating and energy conservation. Our opinions about meat would change from year to year, with some of us going on low-fat diets because of heart trouble, and others embracing high-protein, ketogenic diets. Our thousands of individual opinions, rooted in a myriad of personal circumstances, would appear to ideals-driven analysts to be proof that we are, as Shakespeare's Lysander said of Demetrius, "spotted and inconstant."

This is, essentially, what has happened. For decades, opinion researchers have recorded Americans' answers to questions about political, social, and foreign policies, and have found them wanting. Our answers have not only been inconsistent over time, they have failed to cluster sufficiently at either end of the liberal/conservative spectrum. Liberals are supposed to want fewer soldiers, the right to abortion, and more government aid to minorities. Conservatives are supposed to favor free trade, criminalizing abortion, and building more nuclear submarines. But most Americans don't cluster like that. Some of us want more aid to minorities and a bigger military. Others want less government spending but barriers to foreign trade.

We needn't rely on questions about specific policies to draw inferences about the average American's ideology. Since 1972, researchers have asked broad samples of citizens whether they consider themselves liberal, conservative, or middle-of-the-road. The specific percentages have fluctuated over the years, but not by much. In 2020, 37 percent of respondents either described themselves as moderate, or said that they hadn't thought much about their ideology. If we include those who described themselves as either slightly liberal or slightly conservative, that's 58 percent of Americans. Fewer than 10 percent describe themselves as extremely liberal or conservative.

Sociologists Carl Bowman and James Davison Hunter similarly found, in their interviews with 2,000 Americans in 1996, that the extreme Left and Right constitute about 5-7 percent of the population on either side, and each pole on this spectrum is "self-conscious of the other and, as such, self-consciously antagonistic toward the other." Other studies substantiate this estimate of how many Americans are significantly politically-minded, finding the total percentage of Americans offering opinions that are even remotely ideological growing from 12 percent in 1956 to 20 percent in 2004.

Most Americans are neither highly ideological nor fervidly partisan. A slight majority have political parties to which they are fairly loyal, but they don't appear to think about public policies through a focused, philosophical lens. There are two reasons so many of us have the impression, despite ample contradictory evidence, that America is a battlefield of blue and red fortresses. The first is that these dedicated partisans, possessing the strongest interest in politics and the greatest certainty that they're right, are the ones we most often hear from. The second is that pundits across the political spectrum have advanced the notion that there is, as Republican writer David French claims, a "vast and growing political and cultural gap in the United States, centered around American geography."

A poor understanding of data has never impeded the careers of political writers, consultants, or—as recent presidential elections have illustrated—pollsters. Still, many of the writers advancing the Two Americas thesis are thoughtful and intelligent. They certainly see *something* that alarms them, but if it's really only 20 percent of the population caught up in this red-state-versus-blue-state nonsense, do we need to make a fuss over them? Can't we just let them have their Fox News and MSNBC, provided they leave the rest of us alone? To answer that question, we have to consider American partisans a little more closely.

3

AMERICAN PARTISANS

"If ordinary citizens were to reason ideologically, as political elites presumably do, then the prospects for democratic control would be enhanced."

—Donald Kinder, *Diversity and Complexity in American Public Opinion*

"Dividing the American people has been my main contribution to the national political scene. I not only plead guilty to the charge, but I am somewhat flattered by it."

—Vice President Spiro T. Agnew

Average Americans have, according to political scientists, two strikes against them: they aren't ideological, and they're insufficiently loyal to political parties. Given that so many also appear to be "low-information voters," how then can we trust elections? Scholars have pondered this question for years. Before tackling it, we must briefly consider the minority of citizens who *do* fit the political scientists' profile of responsible citizens—the roughly one-fifth of Americans who score much higher than average on ideological cohesion, political knowledge, and party loyalty.

I want to be clear from the outset that I am not going to argue that everyone who holds strong opinions about the purpose of government and the sources of a well-ordered society is dangerous and deluded. I hold such views, after all, and I am a perfectly normal, rational, and charming person. You can invite me to your dinner party with absolute confidence that I will not harangue your guests, hold forth boorishly with my opinions about gun control, or otherwise make an ass of myself. I certainly believe some ideologically extreme beliefs are poisonous, their adherents opposed to not just our way of life but to humanity itself. That has to do with the content of their beliefs, however, and not the fact that they believe them strongly.

The people I'm going to describe in this chapter aren't simply citizens with deep convictions about government. They're people animated by angry tribalism. They've become convinced that *everyone* who votes for the Other Side agrees with every bit of nonsense espoused by that side's leaders. For example, Glenn Ellmers, a Visiting Scholar at Hillsdale College, wrote that the 77 million Americans who preferred Joe Biden to Donald Trump "are not Americans in any meaningful sense of the term." Not to be outdone, North Carolina congressional candidate Mark Judson tweeted on Memorial Day 2021: "If every single Republican voter magically disappeared tonight - in 10 years the US would have the: best education in the world, most affordable quality Healthcare in the world, most prosperous Middle Class, etc." These ideologues are not alone; our nation's most partisan Democrats claim Republicans are less intelligent than average, while strongly partisan Republicans say Democrats are unpatriotic. The people who express such opinions are more prone to believe untrue things about people in the other tribe, while overlooking uncomfortable truths about the leaders of their own tribe.[†] Worse still, they're willing to modify their opinions about public policies in order to match what their party leaders tell them.

---

† Like many writers before me, I will sometimes use "tribe" to denote groups whose members have deep allegiances to one another, and deep distrust and antipathy toward non-group members. Occasionally warriors for social justice, playing their relentless little game of Gotcha, will attempt to portray "tribe" as a racially insensitive term. That, of course, is nonsense. If they want to contort language into a minefield, they can do so in their own books. As for you and I, we'll stick with plain language.

Just to be clear, the problem is not firm convictions about government and society. It's tribalism that leads to unclear thought, hateful words, and sometimes bad actions. Think of the people I'll describe in this chapter as that kid who sat up front in your American government class and asked how we could take the Constitution seriously when its authors owned slaves. However bad political ignorance among the rest of us may be, you don't want *that* guy in charge of anything, even if the professor gave him an "A". The danger for our country is that while he and others like him constitute a minority of citizens, they have outsized influence. Worse still, their numbers may be growing.

Their numbers are a concern because they are partisan foot soldiers of the political class. Political scientist Morris Fiorina's definition of the political class is helpful here: "the collection of officeholders, party and issue activists, interest group leaders, and political infotainers who constitute the public face of politics in contemporary America." These people are the string holders, the shot callers, the chieftains and shamans of our political tribes. They're often the most extreme ideologues and partisans in America.[†] Some, however, are very little of either. They're fortune seekers, building up their direct-mail fundraising honeypots, their consulting clientele, and their publishing records, whose contact lists are filled with people willing to pay in favors or cash for access to their networks. It's hard to sort out the mercenaries from the true believers, but my suspicion is that we could do worse than heed the wisdom of Frodo Baggins, namely that the pure mercenaries seem fairer than most, but feel fouler.

Partisan ideologues, meanwhile, are the political class's enlistees in its cultural and political battles. I will use the terms *partisan*

---

† Psychologist Jordan B. Peterson's repurposed observation from Carl Jung applies here, which is that while we're accustomed to thinking in terms of an individual having an ideology, in extreme cases it's the other way around; the ideology has *him*.

and *ideologue* interchangeably when speaking about them because in America—among the roughly one-fifth of citizens for whom politics and ideology are very important—party and ideology have become fused. "Democrat" and "liberal" among this group almost always mean support for abortion rights and more generous welfare spending. Likewise have "Republican" and "conservative" come to mean support for a stronger military and lower taxes.

What you don't often hear from pundits, however, is that this fusion doesn't happen for most Americans. They don't fit neatly into the liberal or conservative camps. They may apply one or the other label to themselves, but this isn't a reliable predictor of their opinions on major political issues, nor of how they vote. A critical mistake by pundits was to assume that 66 million votes for Barack Obama in 2012 meant 66 million Americans backed him on everything from Obamacare to Benghazi; and that 74 million votes for Donald Trump in 2020 meant 74 million Americans were enthusiastic about his handling of COVID-19 and immigrants. "The fact that voters ultimately treated Trump as if he were just another Republican speaks to the enormous weight party polarization now exerts over our politics," wrote a horrified Ezra Klein about the 2016 election in his book, *Why We're Polarized*. This is nonsense; all it shows is that voters, when offered deplorable choices, choose the one they find less deplorable. The fact that Ezra Klein found Hillary Clinton immensely preferable to Donald Trump says more about Ezra Klein than it does about the average Trump voter. It's the candidates vomited up by broken party nomination processes who are polarized, not ordinary Americans.

What's troubling about the minority of Americans who *are* partisan ideologues, meanwhile, is the malleability of their principles. Consider how, post 9/11, the locus of distrust for the expanded domestic surveillance powers of the National Security

Administration shifted substantially among both Democrats and Republicans, when Barack Obama replaced George W. Bush in the White House. Depending on which part of the 2001-2016 timeline you're examining, "conservatives" were either strong proponents of allowing the federal government to spy on American citizens, or steadfast opponents of Big Brother. "Liberals," likewise, either wholeheartedly embraced civil liberties, or condoned the use of drone strikes to assassinate American citizens without due process.

This malleability matters because the two major parties tend to stake out positions—especially during the last forty years for reasons that will be discussed below—based more on strategic calculations about fundraising and marginal vote gain than a coherent set of principles, no matter what they tell themselves, the press, and us. No American flip-flopped harder on NSA surveillance, for example, than then-House Minority Leader Nancy Pelosi, who was a staunch opponent during Bush's tenure, but became the linchpin that preserved those very same powers when rising opposition in 2013 almost led to congressional revocation.

Because of partisans' situational morality, I'll only apply labels like "liberal," "conservative," "progressive," etc., when the convictions implied by those titles reasonably align with behavior. While the Democrats who justified or overlooked President Obama's spying on journalists called themselves *liberals*, and the Republicans who supported bombing countries into submission and then attempting to remake them as representative democracies called themselves *conservatives*, going along with that nomenclature would be like agreeing that veganism entails cheeseburgers for breakfast. In such circumstances, therefore, I'll apply a partisan designation, as in: "Too many Republicans happily embrace big government when a Republican is at the helm;" or, "A depressing number of Democrats forget how much they love the Bill of Rights when a Democrat is in charge."

Ideologues and partisans constitute a minority of Americans, and the political class is but a sliver. Nonetheless, that class has amassed considerable control over our political processes, substantial influence within government, cultural, and social institutions and, increasingly, our nation's largest corporations as well. It shapes the narratives by which we understand both our politics and our history. Such elite power is not in itself proof of malevolence. The American Founders, after all, once commanded similarly broad societal influence. Whereas those leaders risked lives and treasure to win American freedom, however, and used their subsequent authority to lay the foundation for a nation of free and self-governing citizens, the modern political class uses its power for its ends and our debasement. It shapes (and reshapes) the content of American ideologies, and it organizes battalions of loyal partisans to vote, give money, repeat its talking points in their communities, and even harass its enemies in an increasingly frequent real-life enactment of Orwell's Two Minutes Hate.

Even though it's not everyday citizens causing America's rising acrimony, they distress both political theorists and political activists nonetheless, albeit for different reasons. Theorists believe the structure that ideology provides is essential to a well-functioning democracy. "If Americans approached the political world with an ideology in mind," wrote Donald Kinder and Nathan Kalmoe in *Neither Liberal Nor Conservative*, "they would see that world clearly, understand it well, and form opinions and make decisions that faithfully reflect their core beliefs." As a consequence, they argued, "strong democracy—government responsive to the articulated preferences of the people," would become "a practical possibility."

Members of the political class, meanwhile, dislike nonideological citizens because political activists are gripped by the conviction that one end of the political spectrum is correct, the other dangerously wrong. They need for us to pick a side. "Opinions and actions justified in ideological terms," write Kinder and Kalmoe, "lay claim to what *all* members of a political community should value." Ideology, in other words, doesn't just guide what you think, *it makes demands on what others should think.* Political elites on the Left and Right believe themselves to be in an existential battle, with too many Americans standing in the middle. Ideology requires battle lines and purity of purpose. No wonder activists and nonprofits tightly aligned with one party or the other pour so much money into websites, social media, ads, and other far less transparent persuasion schemes. Swing voters decide elections. Converts decide the fates of movements.

SELF-DECEPTION AND THE IDEAL CITIZEN

Ideology, political scientists believe, is what Americans need in order to fulfill their potential as citizens, but there's ample evidence that too much ideology and partisanship makes citizens *less* competent. Strong partisans show a greater tendency, for example, to base their judgments of politicians solely on what party they're in. This is the opposite of responsible democratic practice; it's the kind of willfully blind tribalism that enables totalitarians to come to power.

More disturbing evidence of partisan self-deception was uncovered by researchers at Stanford Law School in 2012, when they showed separate groups of subjects an identical video of protestors demonstrating outside a building. Half the subjects were told the demonstration was being staged by pro-lifers against an abortion clinic. The other half were told the demonstration was against military recruiters in a college career-placement office, because of the ban on openly gay service members. The experiment's subjects had sharply different evaluations of whether the demonstrators were breaking the law and should be restrained by police, and those differences stemmed from their preexisting partisanship and ideology. Subjects with strong worldviews, in other words, literally saw the same events differently.

This isn't a result of ideology married to ignorance, either. The people most likely to deceive themselves about political realities also tend, as it turns out, to be the *most* knowledgeable about political facts. In the last chapter, I mentioned that opinions of budget deficits under Bush and Obama were affected by how respondents felt toward each president. That survey data also revealed that respondents with the highest political knowledge were *the ones most deluded about the actual size of the federal budget deficit.* Their partisan fervor made them less reliable judges of facts than average Americans.

Knowledge of current national events, who holds what office, and what party controls which chamber of Congress is correlated with stronger ideology—so much so that many scholars think greater political knowledge leads to stronger ideology. It's entirely likely, however, that the causality runs in the other direction, meaning that strong partisanship induces some citizens to invest more time and emotion in politics. They're not more ideologically committed because they know more about politics; they know more about politics because of their ideological commitment. This explains why more knowledgeable voters are also more prone to self-deception. Their underlying political tribalism drives both.

The vulnerability of partisans to self-deception doesn't just make our national outlook more depressing, and our politics uglier. It literally costs lives. To see how, consider the way partisanship substantially altered responses to two recent American epidemics. First let's examine the 2009-2010 outbreak of H1N1 "swine flu," whose initial similarity to the deadly 1918 Spanish flu prompted the World Health Organization to declare a global flu pandemic for the first time in more than forty years. With growing alarm as cases spread, the US Centers for Disease Control and officials in the Obama administration worked to streamline vaccine production. Their plans ran into trouble during the summer of 2009, however, as H1N1 proved harder to derive a vaccine from than other flu strains. There were also public relations misfires, such as when Vice President Joe Biden announced on NBC's *Today* show that he wouldn't let his family get on airplanes or subways for fear of the disease, one day after President Obama had urged the nation not to panic. Declining public interest over the summer led federal and local health authorities to urge vaccination more aggressively, with New York's State Department of Health even attempting to mandate the vaccine for certain hospital workers.

That fall, Glenn Beck, a rising media star on Fox News with nearly three million regular viewers, denounced federal health authorities. After suggesting the vaccine might be dangerous, Beck declared: "If somebody had the swine flu right now, I would have them cough on me. I'd do the exact opposite of what the Homeland Security says." Beck explained his skepticism as follows:

> I think this thing is going to mutate. It hasn't mutated yet. So, I'd rather have it now, just like in 1916. Those who got the flu in 1916 were the ones that survived 1918. So, I'd rather have it now. I mean, here's my vaccination. Hey, everybody, it's a swine flu chicken pox party.

Beck wasn't alone. An estimated 14 million people heard Rush Limbaugh, on his talk radio program, address Health and Human Services Secretary Kathleen Sebelius regarding the vaccine as follows: "Screw you, Ms. Sebelius, I'm not going to take it, precisely because you're telling me I must." Left-libertarian talk show host Bill Maher, meanwhile, declared that he didn't think H1N1 could kill healthy people.

While we can't know for certain the extent to which opposition from these talk-show hosts and other public figures shaped American opinion, rather than simply reflected how their audiences already felt about vaccines, the Obama administration, or other factors, what's clear is that Americans diverged substantially in their estimates of H1N1 risks based on their political party affiliation. Democrats were 50 percent more likely, on average, than Republicans to be positively disposed toward getting the vaccine. This ideological effect on belief was strongest among those who reported following news about the swine flu most closely, and those who regularly consumed more ideologically segmented sources like cable TV and talk radio.

More troubling is that ideology and partisanship appear to have affected not just opinions about the vaccine, but actual health-care choices. States with higher portions of registered Republicans reported a significantly lower H1N1 vaccination rate, even after controlling for other factors that tend to affect vaccination, like poverty and access to health care. This was unfortunate, because data indicated that the swine flu, while no deadlier on average than other flu strains, was especially dangerous to children and pregnant women. Subsequent research revealed that the US vaccine had an effectiveness on par with previous flu vaccines, with similarly low incidences of adverse side effects. What this means is that many people chose not to provide a viable defense against a potentially life-threatening illness to their children, and that choice was driven partly by partisanship. Politics can kill through more ways than civil war.

Several years after the swine flu, America was shaken by the worldwide COVID-19 pandemic, and divided along partisan lines that were even more pronounced and bitter. Leading Republicans claimed the threat was being overblown by Democrats who wanted to shut down the economy in order to thwart Donald Trump's chances for reelection. Democrats countered that Republicans cared more about corporate profits than lives. The news media, meanwhile, focused relentlessly on deaths, especially of the young, and at one point broadcast pictures of what were purported to be mass-grave trenches in New York City filled with COVID-19 victims.

The effect on everyday Americans was striking. By July 2020, the average American overestimated the risk of death from COVID-19 for people age 24 and younger by a factor of fifty when compared to actual fatality data from the CDC. Democrats' estimates of COVID-19 mortality risk for young people, meanwhile, were substantially higher than those of other respondents. Republicans tended to overestimate risks as well, but their average overestimation was significantly lower, tempered by countervailing claims by some Republican leaders that the threat of COVID-19 was overblown.

COVID-19 had devastating health effects, and combatting it carried extensive costs as well. Our collective misperceptions about its health risks fueled policy choices that profoundly affected lives from coast to coast, including economic shutdowns that destroyed businesses and left tens of millions jobless, millions of children unschooled and in many cases neglected, widespread drug and alcohol abuse, and a staggering $27 trillion federal debt. It also drove individual choices, with some Republicans afflicted by comorbidities disdaining elementary health precautions, and people in need of medical care experiencing greater suffering and fatality due to inordinate fears of visiting the hospital. Political elites generated and amplified those misperceptions because they saw the opportunity for electoral gain.

THE WELL-ORDERED PARTISAN RANKS

We can understand why ideology causes resistance to facts when we recall that Kinder and Kalmoe define it as a structure wherein "ideas are arranged in orderly, predictable patterns," so that "change in one idea requires change in others." To the ideological partisan, accepting the truth of a contradictory fact, or the merit of a countervailing idea, requires the realignment of an entire system of thought. For a die-hard Republican to accept data indicating charter-school performance is little better than comparable public-school performance, for example, doesn't just require her to modify her opinion about this particular school reform, it demands a reckoning with her preconceptions about the value of markets, choice, and a host of other ideological commitments. Likewise for the hard-core Democrat confronted with data indicating that a significant portion of public-school teachers don't score very well on the standardized tests our national education bureaucracy inflicts upon students.

Especially troubling about the grip of ideology is that our strongest partisans have adjusted their views over the past few decades so that their opinions about a host of issues—and their hostilities to contravening facts—have followed along with the evolving views of their political leaders. When I say "adjusted their views," I mean that American partisans have literally conformed themselves, as panel survey data reveal, to the increasingly rigid orthodoxies of elites in the political class. Once you've transitioned from being moderately pro-choice to demanding unlimited abortion with government funding, you're going to react viscerally to suggestions that abortion policy should be left up to voters in their states and communities. When you've traversed the ideological scale from a position of enthusiasm for free enterprise to a conviction that any restriction on trade defies the Constitution, you're going to have no interest in hearing about the massive proportion of critical US medical supplies that are now manufactured in China. As the political class has become polarized, in other words, its followers have become less able to consider how they might be wrong.

Since American ideologues and partisans are foot soldiers of the political class, and they evidence a disturbing inclination to do and believe whatever their overlords require, much depends on whether their ranks are growing. While many pundits write about their numbers as if they're already a majority, the data indicate that by 2004 they represented about one-fifth of the population, up from around 12 percent in the 1950s. All other things being equal, therefore, their growth might be considered insignificant. Using the data from studies I mentioned in the last chapter, that's a paltry 0.17 percent annual growth in the percentage of Americans who are ideologues between 1956 and 2004. At that rate, it would take 186 years before they constitute a majority. With that said, the portion of Americans who describe themselves as extremely liberal, according to the University of Chicago's General Social Survey, has tripled since the 1970s, from two percent to six percent. Those who call themselves extremely conservative have doubled in number from two to four percent. These are still small numbers, but the trend is evident.

The problem is that we don't have reliable estimates of how fast the ideologues and partisans among us are actually growing in number. We don't know whether their growth has been a slow but steadily rising trendline, or if the size of their contingent remained constant from the 1950s until the late 1990s, and is now growing exponentially. Several different growth trajectories are consistent with the data, some of which would yield a decidedly ideological majority by the end of this decade. This possibility looms larger when we consider, in a few chapters, the massive investments our political class has made in a machinery of persuasion designed to turn everyday Americans into partisans.

It's necessary, therefore, to ask what consequences a more ideological America might produce. Is having more citizens who are staunchly conservative or liberal a good thing? Many political scientists believe so (until they're confronted with the possibility that conservatives could grow to outnumber liberals). Might more ideologues further coarsen our discourse, with more family members turning their backs on one another, neighbors ripping down one another's political yard signs, and similar incidents that receive ample attention in mainstream and social media? Darker still, might the intensification of American ideology yield the civil war some experts claim is a growing possibility? In short, will a growing number of ideologues be the body politic equivalent of putting on a few extra pounds, or is it more like arterial clogging? Will it simply make us less attractive, or might it kill us? The answer may turn on what we learn about the majority of Americans who are *not* avid partisans. And as it turns out, that story is more encouraging than we've been led to believe.

4

THE PRAGMATIC AMERICAN

"I would rather be governed by the first 2,000 people in the telephone directory than by the Harvard University faculty."

—William F. Buckley

While American partisans have altered their policy opinions to match the ideologies of the political class, regular Americans have ignored that marching order. Partisans no longer agree with the Other Side on anything, but average Americans don't let team allegiance dominate their views. Even most Americans who are registered as Democrats or Republicans still favor some policies desired by majorities in the other party. Average citizens demonstrate greater independence of thought than the ideological conformists so revered by political scientists.

Political scientists still contend, however, that Americans are in no condition to vote responsibly, let alone engage in self-governance. By evaluating citizens through a unidimensional, ideological lens, they've concluded that there's neither rhyme, reason, nor consistency behind our voting patterns. In the words of Kinder and Kalmoe, "many Americans simply don't know what they want from government."

Is the fact that most Americans don't flock to either pole on the ideological spectrum proof that their opinions aren't held together by an underlying value system? Some opinion researchers have pondered the possibility that force-fitting survey answers to the liberal/conservative spectrum incorrectly casts everyday Americans as flighty and unserious. "Perhaps ordinary citizens' issue preferences lacked 'constraint,'" speculate Christopher Achen and Larry Bartels, "because they had thoughtfully constructed their own personal political belief systems transcending conventional ideologies and party lines?"

Despite more than a hint of derision in this question, there is indeed evidence that when we unpack the liberal/conservative continuum, Americans aren't as scatterbrained as scholars make them out to be. Researchers have separated American opinions about foreign policy and defense, economic policy, and moral issues, and found that we hold somewhat consistent beliefs *within* those issue areas. The problem for theorists is that, when taken in total, those beliefs don't fit onto their unidimensional, ideological spectrum. Many Americans, for example, are very religious and oppose abortion, which political scientists would consider conservative. Yet these same people also embrace government aid to minorities and laws that ensure equal access to job opportunities, which are typically considered liberal positions. Likewise, a significant portion of America embraces free enterprise and limited government spending, but also abortion rights and gay adoption. We're "liberal" on some things, and "conservative" on others, and this drives theorists batty.

The damning reality about Americans, however, which makes political scientists so confident in their negative assessments, is that our political opinions fluctuate from year to year. One year we favor more aid to minorities; two years later we oppose it. We say the government should provide health insurance, then we say it shouldn't. We believe the US should intervene less in foreign affairs, then we're for war. If average Americans *did* have an underlying value structure informing their policy preferences, goes the reasoning, their survey answers wouldn't jump around so much. Maybe there's an ideology that leads someone to be for both free trade and government-provided health insurance, but there's no ideology that leads a person to favor these policies one year, and disapprove of them the next.

Before we throw in the towel on the American mind, however, let's consider a pretend survey question. It asks you to express, on a seven-point scale, your agreement or disagreement with this statement: "People will be better off if they have children." *One* means you very strongly disagree; *seven* means you agree very strongly.

Before you protest that this question lacks all context ("What people?" "How old are they?" "How many children will they have?"), let me remind you that I didn't make the survey rules. Here's a real statement, for example, that the American National Election Studies has used for more than sixty years to evaluate American opinions about foreign policy: "This country would be better off if we just stayed home and did not concern ourselves with problems in other parts of the world."

Let's tease that one out before returning to my hypothetical childbearing question. Imagine a survey respondent in 2002 who has just recently watched President George W. Bush's "axis of evil" speech. Inspired by the urgent imperative to stop weapons of mass destruction from proliferating in the hands of evildoers, he might feel strongly that the US will be worse off if it doesn't get more involved overseas. So, he chooses "disagree" on the survey.

Fast forward to 2012. American soldiers have suffered terrible casualties in Iraq and Afghanistan. Reports of civilian deaths and dismemberments, meanwhile, are staggering. It now appears clear that intelligence failures, even deliberate misstatements, were used to justify our military interventions. No weapons of mass destruction were found, and many of the people we told ourselves we were going to liberate want us out of their countries.

Our same citizen, finding himself once again contemplating this survey question, has significantly cooled toward military interventions. Maybe he still believes some kind of action was warranted against the people who masterminded the September 11th attacks, but he no longer supports wholesale invasions. So, this time he chooses "agree."

This is entirely reasonable logic. One might even argue that this citizen has better judgment—and certainly more humility—than the politicians and bureaucrats who remain resolutely unapologetic for plunging America into a twenty-year war costing $6.5 trillion and more than 7,000 American lives. Yet still this respondent will be judged as inconsistent by pollsters, because he changed his answer to their survey question.

Now, imagine what might go through someone's mind when answering my hypothetical survey question about having children. One respondent has just been around parents yelling at their kids in the local park. Another has an unmarried teenage niece with a six-month-old baby. Still another recently watched her daughter win a state championship in wrestling. Do you think this personal context matters? If it does, do you think the very same people, two or four or eight years later, might give significantly different answers that will have been colored by their recent experiences? If so, does this prove they have inconsistent beliefs about children and parenting?

Of course it doesn't. Ordinary people, when asked abstract philosophical questions, will draw on recent, concrete experience to inform their answers. Cognitive psychologists Amos Tversky and Daniel Kahneman labeled this tendency "availability bias." "Perhaps the most obvious demonstration of availability in real life," they wrote in the academic journal *Cognitive Psychology*, "is the impact of the fortuitous availability of incidents or scenarios." Asked to evaluate abstractions, the natural human response is to draw upon experience, and often our most recent experience is the most accessible. You may hold bedrock beliefs that are proven out in the way you live and how you treat others, yet which don't shine through in opinion surveys that, lacking sufficient context, invite emotion, varied interpretations, and recency to affect your choice of a number on a scale.

With that said, there is a small group of people whose answers to the parenting question wouldn't vary: those with such strong convictions about childbearing that context doesn't matter. Some people have firm religious beliefs, for example, that everyone is called to "be fruitful and multiply," and that God will work out the circumstances. Others believe the world's resources are so depleted that it's imperative for everyone to stop having children before the planet dies.

People who believe a principle should be adhered to no matter what the cost—ideologues, in other words—are likely to be much more consistent in survey after survey than the rest of us. What's more, they'll struggle to imagine how people whose responses depend on context can be anything other than shallow. If they happen to be the scholars constructing the surveys and interpreting the results, well, you get today's near-consensus about American public opinion, which is that most citizens are shortsighted, biased, forgetful, and relatively unprincipled. Not well-suited, in other words, to govern themselves according to the vision of the American Founders.

It's worth noting that a more charitable view of their fellow man might evoke curiosity among scholars about why their surveys indicate citizenship incompetence among a wide swath of Americans. Given a well-established psychological literature revealing the human tendency to explain one's own behaviors (and inconsistencies) with more grace than one generally affords others, we might be justified in saying to the professors who hold such a damning view of everyday Americans: "Physician, heal thyself."

The plain truth is that the machinery of public-opinion surveys, crafted by ideologues, is geared to detect ideology. Ideology is the only mechanism they imagine can drive political opinion in a coherent, predictable direction. There are entire academic treatises on the nature of ideology, its formation and its actualization. The fact that you obey the law, pay your taxes, and participate in the market economy is proof, in some interpretations, that you are embedded in a web of ideology. That discussion is not worth delving into here. The question at hand is whether Americans have shared beliefs that not only lead them to respond to surveys with answers that cut across the academic conceptualization of liberal vs. conservative, but which also explain the variation in their policy preferences over time.

CAN "WE THE PEOPLE" BE TRUSTED?

This isn't just a philosophical question. What's at stake is the American republic. If most citizens really are indifferent, and the remainder blindly partisan, then the faith of the Founders was mislaid, and we are in no condition to govern ourselves. Far better to leave all those policy decisions to the attentive politicos in DC, provided we can find a way to keep them from plunging us into civil war.

In short, where we go from here depends on an honest answer to this question: is there something other than capriciousness and low information that drives the political opinions of average Americans? Something that makes their desires for our country trustworthy?

I believe there is, for two reasons. First, public-opinion scholars assess citizens' knowledge of issues and politics like they're grading a midterm exam. Political scientist James Gibson points out, for example, that President Richard Nixon repeatedly mangled the name of the man he himself nominated to the Supreme Court, William Rehnquist. Coding standards applied by the American National Election Studies would have required pollsters to record Nixon as not knowing his own Supreme Court nominee. So were real survey respondents, when presented with William Rehnquist's name, recorded as not knowing who he was if they answered with something like: "head honcho of the Supreme Court." Using a more reasonable standard of knowledge, Gibson found that 72 percent of responses recorded as wrong were in fact correct. The surveys employed to prove most Americans are ignorant, in other words, appear to be off the mark.

More importantly, surveys of American beliefs about government focus almost exclusively on policy levers. They ask whether respondents believe government should provide health insurance, and whether it should spend more or less on welfare, public health, education, crime—even space exploration. They ask whether courts should be harsher or more lenient with criminals, and whether more or fewer immigrants should be allowed into the country. This is like asking an average person to diagnose his car trouble from the driver's seat. He can no more tell you how much welfare spending is adequate than he can determine how much transmission fluid he's lacking. If you force him to offer diagnoses, he's going to grasp at impressions. Wasn't there a grinding sound last week? Didn't I notice a funny smell?

Ask him repeatedly over the years, and his answers are going to jump around. All his seeming schizophrenia proves is that he isn't a mechanic. It doesn't mean that he has no consistent vision of where he wants his car to go, and how he wants it to get there. Likewise for Americans when it comes to their conceptualizations of government and the common good. Everyday people don't know how much money government at all levels spends on education, or how much it should spend. This doesn't mean they lack coherent opinions about what a child's education ought to look like.

INSTEAD OF SURVEY RESPONDENTS, CITIZENS

Imagine that instead of asking Americans to be government mechanics, we instead asked them to think like citizens. Rather than quiz them regarding what policy levers ought to be pulled, they would be questioned about what outcomes they believed were best for our country. People disagree vehemently about government-provided health insurance, for example, but share a desire to see as many Americans as possible receive the medical care they need. People disagree about whether parents should be allowed to divert public funds to private schools, but share a desire to see every American child receive a suitable education. We're divided over what levers to pull, but not nearly so divided as the political class when it comes to the ends we want to achieve, because we are far more united in our core values than they are.

How do I know? Most directly, I have experienced this reality firsthand—as I suspect you have as well—in many conversations with friends, neighbors, relatives, coworkers, and fellow parishioners whose political opinions vary. Beyond one's own sense from those conversations, hints of an underlying consensus on American values can be found in the same surveys used by scholars to claim American beliefs are incoherent. Occasionally, a question on those broad national surveys reveals—perhaps without meaning to—values and desires of Americans regarding public policy and the common good.

The American National Election Studies, for example, has asked Americans for decades how they feel about government support for people who need jobs. Between 1956 and 1960, on average 58 percent of Americans said the government should see to it that people who needed jobs should get them. Opposing that goal were 26 percent of respondents, with another 17 percent stating either that they didn't know or didn't care. In 1964, however, the percentage of respondents who agreed with this lofty aspiration fell almost by half, to 31 percent. Those who disagreed, meanwhile, rose to 43 percent.

On the surface, this appears to be another example of American ideological schizophrenia. Either that, or a sizable portion of Americans lost their charitable instincts in four short years. A closer look at the question's wording, however, reveals that between 1956-1960, Americans were asked to either agree or disagree with this statement:

> The government in Washington ought to see to it that everybody who wants to work can find a job.

The statement's wording was altered in 1964, however, replacing a simpler declaration with this version:

> In general, some people feel that the government in Washington should see to it that every person has a job and a good standard of living. Others think the government should just let each person get ahead on his own. Have you been interested enough in this to favor one side over the other?

This is a very different question, isn't it? Before, Americans were asked whether they wanted government to help everyone willing to work *find* a job. The revised question, in contrast, asked whether Americans believed government should *provide* everyone a job (no mention of willingness to work), and beyond that a good standard of living. The dramatic change in subsequent survey responses doesn't simply illustrate the sensitivity of surveys to how questions are worded. It illuminates, as demonstrated with greater proof below, a core conviction that informs how everyday Americans think about everything from welfare to immigration, namely that *we should help people who are trying to help themselves.*

This is a widespread and stable value that directly affects how Americans feel about welfare, preferential hiring, aid to minorities, immigration, and other policies. The majority of survey questions about these topics, however, pretend this sentiment doesn't exist. The two most consistently administered and academically rigorous survey batteries in America—the American National Election Studies (University of Michigan) and General Social Survey (University of Chicago)—don't ask Americans to distinguish between welfare recipients who have one child out of wedlock versus three, or immigrants willing to work versus those who subsist on crime or welfare. Yet these are exactly the considerations, as anyone who's talked to regular Americans for even a few minutes about these topics can attest, that determine how generous or stingy most Americans will be. Little wonder responses to survey questions about how much we should spend on social services, or how many immigrants we should allow into the country, fluctuate. Lacking context, respondents base their answers on what's prominent in the news or other media, alongside immediate personal experiences.

Another effect of the aforementioned change to the wording of the jobs question reveals something else about how Americans respond to surveys. When surveyors altered the wording in 1964, the percentage of respondents who subsequently replied that they either didn't know or didn't care rose by more than half, from 17 percent to 26 percent. When the surveyors switched, eight years later, from a Yes/No format to a seven-point scale, the "don't know" responses fell by half. Forty-two percent of respondents, furthermore, placed themselves in the middle of the scale, choosing a three, four, or five.

Between 1964-1972, in other words, ANES administrators forced respondents to consider a false choice: either government guarantees everyone a job and a good standard of living, or it leaves people to fend for themselves. Anyone acquainted with everyday life understands there's a third alternative in which assistance comes from families, churches, and communities. This isn't an uncommon phenomenon in surveys. Ideologically-minded researchers manufacture false choices, and Americans respond by either opting out of the questions altogether, or placing themselves in the middle of a scale when it's available, which gets interpreted as mindless moderation borne of ignorance and shallow beliefs. Americans appear schizophrenic to academics on many policy issues because they're being asked the wrong questions.

Fortunately, some academics have invested in the more painstaking work of asking Americans what they think about government, public policies, and the common good, and recording what respondents have to say in their own words. The findings of these scholars offer a sharp—and encouraging—contrast to the work of pollsters. While survey researchers paint a picture of Americans as ignorant and indifferent, scholars who take the time to actually talk with the subjects of these surveys describe people who sound like they're capable of—and willing to be—the kinds of citizens the American Founders envisioned.

PEELING BACK THE TICKY TACKY

Wellesley, MA, 1995
The American middle class has eluded precise definition, but this hasn't deterred anyone from having an opinion about it. Variously

lauded or decried by academics, journalists, and pop singers, the middle class has been characterized as a bedrock of American values, an enduring source of patriotism, an engine of capitalism and democracy, a stultifying domain of conformity and mediocrity, and a hotbed of intolerance. "Little boxes of ticky tacky [. . .] and they all look just the same," sang political activist and folk singer Malvina Reynolds about a housing development in Daly City, CA, lyrics later popularized by Pete Seeger. Reynolds wrote that doctors, lawyers, and business executives dwelled in those lookalike houses, sipping martinis and intermarrying, but somehow this became a slander of middle-class suburbia. Perhaps those high-end occupations still qualify as middle class; membership has always been a sticky question. According to surveys, a majority of Americans believe they qualify.

One truth that can be observed about the American middle class is that it excludes, by definition, the very rich and the very poor. Historically, its members have taken pride in that. Though they comprise a more diverse array of individuals than neither admirers nor detractors often admit, members of the American middle class have been historically unified in their disdain for the lifestyles of the rich and the poor alike. This is because they share underlying values, even as they differ on matters of faith, family, politics, and other personal matters. It's become easy to overlook this bedrock of values, especially as professional ideologues have parlayed disagreements regarding personal lifestyles and public-policy choices—differences Americans mostly tolerated in one another for decades—into causes for war.

"War" was the word that caught the attention of journalists and politicos in the wake of Pat Buchanan's impassioned speech in a failed bid to unseat incumbent President George H.W. Bush at the Republican National Convention in 1992. "There is a religious war going on in our country for the soul of America," Buchanan proclaimed. "It is a cultural war, as critical to the kind of nation we will one day be as was the Cold War itself." Buchanan singled out abortion, gay rights, and women in combat as bellwethers of the kind of culture Bill and Hillary Clinton threatened to foist upon America. Though his accusations were primarily moral and religious matters, the term *culture war* proved malleable. Everything—foreign policy, taxes, agricultural subsidies—can become a moral matter if you message it correctly. Everyone can be conscripted into the culture war, whether he wants to be or not.

Culture war was perhaps a fitting description of what the political elites were up to, but it quickly gained usage as a description of divides that pundits claimed existed between everyday Americans. Not surprisingly, the purported sides in this war mirrored the deep conflicts within the political class. Half of America, pundits said, wanted things like more liberal welfare policies, open borders, and the removal of religion from public life. The other half demanded elimination of public-support programs, tight immigration control, and more religion in everything from political campaigns to public schools. *Our nation*, commentators on both sides declared, *is coming apart.*

How convenient for them. After all, what use are generals without armies?

Sociologist Alan Wolfe wasn't buying the culture-war narrative, so he decided to get to the bottom of it. After conducting research in communities around his town of Wellesley, MA, Wolfe began to suspect that what actual Americans thought about controversial topics bore little relation to what pundits claimed they thought. He visited a diverse array of middle-class communities in 1995 to hear from Americans in their own words what their principles were, and what they believed their government should and should not do. Though a committed liberal with strong convictions about what American public policies ought to be, Wolfe wanted to hear in unvarnished fashion what average Americans themselves had to say. "Neutral I am not;" wrote Wolfe, "objective I try very hard to be."

What Wolfe found, which he laid out extensively in his 1998 book, *One Nation, After All,* was that middle-class Americans, while by no means monolithic in their political preferences, had a wider and firmer base of shared beliefs than was convenient for those who profited from sowing discord. We were closer to one another in the things that mattered, he found, than the talking heads wanted us to believe.

Consider a topic we're told to avoid because it's so contentious: religion. While political columnists warned that America was becoming either—depending on their partisan stripes—an atheist society or a theocracy, Wolfe found that middle-class Americans welcomed religion in the public square, provided no sect tried to push out others. They varied in the convictions and practices of their own faiths, but generally they believed it was a good thing for their fellow citizens to have *some* kind of faith.

Regarding another "culture-war" topic—immigration—Wolfe found that the middle-class likewise had much in common. Most of them welcomed immigrants willing to work, obey the law, and learn English. They had less animosity toward immigrants than toward companies that sought to flood the labor market with cheap and exploitable workers. University of Chicago polling data in 1994 backed this up, insofar as two-thirds of blacks and whites didn't want immigrants to be eligible for government assistance, yet two-thirds favored either increasing the amount of immigration, keeping it constant, or decreasing it slightly. This was consistent with Wolfe's finding that Americans wanted immigrants who would carry their own weight. Wolfe wrote that when it came to suburban Americans, "what divides them is not politics, but differences over how to best reach goals—a society that respects law, a society that takes care of people, a society that is open to opportunity."

Middle-class Americans evidenced the same moderation when it came to another contentious topic: welfare. Wolfe's interviewees overwhelmingly agreed that government should provide modest support to people afflicted by bad circumstances. They also opposed what they believed to be abuses of the welfare system. They were willing to support a single mother with one child, but they looked askance at the mother with multiple out-of-wedlock births. They wanted to assist Americans looking for work, but they had little patience for those who didn't try very hard to get a job.

Since so many supposed culture-war conflicts (e.g., welfare) opened the door to conversations about race, Wolfe dug into this topic, too. There were plenty of damning realities that pundits could (and still can) point to when searching for evidence of racial division in the US. We tend to self-segregate in our neighborhoods and churches. We experience—at least on the surface—stark racial disparities in economic and health outcomes. Additionally, since the 1940s, blacks have voted overwhelmingly for Democratic presidential candidates, whereas white majorities since the 1960s have tended to vote Republican.

Wolfe indeed found that some interviewees harbored harsh views about the values and behaviors of inner-city blacks, and unabashedly said they didn't want those kinds of people moving into their suburban neighborhoods. The troubling fact for Wolfe, a progressive liberal, was that these views were expressed by blacks. What's more, he found that the majority of black and white respondents denounced racial discrimination, and agreed that equal treatment and fairness should be extended to all Americans regardless of race. They wholeheartedly rejected racial quotas, however, as a means of remedying racial disparities in hiring and promotion. Suburban black and white attitudes

were, in other words, right down the middle of the road, reject-
ing racial prejudice as well as racial preferences.

Wolfe also picked up on something that had often been
neglected by pollsters and pundits: the chief factor shared by
blacks and whites who had the most negative perceptions of
inner-city life and mores was not political party, but parent-
hood. Parents of small children were the least tolerant of crime
and other antisocial behavior. While it was easy for ideological
pundits, who lumped blacks and whites into monolithic camps,
to ignore middle-class blacks' viewpoint while attributing its
prevalence among whites to racism, Wolfe argued for keeping
race in its proper place as an explanatory variable:

> There is much to be gained by treating race as a thing in itself,
> not as a stand-in for other values; if there is one aspect of political
> discussion that distinguishes intellectuals (liberal and conservative
> alike) from the people with whom I talked, it is that the former
> like to read symbolic meaning into all kinds of things—the houses
> people buy, the way they raise their children, whom they have for
> neighbors, even what they eat and drive—whereas the latter tend
> to believe that mundane matters are really mundane matters.

Likewise, Wolfe found intellectuals missed the underlying
root of very real and legitimate anger among middle-class blacks
toward racism: "Black middle-class anger over race is real, but
it is also middle-class anger; it is not a rejection of middle-class
values such as merit, recognition, and reward, but a demand that
those values apply to all."

Finally, regarding the role of women in society, Wolfe
observed families pulled between nostalgia for traditional roles
in families and the workplace, a predominant belief that women
should have the same choices available to men, and the under-

lying reality of economic forces beyond their control. "Most Americans," he concluded, "who know better than conservatives the positive benefits of having women work, also know better than feminists how the family is weakened by it." This conflict was mirrored in observations made by social scientist Daniel Yankelovich in 1982, who found that while a majority of Americans supported equal opportunities for women, two-thirds also craved a return to more traditionally understood family standards and roles. Imagine trying to suss out this nuance with the "feminism" question deployed by the American National Election Studies since 1972:

> Some people feel that women should have an equal role with men in running business, industry, and government. Others feel that women's place is in the home. Where would you place yourself on this scale or haven't you thought much about this?

It's funny how surveyors like to force a choice between stark views, then imply that you can only fail to answer if "you haven't thought much about this." The work by Wolfe and others indicates the opposite, that people who've thought about these deep challenges—primarily by virtue of living through them—are the ones least likely to fit comfortably on academics' liberal/conservative scale.

After talking with citizens across the US about a host of sensitive and divisive topics, Wolfe returned to the question of whether America was in the midst of a culture war: "My answer is yes—*but it is one that is being fought primarily by intellectuals, not by most Americans themselves,*" (emphasis in the original).

Daniel Yankelovich found something very similar, namely that while Americans don't score well on politics tests, or think like philosophers about ideology, they have consistently embraced core values that have informed their choices (when they have been allowed to make them) as citizens:

> The values that unite us (patriotism, self-confidence, pragmatism, community, child-centeredness, acceptance of diversity, belief in hard work, the hunger for common ground) far outweigh those that divide us. Also, many of the apparent 50-50 splits in the polls are not what they seem. When issues like crime and abortion and school vouchers are ideologically framed, they mask pragmatic attitudes in the general public that demonstrate a traditional American willingness to compromise and find practical solutions.

The findings of Wolfe and Yankelovich were echoed later by political scientist Morris Fiorina and his colleagues, whose extensive analysis of decades of survey data led them to conclude, in a 2011 book titled *Culture War? The Myth of a Polarized America*, that: "For the most part Americans continue to be ambivalent, moderate, and pragmatic, in contrast to the cocksure extremists and ideologues who dominate our public political life."

Fiorina found that the rejection of ideological extremes in survey responses was reflected in political-party affiliations as well. As disputes between the two major political parties became more rancorous in the early 2000s, the portion of American voters declaring themselves Independents crept above the numbers declaring themselves Democrats or Republicans. Partisans in both camps have downplayed the significance of this, noting that most Independents lean toward one party or the other and vote for that party with the same frequency as registered party members. The problem with this interpretation is that the data are collected in the weeks before an election, when Independents have mostly made up their minds about which candidates and party they favor. Not surprisingly, their subsequent vote is almost always for the party they told pollsters they were leaning toward. Over multiple elections, however, Independent leaners have alternated between parties at the same rate as pure Independents.

As the political class has become more polarized and spread its acrimony across both parties, more and more Americans are choosing either to opt out or to hold their ground in the center—just as they do on ideologically tilted surveys. As political theorists Peter Lawler and Richard Reinsch have argued: "Both parties decline to incorporate the serious concerns of their voters on a range of issues including immigration, trade, foreign policy, and social and cultural issues, each party preferring instead its own consensus, one derived from a particular corridor of economic and cultural power."

A PRAGMATIC TRUST

Returning full circle to the question of the American mind, rooting beneath superficial analyses by pundits, journalists, and other ideologues reveals that most Americans believe they should do what works for their communities and families. They believe in pursuing the common good, and they share some decent ideas about what that is. They don't want to upend society in pursuit of utopian visions, nor constrain their options to suit any ideologue's sense of philosophical purity. They value rights and freedoms, but they also believe in using government to take care of the vulnerable and needy. They favor free enterprise and believe in pursuing the American dream, yet they distrust big business. Most of them also distrust big government. They're patriotic, but wary of warmongering. They believe in God, but don't need their neighbors to believe in Him the same way they do.

Just as encouraging is the evidence that widespread claims about declining trust among average Americans are as overstated as claims about red states versus blue states. The journalist David Brooks exemplified the received wisdom from academics and public intellectuals, when he wrote in *The Atlantic* in 2020 that trust among Americans was not only "in catastrophic decline," but was being replaced by "explosive distrust." Similarly, philosopher Kevin Vallier claims that America is the only established democracy where social trust is declining, dropping from half of Americans in 1970 who said people could be trusted, to less than a third today. These claims are based on trends in a question asked for decades on the General Social Survey from the University of Chicago: "Would you say that most people can be trusted or that you can't be too careful in dealing with people?" In 1972, 46 percent of Americans responded in the affirmative, but by 2019 that number was 32 percent. As with other assessments of public opinion, however, this appears to be another case of researchers seeing what they want to see.

Astute readers will note, for example, that the tacit alternative offered in this trust question is that we should exercise great caution when dealing with people. The question, in effect, juxtaposes apples and oranges; the first part is about the character of "people," while the second part is about the respondent's prudence in an uncertain world. I'm going to go out on a limb and speculate that you, like me, agree with a trust statement like this: *I believe most people are trustworthy, but because some people are untrustworthy some of the time, I also believe you must be careful when dealing with people, especially strangers.* I'll bet further that most of our neighbors, friends, and family agree with this statement, too. So, what happens when researchers come calling with their convoluted question? Will they get a reliable measure of the absolute level of trust in American society, or will they get data that only looks definitive because they've made people choose between two artificially opposed options?

The sociologist Robert Wuthnow divided this complicated question about trust into two separate questions, and gave both of them to a representative sample of Americans. He found not only that 62 percent of them believed most people could be trusted, but that two-thirds of those trusting respondents *also* believed that you couldn't be too careful in dealing with people. By fusing these two very different questions into one, researchers have effectively obscured the true level of Americans' trust in one another.

A key question used by pundits and scholars to prove a lack of trust among American citizens is highly suspect, but its defenders argue that even if the question is confusing, it still indicates declining trust, because more people now choose the "you can't be too careful" option than was the case forty years ago. Perhaps that does indicate declining trust—or perhaps it indicates rising fear of what happens if you trust the wrong person. Americans today may have no lower an opinion of average people than they did in the 1970s, only a greater concern with avoiding creeps—an understandable phenomenon given the dark turn our national news has taken in the past several decades.

Trust in *government*, meanwhile, has fallen significantly, which political scientists and pundits take as further proof of declining trust in society overall. We must be mindful, however, that too much faith in government would be a problem. It's the strongest partisans, after all, who trust their political leaders so much that they're willing to follow them off a cliff. Imagine the results if we could poll Alexander Hamilton, James Madison, and the rest of the Constitutional Convention to see, as ANES asks, whether they trust the government in Washington, DC, "just about all the time," "most of the time," or, "only some of the time." Their answers (which are eloquently explained in *The Federalist*) would scandalize the modern political class. Only politicians and political scientists interpret American distrust of Washington as a threat to society. The average American's willingness to trust government is captured by Ronald Reagan's stance toward the Soviet Union: "Trust, but verify." It's a pragmatism that gets obscured by ham-handed survey methods.

While there's little evidence that Americans are experiencing the "catastrophic decline" in trust toward each other posited by David Brooks and others, it does appear that we're losing confidence not just in government, but in the political judgments of our fellow citizens. The portion of survey respondents who say they have little or no "trust and confidence in the wisdom of American people in making political decisions" rose from 35 percent in 1997 to 59 percent in 2019. Some of what's driving that is a growing belief, indicated in the same survey, that Americans are overly swayed by social media and fake news. The constant red-state-versus-blue-state narrative doesn't help either. We're repeatedly told that the reason our political system is broken is because We the People are broken. Many of us have begun to believe it.

Even though it doesn't have the actual word in it, a better question to determine Americans' level of trust might be this, from the same survey: "Do you think most people would try to take advantage of you, if they got the chance, or would they try to be fair?" Based on this, we have seen a modest decline in the numbers of Americans who trust others to be fair, from an average of 60 percent in the 1970s to an average of 51 percent since 2010. It's worth noting that the downward trend began in the 1990s which is when the political class really kicked its strife-making machinery into high gear.

Summing up, even though Americans disagree about political parties and the specifics of some policies, our disagreements are frequently exaggerated and misinterpreted. The red-state-versus-blue-state narrative overlooks the fact that tendencies to vote for a party do not equate to fervid support for that party. Americans appear to be more extreme because the candidate choices foisted upon us by a polarized political class are more extreme. We appear to have sorted ourselves geographically behind red and blue walls, but the "Big Sort" posited by journalist Bill Bishop, and popularized by everyone from Bill Clinton to David French, doesn't stand up to serious scrutiny. Most Americans don't embrace politics deeply, have grown less supportive of the two major parties as they've become increasingly polarized, and care more about making America work than beating the Other Side. We have much in common, and more goodwill and trust toward one another than national pundits care to see. Elites in the political class want us to pick a side, but the side most of us want to pick is that of our families and communities.

To understand why the political class wants so badly to divide us, it helps to know that a majority of Americans are united not just by values, but a desire to see politicians compromise to solve problems. Unlike partisans and the political class, most Americans care more about consensus and peace than getting every one of our favored policies implemented. Americans don't want a civil war. They want to work together, to get along, and to reach consensus. The pragmatic American center is easily overlooked because its members are working and raising children, but it still holds.

For now.

While the majority of Americans aren't partisan ideologues, it's quite possible, as I mentioned earlier, that the contingent of dedicated ideologues and partisans is growing under our noses. They constitute at least 20 percent of the American body politic, if not more. Even if their numbers aren't growing quickly, their animosities are deepening. Partisans despise each other today;

thirty years ago, most of them did not. Indeed, their animosity has grown considerably in just the past few years. The Pew Research organization found in 2019 that 79 percent of Democrats felt "cold" toward Republicans, up from 61 percent in 2016. Eighty-three percent of Republicans felt similarly toward Democrats, up from 69 percent in 2016. Additionally, a growing percentage of partisans in both parties consider members of the opposing party to be more immoral, unpatriotic, and closed-minded than other Americans.

Meanwhile, nearly three-quarters of dedicated partisans in both parties say they disagree not just over politics, but basic facts. There's little possibility of consensus or compromise when the two sides can't agree on whether a problem even exists, or what its causes are. Among the most extreme partisans, nearly 25 percent of liberals and 20 percent of conservatives say it's essential that they do not live near people on the other end of the ideological spectrum.

These partisans are by no means a majority, but as sociologist James Davison Hunter notes, most wars are waged by societal minorities. Partisans, by virtue of their greater commitment and influence, have an outsized influence on the direction of our communities. Most Americans, Hunter writes, are "not self-conscious partisans actively committed to one side or the other. [. . .] But the options they ended up with were framed by elites in the parties and special-interest organizations, their respective institutions, and the rank-and-file supporters who formed the grassroots support." The political class frames the conflicts, and their partisan foot soldiers array themselves for battle. Even though most Americans are in neither group, these battles are being waged over our lives and livelihoods.

The opinions, values, and attitudes of regular citizens give ample reason to believe that Americans are fully capable of the self-governance envisioned by our Founders. A spirit of compromise, a pragmatic mindset, the instinct to live and let live are abundant in Middle America, but these qualities have all but disappeared from the American political class and its partisans. There's simply no middle ground when every political decision, from auto fuel-economy standards to capital gains taxes, is cast in good-versus-evil theatrics, and evaluated not for its effects on everyday Americans, but according to what advantage or harm it might confer on political friends and foes.

How was American politics transformed like this? How did our political class become so invested in conflict, and our partisans so angry? Some of the responsibility lies with the very people who are today so confident that everyday Americans aren't capable of being good citizens. Understanding what they did will help us chart a path out of the mess they created.

5

SCIENTISTS, MAD AND POLITICAL

"The logical evolution of a science is to distance itself increasingly
from its object, until it dispenses with it entirely."
—Jean Baudrillard, *Simulation and Simulacra*

"Instead of assuring the people that they passionately want what we
want, it would be better for us to ask ourselves whether they want
something different."
—Alexander Herzen, *From the Other Shore*

In the beginning, the conspiracy was intentional. It was engen-
dered in plain sight, borne of a desire to bring to life something
its authors believed would benefit America. They weren't mad
scientists, they were something far worse: political scientists. As
a recovering and repentant political scientist myself, I hasten to
note that my academic discipline has probably made fine con-
tributions to civil society, though none come to mind. Just as
Dr. Frankenstein likely had many laudable creations that went
unremembered because of that single mishap with a corpse,
the field of political science is rightly identified with its own
destructive creature: Woodrow Wilson. Eugenicist, segregationist,
censor, hater of small towns and free enterprise and free people,
meddlesome, puritanical; an imperious, fancy-pants, sourpuss
nicknamed the "schoolmaster in politics," Wilson was the only
US president ever to hold a PhD in political science.

With any luck, he'll also be the last. There are certainly many well-meaning, caring, decent political scientists in the world, but there are many more Labrador retrievers with the same qualities, most of whom are no less qualified to serve in the White House.

This is no mere *ad hominem* attack on Wilson and his progeny. It's an exceptional *ad hominem* attack, and well-deserved. Sometimes, who the man is determines what he does (Wilson, an inveterate Calvinist, no doubt would have agreed). That said, Wilson isn't the monster in this story after all, he's just the first of many Dr. Frankensteins in my old profession. Like Dr. Frankenstein in his eerie laboratory, Dr. Wilson concocted, in his ivory tower, a theory about what American politics should become. His vision proved so seductive that future generations of political scientists set about hammering it into reality. Somewhere along the way, however, what was intended to be a living and reasonable creature became something else entirely. It's this undead creation that set us on the path to our present and widening state of disunion.

Wilson's theory was that America should have political parties with much sharper ideological distinctions, in order to elicit from voters a mandate for one party. Wilson despised federalism and the separation of powers between executive and legislative, and harbored the conceit that he could have performed a nation-building job superior to that of Alexander Hamilton and the Philadelphia gang. Wilson's aim, so long as he was stuck with the antiquated machinery left to him by the Founders, was to inject enough ideology into American life to turn elections into national referenda, thereby empowering one party, through uniform control of the presidency and Congress, to implement its agenda from top to bottom without interference from the minority party. That agenda, of course, was Wilson's.†

---

† Wilson and every progressive to follow him seemed incapable of imagining what a system like that would mean if the voters—whom they don't really trust in the first place—give their mandate to a party with very *different* priorities.

Wilson had limited luck with his grand plans, but his creation lurked in the shadows, nursing its wounds as Democrats followed in his footsteps, eager to expand the power of Washington, DC, in order to control everything from the price of chicken to who would win the Greek Civil War. They met with opposition not just from Republicans, but from conservative members of their own party. It was the latter who were especially galling, because they required frequent finessing of policy decisions, bargains between regional and economic factions, and constant exercise of a practice utterly detestable to idealists: compromise.

Dr. Wilson's monster shambled into fleeting view in the late 1950s, shrouded within the pages of a mostly neglected report presented to the American Political Science Association (APSA) by a committee of its accomplished members, titled: "Toward a More Responsible Two-Party System." Taking their inspiration, as had Wilson, from the socialist parties of Europe, the committee sought means by which political leaders in the US might offer the masses what they hoped would be compelling policies geared toward national control of the economy. These policies, they believed, would be the surest way to provide sustenance and jobs for a wide swath of American society while warding off the ravages (still fresh in their minds from the Great Depression) of economic downturns.

Their recommendations were well-intentioned, and their reasoning not without merit. Insofar as the political party out of power lacked the ability, they argued, to offer policies that differed in clear and significant ways from the policies of the party in power, and similarly lacked the internal discipline to deliver on its promises should citizens vote it into power, then voters effectively had no real choices. Politicians asking for citizens' votes could promise nothing in return, rendering a choice between Candidate A and Candidate B meaningless. So long as America's major parties, explained committee member Evron

Kirkpatrick, continued to be "neither cohesive, programmatic, or responsible, democracy does not exist in the United States."

Solutions offered in the APSA's report included abolishing the Electoral College and stretching House of Representatives' terms to four years, both to increase the likelihood of single-party control in Congress and to give the ruling party more time to implement its agenda. The report also proposed giving national party leaders more power to select and promote state and local candidates, the better to enforce party orthodoxy. In a similar vein, the report recommended short ballots akin to those employed in European parliamentary systems, wherein voters would be able to choose between candidates for top political offices, but party leaders would select who would hold lower-level offices. The objective was to drive conservative officeholders from the Democratic Party, replacing them with liberals more attuned to the desires of party elites and political-science professors. Given the balance of party power at the time, this promised liberals an untrammeled ability to implement the wide-scale federal programs and oversight they craved.

Beyond the immediate goal of ensuring Democratic ascendancy, the APSA report's authors wanted to make "policy the central concern of voters, parties, legislators, and government." This may sound tautological—after all, isn't politics just a store from which voters buy policies? What frustrated reformers, though, was how the system bequeathed by the Founders required a proposed law to navigate numerous junctures, where compromise between factions was necessary. The reformers sought far-reaching, radical changes in areas ranging from national economic planning to reforming the voting laws in southern states. These changes required pure, powerful, unadulterated policies. The system erected by the Founders, however, required deliberation, incrementalism, and compromise. By making policy the central concern, reformers aimed to avoid grubby compromises. They wanted voters to choose between ideological platforms, then get out of the way so that the technocrats, licensed by a national mandate, could get to work.

By arguing that voters be given two stark choices, with immediate implementation of the winning platform, the reformers advocated plebiscitary democracy. Though today's political leaders claim to see mandates in even the slimmest of electoral margins, the Founders did not intend for winning majorities to cram policies down the throats of the losers, but instead that elected officials should seek what Alexander Hamilton called a "deliberate sense of the community," by which he meant elected representatives would grapple not only with problems, but with one another's ideas and interests, until they reached consensus. In this vision, a premium was placed on generating as much support for a law as possible, because maintaining comity among fellow citizens was just as important as passing laws—and in some respects *more* important. The Founders' vision required policy advocates to frequently settle for less than they wanted.

Our constitutional separation of powers and all the compromises it required was, therefore, intolerable to reformers. They had a nation to reorder, a world to lead. As a result, they looked askance at federalism because it permitted local variation, with some communities and states preferring stronger safety nets, or freer enterprise, or different school standards, than others. The reformers sought optimal, scientifically validated rules, and their logic demanded that everyone abide by them. Federalism sacrificed efficiency and equity on behalf of local self-governance.

Like Woodrow Wilson before them, reformers in the 1950s made no secret about the imperative of sweeping aside these constitutional principles in order to fashion a nation-state capable of micromanaging the economy and projecting military might around the globe. They reasoned that the Founders, not realizing that wiser men with sophisticated tools would one day be in charge, had foolishly mistrusted Big Government. With a brave new world being midwifed, this was no time to wax nostalgic for men who had used muskets and believed leeches to be medicinal.

THE BRIGHTER SIDE OF PARTIES

Not every political scientist agreed with the APSA report's recommendations. Some noted that realistic solutions to complex national problems couldn't be neatly packaged into party platforms. Voters wouldn't be choosing, therefore, between clear policy alternatives; they'd be basing their votes, as they always had done, on preexisting party loyalties, group identities, and estimations of candidate competence and trustworthiness. If debates about complex problems boiled down to a simple pro versus con, noted Evron Kirkpatrick, "the prize goes to the best argument, not to the best solution."

Other critics noted that there already *were* substantial policy differences between the two major parties. The 1952 Republican Party platform stridently distinguished itself from the Democratic Party on highly salient issues like the Korean War, communist agents in the US Department of State, and the power of labor unions. It denounced Democrats for working "unceasingly to achieve their goal of national socialism," and promised to "put an end to corruption, to oust the crooks and grafters, to administer tax laws fairly and impartially, and to restore honest government to the people." Claims of a single blob masquerading as two separate parties seemed a tad exaggerated. The *real* complaint of reformers was not that the Democratic Party was indistinguishable from the Republican Party, it was that the party wasn't left-wing enough to suit them.

There was a deeper danger, meanwhile, lurking within the reformers' agenda. Even at just this theoretical stage, some thinkers could see how, if implemented, it would eventually set Americans at one another's throats. They counterargued that there was a deep societal benefit in having varied factions represented in *both* major parties. Social scientists call these "cross-cutting cleavages," in which citizens' shared interests offset their conflicts. People on opposite sides of the table negotiating a new union contract, for example, might be combat veterans, or attend the same churches, or have children in the same schools. Members of families in a racially transitioning neighborhood might work in the same plant, or be supporters of the same city councilman. Demonstrators for and against a war might be mothers of soldiers, or veterans themselves. Even when these commonalities don't reduce the heat of a particular conflict, they humanize opponents, and create a likelihood that people won't find themselves on the opposite side of every issue.

Historian Clinton Rossiter observed in 1960 that America's political parties "are weak agents in the struggle for power because they have been strong agents in the course of our rise to nationhood. It has been their historic mission to hold the line against some of the most powerful centrifugal forces in American society." Rossiter described all the ways political parties, precisely because they weren't sorted into ideologically distinct tribes, brought together citizens of different classes, regions, and ethnicities, and invited them to strive alongside one another for Hamilton's "deliberate sense of community," all before a single public official was elected or a legislative vote cast. "In all these ways and in many more," Rossiter wrote, "the parties have softened the rough edges of America's fabulous diversity."

Political parties oriented more toward accommodating multiple group interests rather than advancing a singular ideology, in other words, were integral to democratic consensus building in a diverse country like America. "The old parties brought leaders of major policy demanders into a big room and gave them the incentives and the institutional means to find common ground." Most of this deliberative decision making, furthermore, took place at the state and local level, where everyday citizens had greater access and influence. It seems odd to us now, but political parties were once a source of unity, rather than division. Indeed, Rossiter and others have argued that the collapse of the Whig Party, which might otherwise have achieved compromise, was one of the precipitating events of the American Civil War. Rossiter lauded the political culture that evolved in the aftermath of that tragedy, in which "the parties have been the peacemakers of the American community, the unwitting but forceful suppressors of the 'civil-war potential' we carry always in the bowels of our diverse nation."

It's hard, from our contemporary vantage point, to understand how anyone could consider America's two major political parties to be sources of stability and cooperation, given how they appear hell-bent on destroying one another now. The truth is they no longer resemble the parties of Rossiter's day. "The trouble began," congressional scholar Nelson Polsby quipped, "when we political scientists finally got our wish: 'responsible' political parties instead of broad, nonideological coalitions. The idea was, of course, completely nuts from the start."

A HIDDEN IDEOLOGY

Nuts or not, the 1950 APSA report gained little immediate traction. A few Democratic Party leaders did take notice, however, since it aligned with their own frustrations. They began politicking to develop intraparty consensus around a bold set of policy prescriptions that would be aggressive on social spending, and tackle the deplorable state of African-American civil rights in the south. They aimed to drive segregationist Democrats from their ranks and offer Americans a clear choice between moral principles. What they didn't comprehend was a reality grasped by politicians who had spent far more time around everyday American voters, which was that overtly ideological agendas did not sell well to regular people. Lyndon Johnson, canny Texas politician that he was, understood that "what the man on the street wants is not a big debate on fundamental issues; he wants a little medical care, a rug on the floor, a picture on the wall."

Rather than make the Democratic Party more openly ideological, Johnson preferred the opposite tack, positioning his Great Society as a widely supported dose of American common sense. He aptly noted that Republicans who might otherwise support his agenda would certainly never do so once they perceived it to be part of an orchestrated effort to get Democrats elected. Johnson muffled, therefore, idealists who wanted to enforce more left-leaning dogma throughout the Democratic Party. He also labored "obsessively to maximize the margin of victory as a way of securing a cross-party veneer and a seemingly universal support base for his policies," wrote Sam Rosenfeld in *The Polarizers: Postwar Architects of Our Partisan Era*, and to enlist support from all socioeconomic sectors "in a tableau of establishment consensus on behalf of an activist liberal state."

Johnson wanted consensus for his "activist liberal state," the particulars of which entailed a government with powers concentrated in Washington, DC. Massive new social programs, addressing racial strife, and escalating a Vietnam War inherited from Kennedy all entailed widescale federal power. Viewed from this vantage point, it was clear that Johnson was indeed peddling an ideology, as had Kennedy before him, alongside nearly every president stretching back to Wilson. Their ideology was revealed in the imperative—that underscored the New Deal, the Fair Deal, the New Frontier, the Great Society, and every other initiative presidential speechwriters chose to Capitalize for Added Effect— of expanding national power to fine-tune the economy, pursue egalitarianism, and promote American-style democracy around the globe. Many in the political class didn't think of this transformation from the original American vision as ideology, however. To them, it was merely a reflection of the emerging truth that, in the words of Dwight Eisenhower: "Government is a friend."

This was, and remains, the heart of the matter. It was the reason, even as liberals searched for means to circumvent the Constitution, that disparate bands of free marketeers, anti-communists, and traditionalists began fusing into a conservative movement seeking the very same clarification of ideological choices sought by their opponents, albeit for very different purposes. Eisenhower was, to them, Tweedledum on the Tweedledee-heels of Roosevelt and Truman, proof that Republican party leaders had no stomach for overturning, in the words of conservative theorist Frank Meyer, "collectivism at home, camouflaged as humanitarianism," and "appeasement abroad, camouflaged as containment." The transmogrification of the 1952 fire-and-brimstone Republican platform into a kinder, gentler statement in advance of Eisenhower's reelection bid, boasting that millions more Americans had been added to union rolls and federal-support programs, touting the creation of the first new federal agency in forty years, and calling for an equal-rights amendment to the Constitution, only served to confirm conservative convictions that Republicans had become the "me-too" party. Meyer, like his liberal counterparts, suggested "a new alignment of parties, giving the voters in 1956 at last a real choice of the kind they have not had for many years."

Contra Eisenhower, Kennedy, and Johnson, conservatives

believed not that America's parties had transcended ideology in commonsense service to the common good, but that they had been captured by a singular worldview which ruled out discussion of fundamental matters like rights, the pursuit of equality, and the role of the state because these were, as the conservative theorist Willmoore Kendall observed, "issues about which, nowadays, reasonable men could not possibly disagree." Kendall described this seeming intellectual hegemony as "an elaborate pretense" which enabled well-meaning policymakers to believe that "the Conservative position has to be ignored, has to be treated as nonexistent, because to treat it otherwise would, for them, itself be intellectually dishonest, itself be a conspiracy against the public good." The only way to break free from this Establishment groupthink, reasoned conservative intellectuals, was the same medicine sought by far-left liberals: party polarization that yielded distinct alternatives to voters.

A NOTE ON POLARIZATION

Let me set the record straight about political polarization, which is fundamentally—sometimes intentionally—misunderstood in current discourse. Polarization refers to the separation of ideologues or partisans along one of those scales in which most Americans aren't overly invested, but which matter a great deal to Americans who are very politically engaged, and matter even more to our political class. Increasingly, the ideology and partisanship scales in America have fused into one, with Democrats and liberals becoming virtually synonymous since the 1990s, and likewise for conservatives and Republicans. Not only are these groups clustering more predictably at the left and right poles of the ideology/partisan spectra, members of the political class are moving them farther apart from each other.

The angst both liberals and conservatives felt in the 1950s, as they pondered those hypothetical scales, was that Establishment politicians in both parties were clustering in the wrong place. Liberals wanted Democrats to slough off conservative party members and shift leftward. Conservatives, on the other hand, believed both parties had been drifting left for some time, all the while pretending to represent the interests of everyday Americans. They, therefore, sought to establish a cohesive program that would draw people rightward.

As a consequence, liberals and conservatives began working in the 1950s to polarize political parties and, they hoped, voters. And they were successful; the ranks of partisans are now as far apart as they've been at any time since the Civil War. While much of this book describes the harmful consequences of polarization as a deliberate manipulation deployed by our self-serving political class, Willmoore Kendall's observation above nevertheless illuminates an important point that is easily lost when every commentator from Ezra Klein to David French characterizes polarization as inherently destructive: *sometimes the absence of polarization is even worse.*

Think about it: who wants their potential leaders to be drawn solely from Stalin's Politburo, or the Chinese Communist Party, or the editorial board of *Teen Vogue*? As General George S. Patton reportedly said: "If everybody is thinking alike, then somebody isn't thinking." Polarization, it follows, can sharpen the mind and invigorate the body politic. Political theorists, while not too keen on General Patton, have long recognized the valuable service a "loyal opposition" can provide. Opposition can only exist where there's polarization, and since opposition is a valuable means of keeping political rulers in check, polarization must therefore be valuable, too.

What's essential to make polarization beneficial rather than destructive, however, is the modifier in "loyal opposition." In the American system, this entails loyalty to the Constitution and the people. Indeed, such patriotic loyalty may even *demand* polarization. Hank Morgan, Mark Twain's protagonist in *A Connecticut Yankee in King Arthur's Court*, explains it like this:

> You see my kind of loyalty was loyalty to one's country, not to its institutions or its office-holders. [. . .] I was from Connecticut, whose Constitution declares 'that all political power is inherent in the people, and all free governments are founded on their authority and instituted for their benefit; and that they have at all times an undeniable and indefeasible right to alter their form of government in such a manner as they may think expedient.' Under that gospel, the citizen who thinks he sees that the commonwealth's political clothes are worn out, and yet holds his peace and does not agitate for a new suit, is disloyal; he is a traitor.

If we believe political actors have bad ideas or poor intentions, in other words, loyalty to the Constitution and our country demands we say so, in clear and direct language. What we have to say about the negative effects of our opponents' positions may be harsh, and certainly not to their liking, but it's entirely possible to stake out a polar-opposite position without demonizing the other side. One might even say that the more compelling your argument, the less you need dwell on your opponent at all.

It should be clear by now that polarization is not what's pulling America apart at the seams. What threatens to destroy us, rather, is the fact that so many members of our political class who engage in polarization as profession and sport long ago abandoned any pretense of fidelity to truth, the Constitution, and we citizens, who are the beneficiaries and guardians of that Constitution. Worse still is how the political class not only behaves disloyally, but encourages us to do the same. It strives to elicit the worst in us, because our animosity is its gain.

Perhaps in these acrimonious times it's hard for some readers to imagine how polarization can be anything but ugly, but we have to set aside the notion that the way to national healing is to disagree less. The way forward, rather, *is to disagree better.*

I gather with a group of men once a month to talk about ideas, books, and notable figures from our shared faith, which is Christianity. We're an ecumenical group—Baptists, Presbyterians, Anglicans, Catholics, Eastern Orthodox, and nondenominationals—and we're politically diverse as well. A couple of our number are libertarian, another is an avowed socialist. Some of us are unashamed Trump supporters, others have despised him since *Home Alone 2.* Unlike most Americans, we tend to be more politically engaged, and ideologically aware. We are, in fact, quite polarized.

And yet, we get along fine. Better than fine, in fact; we enjoy one another's company. Do we argue? Of course. Do tempers flare? On occasion. But what binds us is far more important than what separates us. Sometimes we are loyal allies, other times we are loyal opponents. What doesn't change is the *loyalty.* It doesn't mean we let each other get away with nonsensical arguments; in fact, it means the opposite. But it also means that we really, truly listen to the guys we disagree with, because they are worth it to us. Listening to them is worthwhile.

This is what's missing among too many of our country's partisans and political elites. Not loyalty to a government or a party, but loyalty to their fellow citizens. They stopped listening a long time ago.

We've come to think polarization necessitates animosity, but it doesn't have to. Disagreement is a much-needed strength in a community, but only if it's rooted in love and humility. A love for our country, our Constitution, our neighbor. The humility to keep in mind all of the times we've been wrong, all the times we have learned from someone we assumed had nothing to teach us. At the end of this book, I'll offer some ideas for what you and I can do to retake our country from the political class, but here's an idea we can all work on right now, today: love your neighbor more, and your pride less.

6

THE MONSTER COMES TO LIFE

"Accursed creator! Why did you form a monster so hideous that even
you turned from me in disgust?"

—Mary Shelley, *Frankenstein*

THE WAR AGAINST THE ESTABLISHMENT

Though they had what they believed to be valid reasons, the
orchestrators of American polarization unleashed a destructive
force upon our republic. With intentions likely closer to "loyal
opposition" than not, conservatives and left-liberals in the 1960s
began pressing harder on the parties in an effort to polarize them.
In his book *Why Americans Hate Politics*, E.J. Dionne described
the similarity in their efforts:

> In retrospect, it is striking that the New Left and the rising right
> saw the enemy in almost exactly the same terms. The New Left
> despised 'Establishment liberals.' The right hated 'the liberal
> Establishment.' Yet the slight difference in labeling also revealed
> much—each group put the most important word first. What the
> New Left disliked about liberals was that they represented the
> *Establishment*; what the right disliked about the Establishment
> was that it was *liberal*.

Liberals believed a more leftist platform could maintain the
dominance the Democratic Party had enjoyed since Roosevelt's

time, while dramatically expanding federal authority. Conservatives believed Americans needed to be awakened to the reality that their country was being stolen out from under them. The first camp wanted to usher Big(ger) Government ("Government is your friend!") through the door; the second wanted citizens to know Big Brother was already at the supper table. Both camps believed a majority of voters would support them if offered candidates who were untainted by compromise.

Powered by superior energy, organization, and a growing web of associated interest groups, both camps would soon seize opportunities to do just that. Over a span of eight years, activists in both major parties managed to field an ideologically distinct candidate in a presidential election. And in both cases, those candidates were thrashed by the largest electoral vote margins since Franklin Roosevelt ran Alf Landon out of politics for good in 1936.

Conservatives went first, ushering Barry Goldwater through a byzantine party nomination process to the great surprise of the Republican old guard in 1964. Goldwater, who despised racism but believed states' rights should be respected, who was personally generous but believed social welfare destroyed families, and who advocated vigorous confrontation with the Soviet regime wherever its rulers attempted to wield influence, electrified activists on the Right. Here was a Republican who didn't apologize for being conservative, or try to change the subject to what he agreed about with liberals.

Johnson's people made mincemeat of him. The chief message of the Johnson campaign could be summarized in the most infamous political advertisement ever made: the Daisy Ad, which featured a little girl standing in a field, plucking petals from a daisy, as a rocket launch counted down in the background, culminating in footage of an atom-bomb explosion. "The message," according to political historian Robert Mann, "was clear if only implicit: presidential candidate Barry Goldwater was a genocidal maniac who threatened the world's future." This was the harbinger, wrote Mann in *Smithsonian* magazine, of emotion-laden, negative political advertising in place of thirty-second candidate speeches about their qualifications. "Voters don't oppose a candidate because they dislike his or her policies; they often oppose the policies because they dislike the candidate." Campaign managers took that lesson to heart.

Left-wing activists, meanwhile, got their opportunity to field an ideologically distinct candidate not long after, in the person of George McGovern. A principal leader (and beneficiary) of reforms that radically undercut party insider control over the Democratic presidential nomination process, McGovern not only intended to end the Vietnam War and give blanket amnesties to draft dodgers, he wanted to cut US military spending by more than a third. His own vice-presidential running mate secretly tagged him with a slogan Republicans would use to great effect: that he was the candidate of "Acid, Amnesty, and Abortion." It wasn't entirely fair; McGovern favored abortion rights, for example, but wanted to leave the matter up to state law, which would place him—as would some of his other policy preferences—firmly to the right of most Democrats today. In 1972, however, McGovern's positions were decidedly to the left of most presidential candidates up until that time.

Like Barry Goldwater before him, George McGovern was crushed at the voting booth. You'd think these experiences might have quashed any further activist talk about moving the parties to more extreme points on the ideological scale, but both camps were undeterred. The McGovern-Fraser Commission reforms, enacted by Democrats but which spread to the Republican Party by dint of state election law changes, had had the effect, as reform author James O'Hara noted, of creating "a system that was open to capture by an aroused minority." Data over subsequent decades reveal that the activists who work in and support state political parties are most divergent from the beliefs of regular voters in states that most thoroughly embraced McGovern-Fraser reforms. "We can see in the differential application of state party reforms," wrote political scientists Byron Shafer and Regina Wagner in *The Long War over Party Structure*, "that the states that went furthest in the direction of muting local party officials and opening the door to activists evidenced greater polarization not just between parties, but between party activists and their own rank and file."

The effort to sweep aside Establishment players was not confined to party activists. Following landslide Republican midterm losses in the wake of Watergate, these efforts spilled over into reforms of Congress. Democrats took away committee chairmanships from opponents of civil-rights legislation, and forced powerful committee chairs to more equitably share subcommittee control. Long-time congressional insider John Lawrence wrote in *Politico* that the new members "wanted to send a clear signal to voters back home that they had not simply become a part of the congressional muddle they had been elected to purify."

These congressional reformers quickly fell in with liberal stalwarts from the party-reform movement. They came to believe the ongoing battle to transform the Democratic Party required a similar transformation of congressional processes. "It is not coincidental," wrote Sam Rosenfeld in *The Polarizers*, "that a transformative period of reform in Congress took place alongside the McGovern-Fraser reforms. The two movements shared key personnel, motivations, and theoretical premises about the function of parties."

Capitalizing on their numbers and momentum, and eager to show voters stark differences between themselves and both

Republicans and hidebound southern Democrats, the new congressional majority made a decision that would reward, in the words of long-serving Senator Carl Hayden from Arizona, "show horses" rather than "work horses." It's fitting, then, that young congressman Albert Gore, Jr. ushered in the new age of televised congressional proceedings, promising:

> Television will change this institution, Mr. Speaker, just as it has changed the executive branch. But the good will far outweigh the bad. From this day forward, every member of this body must ask himself or herself: 'How many Americans are listening to the debates which are made?' [...] The marriage of this medium and our open debate, has the potential, Mr. Speaker, to revitalize representative democracy.

Congressman Gore offered his prognostication about the fruitful marriage of television and congressional debate as the Speaker gaveled him for exceeding his time limit. Here was another harbinger, perhaps, of things to come. It was certainly the case that members of Congress would begin to ask themselves, as Gore predicted, who was listening. And more than ever before, they would be tempted to ask further: *What do they want to hear?* Senator Jesse Helms predicted the outcome in 1974:

> "It is not difficult to envision Members scrambling to the floor to get before cameras in order to impress the voters back home instead of persuading other Members, producing much oration and little debate. What is more, oratory would become the chief, if not the only, criterion of legislative ability, to the disadvantage of those members who contribute their valuable skills and knowledge in countless other ways. Not every member of Congress wishes to strut upon the stage of public acclaim."

Coinciding with this reform that would turn every moment at the microphone into a potential news or fundraising clip, was the penchant among new congressmen to cast their agenda in the language of *rights* rather than priorities and tradeoffs. Congressional veteran John Lawrence described the effect as follows:

> These new legislators articulated their agenda not merely as policy objectives but as constitutional and ethical "rights" with a profoundly moral dimension: a *right* to an abortion, a *right* to clean water and air, a *right* to consumer safety. Elevating policy goals to the status of rights would prove to be a crucial step in the evolution of ideological partisanship in the United States. The application of such a moral dimension to the framing of public issues served to diminish the attractiveness of compromise in pursuit of a common objective.

Lawrence noted that compromise was particularly frowned upon by proliferating "interest groups that rated, financed and provided grass-roots supporters for their campaigns." All this rights-language wouldn't remain limited to idealistic Watergate babies, either. As Lawrence noted, the practice "increasingly appeared among conservatives as well: a *right* to gun ownership, a *right* to life for unborn fetuses, a *right* to lower taxes, a *right* to less government, a *right* to freedom from government regulation."

Members of Congress sorting themselves into ideological camps, performing in front of television cameras, and discovering that casting policy differences in moral terms gave them a rhetorical edge, easily fell into a pattern of escalating partisanship. Even when the "work horses" met behind the scenes to negotiate trade-offs that might enable legislation to move forward, they had to worry about ambitious "show horses" framing their labors as back-room dealing that undercut partisan principles (which, of course, it always had been). Partisans on both sides became adept at amendments that forced opponents to make controversial votes on topics like abortion and flag burning that could later be used against them in elections. "When we had committee meetings," reminisced former Republican Minority Leader Bob Michel of Illinois, "we'd sit at long tables, the majority and minority across from one another, and so we'd have to talk and work things out. Now they have these long daises, with the majority on one side and the minority way over on the other, and no one gets to know one another."

The small increments of time traditionally reserved for members to read statements into the congressional record honoring constituents for various accomplishments, meanwhile, became staged mini-dramas, in which media-savvy members could lambast the other side for its venality and treachery. Journalist Joe Klein recounted in the *New Yorker* the moment in 1984 when Democrat Speaker of the House of Representatives Tip O'Neill, infuriated that a Georgia upstart named Newt Gingrich had challenged several House members by name during a late-night televised speech which cameras did not reveal was to an empty chamber, came down to the floor to confront him. "You deliberately stood in that well before an empty House," O'Neill thundered, "and challenged these people, you challenged their Americanism, and it's the lowest thing that I've ever seen in my 32 years in Congress!" Gingrich's congressional ally Vin Weber from Minnesota reflected on that event to Klein:

> The Democrats were arrogant to the point of corruption, and Newt's idea was to expose the arrogance and corruption for what it was. It was guerrilla war, and I don't think we could have won the House in 1994 without those sorts of tactics. But the victory

came at a price, and the price was a loss of civility. And we are paying for it now.

Gingrich himself, though nowhere near as recalcitrant as Weber, likewise portrayed his party's position as a bind that only polarization could cut through. "If voters see a race as a nice-guy Republican against a nice-guy Democrat," he told journalist E.J. Dionne, "we lose."

DESTROYING DEMOCRACY TO SAVE IT

Along with amplification of the most strident voices came centralization of the very power reformers had set out to redistribute. While reformers had intended to democratize congressional processes through greater transparency and access, they effectively wrested power from the old guard and placed it in the grip of even more intransigent partisans. Congressional Democrats had certainly broken the monopoly of powerful committee chairs, but they simultaneously centralized authority over committee assignments and the flow of legislation in the hands of the Speaker—a move that paid dividends for Democrats under first Tip O'Neill and then Jim Wright, but gave the same upper hand to Republicans once Newt Gingrich was at the helm.[†] Congressional leaders further centralized power by tripling their own staffs while slashing committee and individual staffs in the House, and trimming them in the Senate. Both parties fell into a pattern that can be seen today, wherein the minority decries the dictatorial rule of the majority, then

---

† The danger of centralizing power, of course, is that it tends to fall into the hands of the people most interested in having power, who are almost always the last people we want to have it. This is something the Founders easily understood, but which successive waves of Congressional leaders, preoccupied with shaving away checks and balances in order to eke out narrow policy victories, seem intent on ignoring.

immediately sets about deploying the same uncompromising tactics when it retakes the reins.

Despite the appearance of more democratic nomination processes, meanwhile, both Democratic and Republican party insiders, having run off local politicians, consolidated their control via mechanisms like "money primaries," wherein potential presidential candidates proved their ability to attract top fundraisers and donors, and built intraparty support by distributing the resulting lucre. While decades of reform were supposed to have made the parties more accountable to voters, exhaustive analysis of the factors affecting presidential nominations between 1980 and 2004 found that endorsements by powerful party players remained the key determinant of a candidate's success in what's widely known as the "invisible primary."

The slate of candidates presented to voters in primary elections today, in other words, appears to be nearly as well-orchestrated by the political class—albeit with more competition and jostling between a larger array of them—as the rosters of old. As the icing on the cake, the Commission on Presidential Debates ensures that nobody who wants to play outside the two parties' system has a chance of appearing on a national debate stage.

Having set out with the idealistic-sounding intention of making American political parties and Congress more accountable to a broader array of citizens, reformers in both parties accomplished something quite different. Political scientist Seth Masket describes how the displacement of traditional local party machines by "informal party organizations" (IPOs) shifted power from local leaders to ideologues: "Machines distrusted ideologues; IPOs rely on them. The result is extreme candidates and highly polarized politics." Reformers didn't make the two major parties more representative of *broader* interests, they made them more responsive to *activist* interests. Democrats embraced feminists and white-collar racial minorities, but demoted pro-lifers, soldiers, and most important for their future, the working class. "These zealots," observed Al Barkan, executive director of the AFL-CIO's Committee on Political Education, "were running off on their own crusade, and they weren't much concerned about what would happen to the American working man in the process." The Democrats' old governing coalition, party-reform historian Byron Shafer observes, "was based in blue-collar constituencies, while the newer version was white-collar from top to bottom." Republicans, meanwhile, welcomed social conservatives into the fold, but turned a deaf ear to environmentalists, minorities, and millions in manufacturing jobs imperiled by free-trade absolutism. Both parties appeared to abandon rural America except as a locale for campaign photo shoots.

Worse still, they destroyed the "cross-cutting cleavages" which once dampened partisan conflict, and this in turn enabled them to drive their parties farther and farther apart ideologically. In 1980, you might have been able to infer quite a bit about someone by learning he was a strong Republican or Democrat. You could have predicted with some accuracy that he was for or against higher corporate taxes, or more military spending, or more protections and financial support for minorities. He would not have been nearly as predictable as his counterpart today, however. There used to be many more Republicans who prioritized environmental protections, for example, and Democrats who believed in gun rights. If you meet a strong Democrat or Republican today, in addition to being highly confident that he is in lockstep with his party leaders on every position—even positions that are the opposite of what they had advocated a few years ago—you can be certain he harbors much more animosity toward the other party than his predecessors did. What he sees on the other side, unlike his counterparts of old, are people who oppose every solution he believes will make America better. It becomes easy, in such a world, to conclude one's political opponents must be stupid and evil. How else could they be wrong about *everything*?

Opponents of the 1950's project to infuse ideology into party politics warned about all of this, but the temptation for party ideologues was too strong. The political scientists' Frankenstein monster is now rampaging through our communities, only unlike Mary Shelley's fictional monster, this one induces us to destroy ourselves.

Not only did the political class turn partisans into bitter enemies, they concentrated the stakes by relentlessly nationalizing our parties and politics. Local party leaders, their influence over presidential nomination processes all but eliminated, were displaced by independently organized political candidate operations, and made subservient to national headquarters that were better organized, staffed, and funded. "Like other political groups," wrote political scientist Daniel Hopkins in *The Increasingly United States: How and Why American Political Behavior Nationalized*, "the two major political parties were transitioning from organizations with large memberships and physical presences in many communities to professionalized organizations located primarily in Washington, DC."

Local public officials and locally-minded congressmen, who felt a responsibility to represent their constituents' parochial interests, were displaced by movement-minded politicians who built volunteer and donor bases of partisans. Party leaders and their allies likewise focused on national political strategies that pleased their activists and donors.[†] Sam Rosenfeld summarized the consequences of party nationalization and ideological sorting

---

[†] Ironically, the focus on national policy and conflict has ultimately made our political system *less* capable of fixing long-term national problems, from health care to the costs of education.

as follows: "Organizations that were once deeply and tangibly rooted in ordinary people's lives, even as their ideological content was fuzzy to the point of irrelevance, now exist for most Americans as abstract ideological designations and vehicles of collective antipathy."

The nationalization of power—a continuation of New Deal thinking—necessarily meant the further destruction of citizen self-governance. Political elites already operated as if ignorant of the American Founders' ethos. The authors of "Towards a More Responsible Two-Party System" likewise seemed to have no awareness of how deeply the role of American citizenship had been altered over their lifetimes when they wrote: "For the great majority of Americans, the most valuable opportunity to influence the course of public affairs is the choice they are able to make between the parties in the principal elections." A real reform effort would have been to set about rectifying that, by returning to states and communities the power they'd once had. But the reformers believed it was the job of the political class in Washington, DC, to rule the country. The role of citizens was to show up every few years to select their masters.

Little surprise, then, that reforms enacted in the name of access, transparency, and democracy yielded a system in service to the political class. Sam Rosenfeld summed up the result:

> It was the work of ideologically driven activists, factional fighters, and strategic party elites to make such linkages between parties and issues possible. And it was the further work of many of these same actors to reform the parties as institutions to render them more permeable by, and accountable to, issue- and ideology-driven activists like themselves. [...] These were the men and women [...] who worked over the course of decades to remake the parties in their image, and ultimately succeeded."

This ideology of nationalized politics and control was what bound liberal reformers to the Wilsonian reformers who had preceded them. Both groups believed that the future of America was control from Washington. The states, in this viewing, were merely organizing vehicles for unified national agendas. Insofar as their leaders represented local interests, therefore, they were obstacles. "The national and state party organizations," wrote the authors of the 1950 APSA report with disapproval, "are largely independent of one another, each operating within its own sphere." That is, of course, literally the purpose of federalism, but as we've already seen, reformers had no use for that antiquated concept. Federalism impeded progress, so federalism would have to go.

All the foregoing yielded the final, essential spark that gave the political scientists' mad creation life: though they had set out to replace blind party loyalty with distinctive principles, the reformers instead married ideology to parties, leaving both the worse for it. Ideology became malleable in service to partisan victory, and partisanship became more venomous with the transmogrification of policy disputes into disputes over values. The consequence of all this were political battles "colored by a slash-and-burn, polarizing style of attack," wrote Sam Rosenfeld, "precisely *because* the binary lines of ideological conflict would align so closely with the partisan lines of campaigns." The political scientists' Frankenstein monster was loosed among our villages.

The unholy fusion of party and ideology in the chest of the political scientists' Frankenstein monster, roaming across a political terrain that rewarded individual ideologues and discouraged compromise, helps explain why members of the political class became polarized, and beyond that, came to despise each other. But it took more to draw everyday Americans, even that roughly one-fifth who are committed partisans, into the hate cycle. Political scientists—of the applied sort this time, rather than theorists—once again figured prominently.

7

THE AMERICAN PANOPTICON

"We are neither in the amphitheatre, nor on the stage, but in the panoptic machine, invested by its effects of power, which we bring to ourselves since we are part of its mechanism."
—Michel Foucault, *Discipline and Punish*

WAG THE DOG

Des Moines, IA, 1987
It was early evening on October 27 and fifty undecided, registered Iowa voters sat in a hotel conference room, each holding a device that looked like an old-school thermostat with a knob at its center. They were being paid $25 apiece (nearly $60 in 2021 dollars) to watch a debate between six contenders for the Republican presidential nomination. The frontrunner and putative heir to Ronald Reagan's legacy, Vice President George H.W. Bush, had rolled into his adopted Texas hometown voicing complaints about what he considered misleading ads by two opponents, Pat Robertson and Jack Kemp. Fed up with Bush's complaints against him, Robertson had labeled Bush a "whiny loser."

The Iowa observers had been hired by Columbia Information Systems, Inc., (CIS), which had received $9,000 from Vice President Bush's campaign staff for this session. The company was conducting similar research for Bush's people in Atlanta and Portland, OR. The participants were instructed to turn their dials to the left when they heard things they disliked, and to the right when they heard things they did like. The further they turned their dials, the more they liked or disliked what they heard. Wires ran to a computer in the corner that captured their reactions to produce graphs which looked like EKGs. Analysts later ran those graphs alongside a tape of the debate to isolate how various members—be they young or old, male or female, Democrat, Republican, or Independent—responded to every particular part of the statements made by each candidate.

Over the course of the night, the viewers in this Iowa hotel room turned their dials to the left when Alexander Haig and Pete duPont attempted to boost their failing appeal by harshly criticizing frontrunner Bush. Then, they turned their dials hard to the right when Bush, asked by a moderator to detail which of President Reagan's positions he disagreed with while serving alongside him, declined to do so, declaring: "In our family, loyalty is a strength, not a character flaw." Cheers from the crowd in attendance corroborated the electronic readouts examined by CIS technicians at the debate's end.

Political campaigns weren't the first to use response-tracking devices to capture people's opinions; television stations, Hollywood movie production companies, and even WWII propaganda filmmakers had deployed similar devices to document viewers' responses. Perhaps because of the fluidity of their principles, however, and their incentive to obscure rather than clarify their positions on issues, it was politicians who would have special use for these tools, and in particular their potential to identify exactly what voters wanted to hear. "It's like an X-ray," said pollster Frank Luntz, "of someone's thought process."

Word about this new technology spread rapidly through the community of political insiders, and opinions varied widely. Some considered it a means of helping candidates understand more fully what the people wanted, enabling them to be more responsive to the interests of their constituents. Others viewed it as the harbinger of dystopia, a new era of techno-manipulation and mind control that would eviscerate the American polity. "It's a prime illustration," said Duke University political science professor James David Barber, "of the deterioration of political discourse in this country, the substitution of sentiment for reason."

Interest ran high, however, among political operatives who cared first and foremost about winning. Within years, every major campaign was dial-testing messages to see what resonated with voters. Firms like CIS raked in millions, drawing competitors with similar technologies. Veteran campaigners like Roger Ailes, on the other hand, turned up their noses. "I still don't know how the graph works and I don't care," he said. "I don't paint by numbers."

Ailes had a point. The Perception Analyzer Dial couldn't tell politicians what to say, only what resonated with particular audiences after it had been said. Politicians with a keen ear and eye already had this ability, though not always to their benefit, as Democratic presidential contender Joe Biden had learned just several weeks earlier. After giving a speech at the Iowa State Fair during which he not only plagiarized a speech by British Labour Party leader Neil Kinnock, but went so far as to mimic Kinnock's mannerisms, Biden was outed by the *Washington Post,* effectively ending his campaign.

Nor could this new technology be a substitute for political instinct, as was illustrated during the Houston debate, when George Bush addressed duPont as "Pierre," knowing full well his opponent had worked for years to make voters forget his given name, dripping as it did with snooty privilege, in favor of the folksy, fabricated nickname "Pete." Likewise it was pure instinct, charisma, and a summertime unemployment peak of 7.8 percent—not dial-testing—that fueled Arkansas governor Bill

Clinton's victory over George H.W. Bush four years later. By the same token, dial responses during the Houston debate presaged, by virtue of the flat-line response every time Bob Dole opened his mouth, Clinton's eventual trouncing of Dole by 220 electoral votes in the 1996 presidential race.

While dial-testing couldn't fashion an effective politician out of a brick, it would prove to be one more edge in a campaigner's arsenal. It was the reason Bill Clinton began to insert, for example, the word "responsibility" into his public remarks, burnishing his credentials as a centrist. Clinton's nemesis, Newt Gingrich, used similar technology to develop a list of words Republicans could use to make their positions sound appealing, and to demonize their enemies. "We have heard," read a memo released by the political-training organization GOPAC to its members in advance of the 1990 midterm elections, "a plaintive plea: 'I wish I could speak like Newt.' That takes years of practice." In lieu of 10,000 hours honing a Newt-like vernacular, the memo advised Republicans to give "extra power to your message" by using words like: *prosperity, moral, precious, children,* and *tough.*

Rhetorical fine-tuning aside, the Perception Analyzer Dial and similar technologies became the vanguard of sophisticated methods for probing voters' minds and manipulating their emotions. If those new technologies had been used simply to mask politicians' true intentions behind words that were palatable to voters, they would have been bad enough. But the real damage, which few foresaw as analysts pored over data from the Houston debate, began when an array of campaign tools was deployed to destroy political opponents, make compromise a death sentence for aspiring politicians, and turn Americans against one another. "Often we search hard for words," continued that GOPAC memo, "to define our opponents. Sometimes we are hesitant to use contrast. Remember that creating a difference helps you." What were some of the "contrasting" words the memo recommended candidates apply to their opponents? *Sick, pathetic, lie, traitors, disgrace, steal,* and *bizarre.*

AMERICAN PANOPTICON

The Perception Analyzer Dial and other tools to isolate emotion-triggering words were creepy and cynical at the time, but now they're quaint. Today's political campaigns employ psychologists skilled at preying on human fear and frailty. They hire data analysts to sort through detailed information about you and me—not just people like us, but *us specifically.* "The hyper-targeting of users," wrote *Atlantic* editor Adrienne LaFrance of Facebook, "made possible by reams of their personal data, creates the perfect environment for manipulation—by advertisers, by political campaigns, by emissaries of disinformation, and of course by Facebook itself, which ultimately controls what you see and what you don't see on the site."

Thanks to profit-oriented customer tracking and data mining by corporations like Facebook, Google, and their ilk, every political candidate interested in your vote—or in convincing you that your cause is hopeless and you should stay home on election day—knows not just your political party registration, but the value of your home, what products you buy, where your children go to school, what videos you watch, what ads you click, who your friends are, where you've worked, what legal troubles you've had, whether you buy birth control, how much debt you carry, and a host of other intimate details.

Not only that, political operatives can grab your phone's identifying code when they see you in locations of interest. If you've attended a political rally, a gun show, even a large church, they can reach you with messages designed to influence your thinking. Thanks to their psy-ops experts, they know exactly what mind-worms to deploy, often while disguising the fact that what they're showing you is, for all practical purposes, a political advertisement.

If political ads, texts, and pop-up propaganda videos were slung at us without augmentation, their effect might remain muted. Americans are accustomed to full sensory assault from Madison Avenue necromancers trying to manipulate our choice of everything from car insurance to breakfast cereal. We're used to being sold things; it's the American way. And being freedom-loving consumers, we aren't *forced* to buy anything, or to like pizza when we really prefer eggplant. Companies offer us goods in exchange for cash (or debt), television stations offer us entertainment in exchange for our attention to those companies' advertisements, and politicians offer us promises in return for votes. Sure, advertisers can create an itch for a new SUV, or a Sunday night football game, but we know the risks when we look at our TVs and computers and smartphones. As Robert Orben, the comedian, magician, and speechwriter for Gerald R. Ford liked to say: "Most people want to be delivered from temptation, but would like it to keep in touch." Maybe that's all most advertising is: a mild temptation, occasionally entertaining, often irritating.

But what happens when we no longer realize we're being sold something? And when the sellers aren't slick-suited, business-school marketing guys, but our friends, co-workers, family, and all the people connected to them? As the internet has radically increased communication points between people, everyone from copywriters at innocuous-sounding nonprofits to our own social media "friends" has received a window on our thoughts, and we on theirs. Those among us who are most interested in politics offer one another ideas, convictions, and outrages. Some within this subgroup become—in some cases wittingly, but more often unwittingly—aiders and abettors of efforts by the political class to extend its ideological combat into our communities. The engineering that undergirds social media platforms is optimized for that purpose. New technology has not only given the political class powerful tools of manipulation, it has yielded something far worse: self-fueling animosity machines. And we are the fuel.

NOT SO BRAVE, NOT SO NEW

Technology enthusiasts might be forgiven for not seeing what was coming as the World Wide Web extended its strands. There was reason for optimism as the internet steadily brought every major reputable news source and research institution online, enabling them to make facts and findings accessible to potential audiences that were orders of magnitude larger than before. Likewise for the considered opinions of tens of thousands of individual experts in every manner of science, economics, and data analysis, all of them available via websites, blogs, and, in more recent years, social media streams. Thousands of lectures by the world's foremost authorities became available to anyone with electricity and a modem. Datasets on everything countable. Art, film, literature—more and more of it attainable regardless of one's pedigree or formal association with an institution of higher learning.

If an optimist in 1980 had predicted that within twenty years nearly everyone in America would have instantaneous access to the unfiltered opinions and analysis of thousands of experts, all of them subject to public critique and fact-correction by competing peers, searchable by topic, and delivered straight to everyone's phone, she might have been forgiven for assuming that this would yield an increase in the average citizen's command of the facts, and a precipitous decline in the traction attainable by rumors, gossip, and "fake news." She might have assumed a new era of enlightenment was dawning. Wisdom, tolerance, and understanding would finally reign from coast to coast.

More pessimistic observers of human nature (we prefer the term "realists") could have predicted what happened instead. A proliferation of media choices emerged, first in the form of cable TV, next the internet, and then social media—each more capable of being tailored to individual predilections and convictions than the one before—that enabled users to fine-tune not just their news consumption, but their entertainment and even friendships (or, "friendships") to suit their political, religious, and social leanings.

Unsurprisingly, it's the strongest partisans on the Left and Right who've ended up with the most politically homogenous social networks. They gravitate to people who think like them. This needn't be intentional; social-media algorithms are designed to identify what we like and where it comes from, and to offer us more of the same. You needn't close your mind on purpose, the algorithm will do it for you. The people really into politics are the ones clicking politics-related material, and thereby having their newsfeeds fine-tailored, yielding more content that confirms what they believe to be the pertinent facts, and more revelations about the nastiness of their opponents. In that kind of set-up, groupthink is the default. It's cultivating diverse inputs that takes intentionality. To do that, however, we have to be aware of what the algorithm is up to before it sucks us in.

A theme in this book is *unwitting conspiracy*, which arises as individuals in the political class pursue their self-interest within the context of the incentives and technologies that dominate their world, collectively behaving as if they've conspired to spark civil war and destroy American self-governance. The outcome is just as bad as a real conspiracy, it just doesn't make as compelling a screenplay.† Another theme is the *nationalization* of American attention, so that our minds and hearts are drawn away from our communities towards the DC national stage instead, reducing our citizenship role to that of *spectator, voter, meme-spreader, couch potato.*

The algorithms driving social media and entertainment platforms facilitate both animosity between citizens, and nationalization of our attention. Their owners are, in the words of law professor Kate Klonick, our "new governors," and they are "responsible for shaping and allowing participation in our new digital and democratic culture, yet they have little direct accountability to their users." Jon Askonas and Ari Schulman, who write frequently about technology and society, explain in *National Affairs* how Facebook, for example, in its quest to acquire as many users as possible, altered its focus on small, moderated communities of shared, apolitical interests to make a "news feed" central, giving hot takes, memes, and outrage a viral edge. The odds that anyone outside your network of old school buddies is going to care about the retirement of a beloved English teacher is nearly zero, so this kind of community-focused information doesn't travel far. The odds that at least one of your buddies wants to repost a meme making fun of the US president, on the other hand, is nearly 100 percent, which means that's the kind of content that proliferates across user subnetworks. Given the regrettably fallen nature of man, the more controversial or outrageous or titillating that content is, the more clicks it will get. It might even go viral.

Which feels good, as I can attest from personal experience. I haven't *exactly* gone viral (yet!), but I *did* once get retweeted by a minor actor from a 1990s sitcom. My tweet activity went up astronomically for the next few hours, as I chased the lightning.

---

† A little tweaking, however, could get us there, so if you're reading this and your name happens to be Brad Pitt or Sophia Coppola, call me.

What's true across human history is that when the rewards for an activity increase, people will do more of it. Thus did Facebook, Twitter, Instagram, Reddit, and the rest of them spawn legions of shit-posters, trolls, meme spreaders, and reply guys.

Being exposed to fools is the price of admission to "free" social media sites, whose business model is to appropriate user content, intersperse it with paid material, launch into virality as much digital slurry as human minds can consume, and sell our personal information out the back door to credit card companies and political campaigns. Little of this content impinges on American democracy, because most social media content isn't political, and most people aren't overly invested in partisan battles.

Thanks to the algorithms, however, highly partisan Americans get more than their share of belief-confirming political content, and the evidence is clear that it warps their perceptions. The Pew Foundation has found, for example, that significant consumption of social media yields greater misperceptions of reality. More troubling still, this effect is highest among Americans who rely chiefly on social media for their news—a proportion that has unfortunately grown, since the advent of Facebook, Twitter, and other channels, to one-in-five Americans, while growing numbers—especially among the young—access social media daily.

Social media platforms weren't deliberately engineered to produce clans of groupthink that hate other clans, but that's been their effect. "Algorithmically tweaked environments feed on user data," writes Adrienne LaFrance, "and manipulate user experience, and not ultimately for the purpose of serving the user." The consequence has been perfectly normal, peaceable neighbors tacitly choosing sides in an engineered ideological melee where every click summons more of what they want to see. "The platforms," write Askonas and Schulman, "are rotten to the core, inducing us all to become noxious versions of ourselves." They are "rather close to a form of mass voluntary intellectual pornography: a marketplace that lauds the basest instincts, incentivizes snark and outrage, brings us to revel in the savage burn."

Mercifully, all this political content that consumes partisans appears to have little effect on how the rest of us vote. But because what they're focused on is the *national* battle between Democrats and Republicans, that's what spreads into our social-media timelines. No matter how carefully we attend to local friendships and connections and care about the governance of our communities, the nature of social media machinery interposes DC-focused political content. It may not change how we vote, but it reinforces the nation-state ideology of the New Deal and the Great Society and the New World Order and the smart bomb. It cultivates a mindset that Washington, DC, runs everything, as it always has and always will, forever and ever, amen. This is a mindset that strangles self-governance in the cradle.

THE PARTISAN WHIRLPOOL

It's becoming clear that some very well-populated corners of the internet are evoking among partisans the tribalism we thought our modern society had left behind. They function as whirlpools, sucking their victims into groupthink, directing their ire at people in other groups. Political scientist Matthew Levendusky examined the effects partisan news media have on the attitudes of viewers. News organizations openly allied with one or the other major political party, Levendusky reported in the *American Journal of Political Science*, "present the day's news as a partisan struggle, with clear references to the political parties and their positions." The effect is to pull viewers into the drama, stoking anger at the other side. Instead of honestly considering opponents' arguments, partisan viewers rehearse counterarguments that solidify their certainty that partisans on the other side are not only wrong, but have bad intentions. The effect of consuming partisan media, Levendusky found, lingers well after subjects have forgotten the particulars. They no longer recall *what* they disagree about, in other words, but they retain the emotional conviction that the other side is *wrong*.

Author and legal scholar Cass Sunstein explored what happens when people confine their engagement on issues and ideas to tailored networks of likeminded people. He began by observing a naturally cloistered group laboring to reach consensus: the courtroom jury. What he found was that jury members most adamant about punishing a defendant tend to move others in their direction, rather than having their views tempered by the less vindictive (and less emotional) majority. The same phenomenon, he argued in his book *Going to Extremes: How Like Minds Unite and Divide*, arises in social networks of likeminded people. The most extreme members tend to speak more frequently and forcefully. Sunstein calls these people "polarization entrepreneurs." Absence of vocal opposition leads other group members to assume everyone else agrees with the outspoken extremists, which makes their positions seem reasonable.

The political scientist Elizabeth Connors found a similar dynamic within in-person networks of friends, neighbors, and co-workers. While American opinions about politics and policy are often rooted, as discussed earlier, in underlying values, those values are themselves subject to social influence. This is unsurprising to anyone who knows humans—we can't help but evaluate our views through the eyes of other people. If we sense that a large majority of people we know care about police brutality, say, or the integrity of elections, we're liable to care—or at least feel tempted to *say* we care—about those things, too. This phenomenon can be beneficial when we're connected to a diverse array of people. But when we're not—which is increasingly true for America's most ardent partisans—these networks can become just as toxic and self-deluding as any online cesspool. People begin to align their values to those of the group, and fall in lockstep with their leaders.

To counterbalance platform-fostered polarization, Sunstein calls for engineering that would introduce viewpoint diversity into people's social-media timelines. Contradictory inputs could help shatter the spell of certainty that captivates tribes, reducing the effects their most radical and vocal members have on their thinking. Unfortunately, note Askonas and Schulman, social media companies are headed in the opposite direction, reinforcing their algorithm-driven tailoring to ensure that no user has to see anything that offends him or challenges his beliefs. He'll no longer hear *from* people on the other side at all, only *about* them.

As people slip deeper into ideological whirlpools, they become immunized to facts that undermine their beliefs, more inclined to disbelieve a claim based on the perceived political allegiance of its source, and predisposed to trust claims from people they perceive to be on their ideological side. They not only resist facts that counter their party's line, they become *more* committed to what their side holds to be true; more impervious to inconvenient truths. This is the reality for strong partisans of *all* stripes, much as they all like to believe *their* eyes are open, and the eyes of their political opponents are stitched shut.

Dr. Dee Alsop and his colleagues at Heart+Mind Strategies, a market research firm that convenes focus groups to illuminate citizens' values regarding a variety of topics, found that people immersed in partisan tribalism simply can't participate in reasonable discussions with people who disagree with them. As opposed to the pollsters I've been critiquing, who rely almost entirely on checked-box answers to closed-ended questions to draw inferences about American beliefs, Heart+Mind gives their subjects ample room to say what they believe, in their own words. H+M researchers specialize in understanding what drives disagreement around highly contentious topics, using a method they've pioneered called "triadic illumination." They bring together people who they know from pre-session surveys disagree about a critical issue, but who have many other things in common, like life background, parental and marital status, and economic status. They have participants tell one another about their backgrounds and daily routines, in order for their subjects to realize what they have in common. Only then do participants reveal their opinions about the contentious issue in question. Researchers challenge participants to find common ground, even if just to agree to disagree. As a final exercise, participants are asked to summarize one another's views, which reveals how well they've listened and empathized.

Heart+Mind researchers have found that for a large majority of participants, this proves to be a fruitful exercise. They don't often persuade one another to "switch sides," or even to modify their original positions all that much, but they go a long way toward understanding one another, developing empathy, and recognizing that many people who disagree with them do so in good faith. Perhaps most important, they understand better what values they share with people who vote differently than they do.

That's the case for most participants, but *not* for the most extreme partisans in their subject pool. Heart+Mind estimates that these Americans comprise—confirming what has previously been discussed in public-opinion research—about 20 percent of the population, more or less evenly divided between the Left and Right. Even after these people have learned all the things they have in common with other participants, these shared experiences fall by the wayside once the divisive issue comes up—or even beforehand, because these participants are much more likely to signal (and search for) political allegiances. Their partisan and ideological convictions are their primary motivators, essential to their identities. Anyone who disagrees with them is not only wrong, but ill-informed and quite possibly evil.

Heart+Mind researchers realized they had to screen out altogether these hyper-partisans from their research. "They have a 'take no prisoners' point of view," lamented Allsop, which leads them to dominate any discussion group they're in and to cut off all disagreement. "They're only interested in winning," noted Heart+Mind researcher Erin Norman, "even when they don't know what they're fighting about." One of the focus-group participants summed up the difference between these conversations anchored in rapport, and what happens on social media: "If I tried to speak about any of this on Facebook, I would have spent the last four days arguing with friends, making enemies, and listening to a mountain of ignorance and bullshit. This was pleasant."

8

THROUGH A GLASS DARKLY

"The news elicits from you a variety of opinions about which you can do nothing except to offer them as more news, about which you can do nothing."

—Neal Postman, *Amusing Ourselves to Death*

"They are always sick; they vomit their gall and call it a newspaper. They devour each other and cannot even digest themselves."

—Friedrich Nietzsche, *Thus Spake Zarathustra*

Ideological whirlpools have grim effects on American citizens, so thankfully the people drawn into them—even though their numbers seem larger because they're active on Facebook and vocal at our Thanksgiving tables—constitute a minority of Americans. All the same, their divisions are becoming more bitter, so if the corrosive effects of social media were reined in, might we see a return to normalcy? If progressives get their wish, for example, and ban right-wingers from social media, or if conservatives get Congress to regulate social media companies, might we see the fevers die down as people stop getting their "news" and opinions from hysteria-engineered sources, and return to traditional media? Unfortunately, exchanging reliance on social media and overtly political news platforms for mainstream news sources likely won't make anything better—but not for the reasons many of my conservative friends think.

It's fashionable among those of us who call ourselves conservatives to refer to "the mainstream media" with a roll of the eyes. I've seen the eye-rolling, and at times I've done it myself. By "mainstream media," some people mean the major networks and newspapers, like ABC, CNN, and the *New York Times*. Others, convinced there are few honest dealers in large news media entities, lump those large news organs together with openly partisan platforms like MSNBC. Still others consider "mainstream media" anything—from the *Washington Post* to KCCI 8 News in Des Moines—that isn't overtly right-wing.

My liberal friends roll their eyes at our eye-rolling. In college, many of them read all about this kind of right-wing UFO-spotting in Richard Hofstadter's "The Paranoid Style in American Politics."[†] It's worth considering, all the same, whether there's some justification for all these upturned eyeballs.

When conservatives signal disdain for mainstream media, they intend to convey several beliefs which many on the Right hold to be self-evident: that most journalists are unabashed liberals; that their biases frequently creep into their coverage of American problems and politics; that many journalists deliberately protect the politicians they like and smear the ones they dislike; and, finally, that pervasive media bias prevents regular Americans from waking up to the truth about liberals, taxes, big government, the communists, and a host of other things that conservatives dislike very much.

Is there any evidence for these convictions? The answer to this question is going to make extreme partisans on the Left and Right

---

† Hofstadter's essay spawned a cottage industry, which persists to this day, of applying shakily defined psychological concepts to conservatives in order to show that they disagree with liberals not because they have different conceptualizations of the common good, or a better understanding of the benefits of free markets, or a stronger desire for individual liberty, but because they are mentally ill. The Soviets had a similar approach toward dissidents, only with greater power to rectify their enemies, which is perhaps another reason to concur with William F. Buckley's preference for being governed by random citizens rather than university faculties.

unhappy. To begin with, the suspicion that most journalists are liberals isn't a belief held solely by conservatives; nearly two-thirds of Americans say they can see it in how the news is covered. It's easily ascertained, moreover, in surveys of journalists themselves, as well as by scrutiny of their backgrounds. While most journalists like to call themselves political Independents, implying that they have no political allegiances, we know that they give nearly all of their political donations to Democrats, and that far more of them identify as Democrats than Republicans. Analysis of social media, finally, reveals that the average journalist on Twitter (which is certainly not all journalists, thank God) is ideologically somewhere to the right of Alexandria Ocasio-Cortez, but to the left of Bernie Sanders. Conservative convictions about pervasive media bias make us sound paranoid to liberals, but as the poet Delmore Schwartz once said: "Even paranoids have enemies."

The validity of conservative suspicions that journalists' political leanings creep into news coverage depends, meanwhile, on the journalist and the topic. The *Washington Post's* coverage of transgenderism, for example, has less nuance than Joe Stalin's press releases. After the state of Arkansas passed a law prohibiting doctors from carving the breasts and penises off minor children experiencing gender dysmorphia, and forbidding as well the use of powerful hormones on children, the *Post* published a number of shrill stories that avoided the actual text of the law while implying that hardhearted Republicans intended to punish gender dysmorphic children by restricting their access to medical care. Nobody reads the *Washington Post* for news on transgender issues, however, and certainly not for science; they read it for affirmation of liberal dogmas. Likewise for coverage of abortion in the *New York Times*, or pretty much anything *60 Minutes* airs aside from the second hand on its iconic ticking stopwatch, and probably even that is unreliable. These glaring and relatively ignored journalistic embarrassments aside, however, systematic bias across news organizations is very difficult to prove objectively, because the exercise is based on counterfactuals, ("They covered the story like *this*, but if they weren't so liberal, they would have covered it like *that*"). That doesn't mean that widespread and frequently biased coverage isn't a possibility, of course, but we should recognize how easy it is for human beings to spot anecdotal proof of prior convictions, while ignoring counterproof.

Regarding the third accusation, that many journalists actively work to advance a progressive agenda, this is absolutely true, provided we apply a loose enough definition of the word "journalists" to encompass talking puppets and infotainers like Chris Cuomo and Rachel Maddow. Most working journalists, however, report on things like state legislative races, college football rivalries, and US servicemen returning home. They feel a sense of responsibility to their communities. They receive relatively low pay compared to other professionals, and will never appear on a major cable news network. They are neither your enemies, nor mine.

But let's assume I'm wrong. Everything turns, in that case, on the fourth belief, which is that left-wing media bias sways average Americans to favor the wrong party, vote for the wrong politicians, and in general surrender their liberties with less hesitation than the French Army in 1940. If true, this is infuriating to conservatives, but it's also a consolation, because it means that when citizens reject a conservative tenet, it's not our fault. They're just "sheeple" brainwashed by the liberal media.

Research into whether openly partisan news media do have this kind of pervasive influence on average Americans finds little such effect. The last chapter discussed how viewers with the strongest partisan tendencies are inclined to watch news sources that confirm their views. Political scientist Matthew Levendusky found that these openly partisan media sources, however, don't influence the attitudes and beliefs of average Americans, they simply reinforce the political opinions of viewers who already agreed with them before tuning in. "Like-minded media polarize viewers," he wrote in the *American Journal of Political Science*, "but only for subjects who actually want to watch like-minded media. [...] Partisan media therefore heighten mass polarization not by turning moderates into extremists, but rather by further polarizing those who are already away from the political center."

Morris Fiorina and his colleagues, meanwhile, note that openly partisan news and opinion purveyors have very limited audiences. Before taking some small comfort in the limited blast radius of partisan news, however, it is necessary to consider two disturbing facts. First, the number of Americans relying on more overtly ideological media, be they cable news sources like MSNBC and Fox News, independent talking heads on YouTube, or influential social media commentators, is on the rise, especially among young people. Second, Levendusky shows that while the extreme partisans he studied are a relatively small portion of Americans, they tend to be more politically engaged, thereby exerting inordinate influence on politics and society. "Partisan media polarize active and engaged citizens, who in turn help to fuel elite polarization." He continues: "Even though most voters are moderate and never hear partisan media messages, by affecting a more extreme group of individuals, the consequences of partisan media extend quite broadly." Equally troubling is evidence that while average Americans' political views aren't affected by slanted media, they're losing trust in one another's wisdom all the same, in part because they worry that fake and biased news *is* affecting the judgments of their fellow citizens.

Turning from overtly partisan media platforms to more mainstream news sources, there's also reason to suspect that whatever biases they contain don't substantially alter the average American's voting or political behavior, at least in the short run. The first reason is that most Americans don't follow politics like you and I. Their relative inattention, decried by political scientists, serves as a kind of inoculation against whatever narrative a biased news producer or social media platform engineer might otherwise push into their heads. The second reason is that, as discussed earlier, average Americans have remained consistently middle-of-the-road both in the opinions they express about policy and in their ideological and partisan preferences. If the mainstream media is shifting America to the left, they're taking their sweet time.

If we want to make the case that conservatives are right about the effects of media bias, however, we might return to the culture-war argument advanced by James Davison Hunter, who argued in *Is There a Culture War? A Dialogue on Values and American Public Life*:

> The power of culture is the power to name things, to define reality, to create and shape worlds of meaning. At its most extreme reach, it is the power to project one's vision of the world as the dominant, if not the only legitimate, vision of the world, such that it becomes unquestioned.

In this telling, mainstream news media, largely populated by people with shared values and outlooks that tend to be more socially and economically liberal, function alongside the doyens of other culture-shaping institutions to slowly shift American values and opinions. They help "boil the frog" which, as the saying goes, takes time. This long-term remaking of culture is what, in my view, ought to worry conservatives far more than Rachel Maddow's prevarications. Countering it requires an entirely different approach to governing institutions. I'll argue in coming chapters that a return to American self-governance, rooted in states and communities, is exactly what's needed to stop the hijacking by unelected panjandrums of our cultural institutions' commanding heights.

THE MEDIA SICK CYCLE

While there's little evidence that mainstream news organizations are directly altering American voting choices or ideology, they do have a pernicious effect on how we view our country and its problems. This subtle bias reinforces narratives from irrational and extremist partisans on both ends of the ideological spectrum. Its destructive effect is rooted in a trend many media observers have recognized for years: as the internet-fueled collapse of traditional advertising revenue forced media organizations into a desperate scramble for eyeballs and dollars, what's bad became good. Conflict and tragedy attract attention, and negativity is profitable. Most news media organizations are, after all, profit-oriented business enterprises.

The computational analysis scholar Kalev Leetaru developed techniques to assess positive and negative tones reflected in descriptions of historical events. He observed that gloomy terms cropped up frequently, as should be expected, in accounts of traumatic events like the battles and aftermath of the US Civil War. These dips in sentiment were outstripped, over time, by more positive assessments, as civilizational progress yielded improvements in health, prosperity, and other desirable indicators. As society moved into the modern era, historical accounts encompassing everything from diplomatic relations to scientific discoveries were characterized by rising positivity. Human conditions improved dramatically as the decades passed, and observations of people who recorded these historical changes reflected this reality.

What Leetaru discovered next, however, was remarkable. When he laid these historical records alongside a corresponding time series of sentiments revealed in news coverage by the *New York Times* starting at the end of World War II, the contrast was stark. The bulk of what happened in American society over the subsequent decades was, taken in the balance, quite positive (think about all the advances in medicine, job safety, food production, buying power, and overall creature comforts, just to name a few), but news coverage in the *New York Times* grew increasingly *negative* throughout the 1960s, plunging further as the century came to a close.

This pessimistic viewpoint wasn't just confined to the *New York Times*. Leetaru assessed an index of worldwide media coverage and found an equally visible rise in negativity across an array of news organizations. The very same computational techniques that found rising positivity across thousands of sources chronicling human activities and conditions revealed the *opposite* when those activities and conditions were reported by journalists.

Leetaru also noticed that accelerating news media negativity coincided with the advance of online journalism. "This suggests," he noted, "a fascinating possibility: that the plunge towards negativity of media across the entire world was due to the rise of the Web itself and the increased competition that news outlets now faced." As clicks became the arbiter of news value, shock became essential to media corporation profitability. Just consider how personas like Brian Williams and Sean Hannity notched all-time highs for viewership in the wake of riots after the death of George Floyd in Minneapolis. When Americans kill one another, Big Media profits. No wonder they look for strife wherever they can find it.

Likewise, in their hunger for click-generated revenue, media outlets broadcast shallow, slanted, irresponsible—and occasionally even fraudulent—portrayals of the problems that are inevitable in any large and diverse country. Even as America has become for most—but certainly not all—citizens a safer, healthier, and more prosperous home, we are inundated with tales of crime, disaster, and dysfunction, thanks to large-bore media outlets and their social-media amplifiers.

Perhaps not surprisingly, American perceptions of problems are plagued by similar negativity. Consider crime, an American obsession since at least the days of Jesse James. The US has enjoyed a decades-long decline in the annual rate of violent crime. Five out of every 1,000 Americans were victims of violent crime in 2000; by 2019, that number had fallen to 3.9 per 1,000, a decrease of more than 220,000 violent crimes annually. Public-opinion surveys, however, consistently show Americans believe crime rates are increasing. Since a correlation between news media and general public negativity doesn't prove that the former caused the latter, academics have assessed the data more closely. Their analysis indicates that attention to local news—long guided by the old adage: "if it bleeds, it leads"—does appear to affect public fears of crime. So, too, does consumption of television crime dramas, which made up over a quarter of all scripted shows on broadcast networks in 2010, and account for nearly 20 percent of shows today. Finally, examining Gallup polls alongside crime data reveals that the gap between reality and perception has been steadily *growing* since 2003.

Because beliefs about hate crimes are intertwined with American opinions about race, it's worth looking more closely at this subset of overall crime, where we find a similar pattern of distorted perceptions. FBI data on hate crimes, collected from thousands of state and local law enforcement agencies, reveal there were 0.47 hate crimes per agency in 2019, versus 0.77 in 1996. In other words, the incidence of reported hate crimes declined 39 percent over a twenty-four-year period. It's worth noting that the number of agencies participating in the FBI's hate-crime reporting project increased by 37 percent over that same span of time, however, meaning that a higher tally was quite likely. If you cast more lines in more ponds, in other words, you often catch more fish, but this doesn't mean the total number of fish in the world is increasing. Rather than focusing on the incidence of hate crimes, however, media outlets reported the increase in total hate crimes, framing the change as evidence of rising intolerance and violence.[†]

We find similar perception gaps in other domains. Despite a 34 percent reduction in air pollution—the equivalent of 77 million fewer tons of pollutants per year—from 1970 to 1997, nearly two-thirds of Americans polled in 1999 stated that they believe air quality had declined over the preceding decade. An average 44 percent of Americans surveyed in 1993 and 1994, meanwhile, believed that car pollution was either certain or very likely to increase over the coming decade, with another 32 percent stating they believed it was "fairly likely to happen," all despite the fact that fuel standards and improved engineering have radically reduced tailpipe emissions.

NO SYMPATHY FOR THE DEVIL

Now we come to the central, destructive effect of ideological whirlpools swirling in a sea of relentlessly negative, politics-

---

[†] I want to note that these numbers don't *disprove* the hypothesis of a higher hate crime rate, either. Imagine, by way of illustration, that all the law enforcement jurisdictions which started participating in the FBI's cataloguing effort were home to highly homogeneous citizen bases, in terms of race, religion, etc., such that they have very little opportunity for hate crimes. In that scenario, a falling number of hate crime incidents per law enforcement jurisdiction might conceal an actual increase in incidents among Americans where the opportunity for such crimes present themselves. What I *can* say with certainty is that simply reporting the total number of such crimes while ignoring the incidence rate constitutes journalistic malpractice.

obsessed, national mainstream media. To understand it, let's go back to the hate-crime data, where incidents increased with more reporting, but the rate went down. This critical point was overlooked by nearly all news media accounts, which instead stressed the rise in raw numbers. Any single hate crime is despicable, but for matters of policy and perspective it makes all the difference whether you're seeing more hate crimes because you're looking in more places, or because they're occurring with greater frequency. If we consider the first point, we might be optimistic that current policies are having a positive effect. If we ignore the first point, however, and see only an increase in reported hate crimes, we'll conclude that our policies *aren't* working. We might therefore become open to more interventionist—perhaps even radical—federal policies. Maybe we'll be tempted to believe the people in charge don't actually *care* about hate crimes. If we're caught up in a left-wing partisan maelstrom, that's certainly what our peers will be saying.

Now, consider how negative framing permeates our nationally-oriented news media. On any given day, no matter where we live, we're getting the worst examples of crime, pollution, racism, police violence, and every other social problem that video-hungry news channels can dredge up, taking their pick from all fifty states. On issue after issue, from hunger to disease to the morals of kids today, we get the impression that things are getting worse. Ideological whirlpools reinforce this in the minds of their captives. These dynamics tempt some people to embrace radical solutions, while people in opposing whirlpools are tempted, because the complaints and allegations are so outrageously out of proportion to anything they've seen or experienced, to believe that the "problem" the other side cares about is a hoax, or at best a small but exaggerated issue that should be far lower on our list of national priorities.

Inundated by negative news and fact-distorting ideological vortexes, two furiously opposed camps have emerged. Each nurses problems and grudges that its members are convinced can only be remedied by upending the system—changing the rules, tearing down the bureaucracy, firing the people in charge, spending whatever it takes. Likewise, each camp believes that the other camp's problems aren't really problems at all, or at least not so terrible that radical solutions are justified.

The radical changes called for, meanwhile, come in two forms: dramatically change the policy, and dramatically alter the political landscape. If we believe the country is being made poorer and more dangerous by immigrants, and that decades of "solutions" by politicians have only made things worse, we become open to building a wall and casting out not only people who cross the border illegally, but the children of people who entered illegally many years ago. If we believe financial turmoil in our banking and housing markets comes not from policies that protect corporate insiders from their own bad decisions, but from the institution of private ownership itself, we become open to government takeover of entire industries.

Similarly, we become more willing to support political candidates who promise these and other radical reforms. We give our votes to people with vested interests in convincing us there's a crisis, and whose solution to our broken political system is to break it further. Little wonder, then, that as the drumbeat of negative news and opinion has widened the gaps for many Americans between perception and reality, opportunistic politicians swoop in with promises to burn it all to the ground.

Which brings us to our present, precarious state of national affairs. American citizens have been fed heightened and dramatized doomsday scenarios about the problems facing America. Entire phalanxes of the political class on the Left and Right specialize in capitalizing on this doom and gloom to persuade citizens that the people running the political party opposite their own are either incompetent to fix things, or worse, actually derive pleasure and profit from keeping things bad. More and more Americans, gripped by the growing (and intentionally cultivated) belief that afflictions like racism and poverty will not be reduced or eliminated without radical alterations in American life, therefore have little patience for moderation, gradualism, and compromise. Worse, they've lost confidence in freedoms established by our Constitution. Why revere the American system when it allows such problems to fester in perpetuity? We see this mentality in surveys that reveal a slippage in positivity, among Democrats in particular, toward what were once widely regarded as bedrock American institutions like free enterprise and freedom of expression.

Americans who maintain traditional convictions of the sort illuminated in Alan Wolfe's interviews across Middle America, meanwhile, perceive the radical drift of their neighbors and political opposites (which are often exaggerated by media accounts and the fact that radicals on the Left and Right tend to be the biggest loudmouths on social media) as threats to their lifestyles and livelihoods. It's one thing to be in favor of fairness and non-discrimination they might say, but another entirely to advocate social reengineering that reverses parental teaching about sexuality and identity. It's one thing to believe in making healthcare more accessible, but another entirely to assert that ardently pro-life nuns be forced to subsidize birth control against their convictions.

Rounding out this vicious cycle, everyday Americans' instinctive resistance to radicalism comes to be seen by the radicalized—ensconced as they are within the feverish confines of their ideological cocoons—as indifference to national problems. They begin to believe that resistance in Middle America stems not from disagreement about the size or nature of the problem, or from differing opinions about how to tackle it, but from indifference to the people affected by it. If voters are unwilling to upend society to deal with the radicals' top priority, it's because they lack some essential element of humanity.

In his book on American polarization, *Divided We Fall*, David French recounted an example of what this looked like during a CNN-hosted debate on gun rights not long after the Parkland, FL, school shootings. Audience members called gun-rights advocates on the stage murderers. Senator Marco Rubio was likened to a mass shooter. "There were millions of gun-owning Americans," wrote French, "who watched all or part of the town hall and came away with a clear message: These people aren't just angry at what happened in their town, to their friends and family members. They hate me. They really believe I'm the kind of person who doesn't care if kids die, and they want to deprive me of the ability to defend myself."

Or consider the deluded earnestness of left-wing media consultant and *Harvard Business Review* blogger Umair Haque, after training his intellect on the dilemma of Americans resisting complete lockdown during the COVID-19 epidemic: "One thing Coronavirus teaches us," he wrote, "is that Americans are genuinely indifferent to mass death." What else could explain Americans' refusal to destroy jobs and livelihoods, stunt the education of millions of children, sever the most vulnerable among us from the lifelines of community and care, and deprive the faithful of their religious services? The only logical explanation, for a smart man sucked to the bottom of his ideological vortex, is that Americans don't care whether people die.

David French, ironically enough given how much he laments polarization, was just as uncharitable on Twitter when he denounced people who resisted governmental mask mandates:

"Anti-masking further exposed the darkness in parts of the right. It's such a small thing to show love of neighbor, but that small thing was and is too much for all too many who claim to be pro-life." The only explanation this intelligent author of a book about overcoming American divisiveness could conjure for his fellow citizens' behavior was darkness in their hearts. Not a desire to resist perceived tyranny, or even simple misinformation about the transmissibility of COVID-19. Nope, it must be the darkness within.

It's not just radicals and disillusioned politicos who encourage base assumptions about their opponents. Every extremist agenda item, from shutting down the economy to defunding the police to ending fossil-fuel consumption, has opponents who are just as willing to set aside empathy. In their minds, it's not that environmentalists really believe climate change is a threat; it's that they want to remake the world economy along socialist principles. Putative police reformers aren't really grieving violence in their neighborhoods, they need the police out of the way so they can usher in a Marxist revolution. *It's right there in the Lenin playbook.* Every contentious political issue today has two sides keeping the vicious cycle spinning, each wounded by the accusations of the other, each convinced the other side must be destroyed.

An essay by the feminist Carol Hanisch helped popularize a saying that radicals took to heart in the 1970s: "The personal is political." With Sunstein's "polarization entrepreneurs" on the prowl, that aphorism has been reversed—all politics have become personalized. Ideologues choose what they want to believe, and they believe the worst of those who disagree. It's a logical step, from there, to conclude that any means necessary to defeat their political opponents is justified. It becomes easy, in these self-fueling partisan maelstroms, for people on both sides to begin thinking of everyday Americans—people they haven't even met—

as enemies. Idiots. Monsters. It's a far cry from the deliberative democracy envisioned by Alexander Hamilton, and it's ugly to see and be around. In fact, one wonders how anyone could stand to be part of it. But one man's garbage dump, as they say, has proved to be another man's castle.

9

THE SPOILS OF WAR

"[…] if they ever fight you, they will have to take all the hard knocks themselves, and someone else will sit quietly by, waiting for the spoils."

—Demosthenes, *On the Peace*

The sickness in American civic life was brought to us, in some ways quite deliberately, by the political class. It's fitting that I write in a season of viruses and quarantines, because these people—many of them residing in the least representative of locations within our national borders, Wards 1-6 of the District of Columbia†—are the super-spreaders of a disease now killing our body politic. If we want to reclaim the rights to govern ourselves in our states and communities, we need to quarantine them inside the DC Beltway. Or better yet, send them home to look for real work.

I said at the outset that they didn't get together and plan any of this—or at least, most of it. But their collective behavior produces the toxins, and they benefit from their poison's effect on the body politic. Understanding how this dynamic works illuminates why DC has become so dysfunctional that there's likely no correcting it, only containing it. This understanding can also point the way toward what we can do as citizens to subdue the political class.

---

† Washington, DC, comprises eight wards. Wards 7 and 8 are predominately African-American, a mixture of poor and working class citizens who labor for little recognition and have no lucrative lobbying jobs awaiting them at the end of the rainbow.

PROFITABLE MAYHEM

"Most of economics," writes Steven Landsburg, a professor of economics at the University of Rochester, "can be summarized in four words: 'People respond to incentives.' The rest is commentary." There's certainly money to be made in politics. This appeals to people neither attractive nor astute enough to make their fortunes in Hollywood or on Wall Street. As campaign spending rises each election season, political consultants take percentages of every ad buy, on top of other fees, raking in revenue that sets new records with every election. The Republican operatives who set up the anti-Trump Lincoln Project reportedly pocketed over $50 million of the $90 million they had raised by the time the FBI opened an investigation into one of their founders for sexually preying on young men. The fact that so many people in DC had known about his behavior for months, yet said nothing, offers an additional lens through which to view the political class. Just being money-hungry would be a moral improvement for these people.

Though not as lucrative, the lesser ranks of downstream political middlemen, like fundraising consultants, partisan pollsters, and direct-mail peddlers, are also swollen with profit from permanent political warfare. There is never a week when engineers of our political machinery aren't raising either money or their wetted fingers to the wind. Politics-focused news organizations raise considerable sums as well, with Fox News, MSNBC, and CNN raking in hundreds of millions in advertising dollars during recent election years.

Leaving aside carnival barkers and turning to the politicians themselves, we find that over a timespan that includes the Great Recession of 2007-2009, the average US Congressman enjoyed a yearly increase in net worth of 15 percent, while most Americans suffered a decline in net worth. In fact, 2014 marked the first time in history when a majority of our elected officials in Washington, DC, were full-fledged millionaires. Serving the public has never been so rewarding.

DRIVING OUT THE COMPETITION

The negativity and cynicism fostered by the actions of the political class and their slavish news media safeguard the civic arena from the kinds of people who represent the gravest threat to modern political elites: leaders who would rather solve problems than build political careers. These people are a danger to professional politicians because they're the leaders we all long for. Having them on the menu would be like offering gourmet meals to people grown accustomed to mud pies and cow flops.

Venal politicians and their behind-the-scenes operatives and handlers, therefore, benefit from the present savagery of American politics in the same way that large corporations can find their long-term profitability perversely enhanced by costly government regulations: both drive smaller competitors out of business and dissuade new, potentially more effective competitors from setting up shop. Good men and women—and believe me, they exist, and we need them in politics—want nothing to do with the people who oversee our national political institutions, from the fundraisers to the party leaders to our pack-minded national journalists. They still have some self-respect, after all, and actual jobs other than politics, and they love their families. Why subject their lives to ruin?

Even if a decent American leader does throw caution to the wind and enters the political arena, voters grown cynical from the antics of the political class are apt to assume she's just like all the rest. Her opponents and their political machinery will set to work twisting every statement, action, and mistake from her past into monstrous proportions. It's what they do. It's their sport. I've met many of them, and trust me, they actually enjoy destroying people. The political class encourages the worst in us, in order to drive away the best among us.

Political toxicity not only keeps away most (but not all) decent leaders, it discourages everyday citizens from getting involved. Pervasive negativity and political conflict undermine American political participation, drive down voting, and make people less attentive to current events. We leave the townhall meetings, letter-writing, and legislative office visits to the crazies. These battles have a depressive effect not only on citizens' participation, but on our psyches, such that the percentage of Americans who believe the future will be worse for the next generation has increased in the past decade from an already pessimistic one-third of Americans to nearly half our population.

HOLLOWING OUT THE MIDDLE

The political scientist Morris Fiorina has shown that those whom a contender for federal office must keep happy to have a successful run—party leaders, activists, consultants, and campaign donors—are at the extreme left and right tails of the American political distribution. They've engineered the success of increasingly polarized candidates, driving moderates, consensus-builders, and compromisers from politics. Their partisan foot soldiers have followed suit, dutifully modifying their issue opinions over time to mirror the left- and right-drifting views of their party leaders. It's important to understand that we're talking now not just about issue extremity, but behavioral extremity. Many Democratic and Republican politicians are decidedly less liberal and conservative than their forbears, but markedly more unseemly in their discourse and behavior. Sometimes, this is a more bitter pill for Americans than extreme ideology.

The nature of American democracy is such that even with ample donors, activists, and partisan supporters, a candidate must still appeal to average voters come election time. What motivates his base doesn't appeal to regular Americans, but as communication scholar Natalie Stroud observes, fragmented media channels mean the politician can whisper one thing to his base while projecting a different image to others. "Without the loyal opposition or a nonpartisan entity checking and counterarguing a partisan version of reality," she writes, "politicians may more readily get away with distortions of the truth."

Talking from two sides of his mouth can only carry him so far, so a politician can also resort to a tried-and-true method of avoiding clear issue positions, which is to cast his opponent as evil and incompetent. This not only animates his base and donors; research shows that when voters get a campaign message emphasizing the *threat* a politician poses to their interests, they become significantly more likely to vote. What's more, according to the twisted mathematics of modern news, viciousness garners more airtime. From press coverage to voter turnout, negativity gets more bang for the campaign buck.

None of this—the negativity, the evasions, the dog whistles to activists—engenders enthusiasm among average American voters. But a candidate doesn't need them to be excited, because his opponent is almost inevitably someone just as appealing to the diehard ideologues on the other end of the spectrum as he is to his. Lost in the middle are regular citizens, who will likely vote according to their party registration but aren't enthusiastic about their party's candidate. Often, they only vote for him because the other candidate is, in their view, worse. This means there's ample room for candidates who more fully reflect the values and desires of voting majorities, but as we see in presidential primaries, these are the people who generally get little interest from party backers, and plenty of disdain from national journalists. As public-opinion scholars Norton Garfinkle and Daniel Yankelovich observe: "Both parties seek to claim the center for electoral purposes, but neither party seems in a mood to build a genuine bipartisan consensus on crucial policy issues." They can't because their bases won't tolerate it.

"In a sense," notes political scientist Carolyn Funk, "politicians have been training the public to be cynical about politics." The political candidates who tend to please activists in each major party have no hope of producing results by working together once in office. Our legislatures, envisioned by the Founders to be the primary creators of law, become gridlocked, inviting rule by bureaucratic agencies and courts. No wonder the percentage of Americans who believe they have little say in politics, and that public officials don't care what they think, has more than doubled since the 1960s.

SILENCING THE MAJORITY

By warding off problem-solving leaders and advancing candidates who have no intention of working with one another across party lines, the political class ensures that solutions amenable to majorities of Americans never get a hearing. For a glimpse of the magnitude of the problem, consider research by political scientist Martin Gilens, who analyzed data from hundreds of nationwide survey questions about public policy from the 1960s to the present day, to assess whether the opinions of everyday Americans actually affect what policies Washington, DC, produces. "Under most circumstances," he reported, "the preferences of the vast majority of Americans appear to have essentially no impact on which policies the government does or doesn't adopt." Policymakers instead cater to the desires of partisans and ideologues who, like themselves, favor freer trade, easier abortion, and cheaper labor than everyday Americans.[†]

Media-fueled viewpoints of our national problems foster the perception that moderate solutions won't work, that what's needed are bold solutions which entail new government powers with no expiration date, and which conveniently leave plenty of room for interpretation and expansion by unelected bureaucrats. Our fragmented national narrative means partisans on either side have strikingly different lists of what needs fixing with their opposing grab-bags of bold solutions. Liberals hear that hate crimes are on the rise, our landscape is being plundered by oil and gas exploration, and systemic racism keeps minorities impoverished. Conservatives hear that immigrants are committing wildly disproportionate amounts of crime, domestic religious persecution is endemic, and terrorist governments overseas are still an existential threat to our way of life. Both groups hear that people on the other side are either orchestrating these varied abominations, or complacently allowing them to occur.

This framing suits the ideologues peddling culture war. The more Americans who look askance at their liberal or conservative neighbors, and who imagine hateful brigades mobilizing in the shadows, the more heroic the ideological politician becomes. It's him, after all, who stands between you and the ignorant fundamentalists that view Margaret Atwood's *The Handmaid's Tale* as a blueprint, or the filthy, commie atheists seeking to turn your children into critical race theorists. It's so much easier to sell his services to us when we believe a substantial portion of our fellow citizens wants to burn the country to the ground.

So long as that hyperbole dominates our political discourse,

[†] My point is not that these policy objectives are all bad, nor that the majority should always get what it wants. I merely want to illustrate how the political class is not accountable to the people its members say they represent.

pragmatism is kept at bay and the desires of party activists get inordinate representation. Our choices are either to completely open our national borders, or to throw out the grown children of illegals who've built productive and law-abiding lives here. We can ban most firearms, or allow 100-round magazines. We can make the federal government our nation's sole provider of healthcare, or do nothing despite the fact that (promises implied in the naming of the Affordable Care Act aside) medical costs are responsible for two-thirds of American family bankruptcies.

Everyday Americans are happy with none of these choices, but that doesn't stop our major political parties from claiming a "mandate" every time they manage to eke out temporary control of the presidency and Congress. What ensues is frequently a flurry of executive orders, administrative reversals, and legislative proposals that often don't reflect the chief concerns of average Americans, which since the 1990s have been dominated by the cost of healthcare, college affordability, crime, and jobs. From privatized Social Security accounts to blocking pipeline construction, recent presidents seem more interested in immediately rewarding the ideologues in their base than rolling up their sleeves to tackle the problems they were hired to fix.

CIRCUMVENTING THE CONSTITUTION

The political class benefits from wars and rumors of war. I don't just mean military conflict, which has served for decades to justify curtailment of civil liberties, neglect of domestic priorities, and presidential peacocking. Every problem is now cast as an urgent national emergency. The extreme tones ideologues use to frame the problems they want us to care about serve not only to drive out both the problems and solutions *we* care about from the arena, they justify circumventing checks and balances. Whereas the Founders intended for passions to cool in our bicameral Congress, and for elected officials to find consensus that reflects broad bases of support, the political class seeks to ram through what laws it can with slim and temporary majorities, and to rely on executive power and lawsuits for the remainder. What all of these mechanisms have in common is that they reflect a profound disregard for American citizens. They are an admission that the trust our Founders placed in the American people is not shared by members of our political class.

Their narrative certainly can't be that they don't trust us, so they claim their urgent national business justifies the lack of compromise, failure to build broad-based support, and Constitutional abridgements that have come to characterize American politics. Presidents no longer try to hide their disregard for the people's representatives. "We Can't Wait" became a literal slogan President Obama's spokespeople used when Congress proved resistant to his plans. "The challenge of making sure that everyone who works hard can get ahead in today's economy," Obama told an audience of supporters, "is so important we can't wait for Congress to solve it. Where I can act on my own without Congress, I'm going to do so." Likewise, President Trump, in defiance of our Constitutional balance of powers, declared an emergency at the US border with Mexico in order to justify reallocating military budget dollars to build a wall the Congress—controlled by his own party—refused to fund at a level he deemed suitable.

This behavior is to be expected in executives when legislatures abdicate their responsibilities, which Congress has done to a shameful extent. Our presidents have grown accustomed to directing our economy and sending our troops into conflict without Constitutional authorization because the people we elect to represent us in Washington have let them. In addition, legislators have kept congressional rules that consolidate power in the hands of party leaders, further reducing the possibility of compromise and making every decision a bitter contest that either ends in stalemate, or in one side being entirely cut out, ensuring half or more of the country doesn't have its interests represented. All of this occurs in the name of urgency. Members of the political class know they're right, and therefore justified, if only to stop the other side from getting what *it* wants. There's no time for democracy when you're in a fight to the death.

10

THE INCREDIBLE SHRINKING LEGISLATURE

Congressman: I actually taught political science years ago, and I didn't know a thing about Congress until I came here. [...]

Kingdon: That's why some of us recently have been coming here to find out how congressmen behave.

Congressman: If we do.
—John Kingdon, *Congressmen's Voting Decisions*

"Unfortunately, the importance of responsibility in a democracy is matched by the difficulty of attaining it."
—Morris Fiorina, "The Decline of Collective Responsibility in Politics"

Hundreds of books delve deeply and thoughtfully into how legislators—in particular congressmen—used to make decisions, how they make them today, what incentives drive their behavior, how information flows, the fluidity of power within legislative chambers, centralization trends, decentralization trends, the unintended effects of reforms, undoing those unintended effects, and so on. Some of those books are written in an accessible, conversational style, others offer diagrams and formulas and read like calculus textbooks. I'm not going to summarize their contents for you. We've made it this far together, and I don't want to lose you now.

In this chapter, I am going to make one very specific and important point: *the danger Congress and our state legislatures pose for American self-governance has less to do with how legislators exercise power than it does with the fact that they don't exercise their powers enough.* It may surprise some readers to hear a self-professed conservative complain about government not being powerful enough, but one's happiness in life, as tightrope walkers and bankers like to say, depends on one's balance.

My peculiar complaint about Congress concerns not its absolute power so much as its power relative to the executive and judicial branches. Congress was indisputably created by America's Founders to be the preeminent branch of our government. It is the branch most representative of the will of citizens. The Founders certainly intended to check popular will, so much so that they split Congress into two chambers with offsetting interests, and bound its powers further with constitutional provisions long since neglected or willfully contorted. But their intention was clear: the power of the United States government to create laws and spend money ultimately resides in the hands of Congress.

Congress has, however, ceded much of its constitutionally assigned power to an overactive federal bureaucracy, and to judges who too often find themselves holding the bag for decisions legislators should make. Increasingly, the rules governing everyday Americans are crafted not by our elected representatives, but by unelected mandarins. Most frustrating is that Congress has not only acquiesced, but actually facilitated this imbalance of power. As constitutional scholar Yuval Levin observes, "the first branch of our government, the legislative branch, has increasingly taken the lead in its own diminution, so that it might be relieved of the burden of taking the lead in anything else."

A few independent and outspoken members of Congress are even harsher. Nebraska's Senator Ben Sasse lambasted his fellow senators during confirmation hearings for Supreme Court Associate Justice Brett Kavanaugh by declaring: "The legislature is impotent. The legislature is weak. And most people here want their jobs more than they really want to do legislative work. And, so, they punt most of the work to the next branch." Senator Angus King from Maine called it "the Great Abdication," claiming President Trump's effort to reallocate $7 billion in funds to wall construction along the Mexican border was part and parcel with fifty years of Congress handing over three of its most essential powers:

> One, the power to declare war. We haven't declared war since 1942. Secondly, the power over trade which is expressly delegated to Congress in the Constitution. But now we're about to delegate the power of the purse. I can't understand any member of this committee of either party countenancing any president taking funds from a congressionally appropriated account to use for another purpose. We may as well just forget about the whole appropriations process. Why not let the president's budget be the budget? Why have Congress intervene at all? But the idea that this Congress is allowing the most fundamental power to be turned over to the executive in total contravention of the whole scheme of the Constitution to me is just unbelievable.

There are several reasons for congressional shirking, many of them rooted in a change that overtook Congress decades ago, and which is tied to dysfunctions driven by the political class. As the 1990s progressed, Democrats and Republicans faced a phenomenon not witnessed since before the Civil War: long-term partisan parity. The numbers of committed voters declaring for each party, the balance of seats in both chambers of Congress, and presidential elections, all began to hinge on tighter and tighter margins.

This had happened occasionally in the decades since Abraham Lincoln's assassination, but Ronald Reagan's election commenced what has stretched into a forty-year run of neck-and-neck battles for control over the presidency, Congress, and the courts. Political scientist Frances Lee reveals how this sustained parity has yielded gridlock, grandstanding, and demonization, as politicians work to gain any edge over their opponents. Consensus-building has fallen by the wayside, because bipartisan solutions might give credit to the other side. Opposing everything that could benefit one's enemies has become the guiding ethos; demonization the default message.

We can see this phenomenon reflected in long-term congressional staffing shifts. Whereas members of Congress had once staffed their offices with experts in various policy domains important to constituents back home, they replaced those capabilities with communications operations staffed by full-time propagandists. Phalanxes of party-aligned nonprofits, campaign bundlers, media operations, and other influencers all helped steer legislators away from what they were elected to do—govern—and ushered them into nonstop fundraising and political theater instead. Though he was widely castigated for it, we shouldn't be at all surprised when twenty-five-year-old, first-time Congressman Madison Cawthorn (R-NC) boasted in 2020: "I have built my staff around comms rather than legislation." He was just carrying to its logical endpoint the example set by his predecessors.

The revolution in persuasion and manipulation launched by political campaigns in the 1990s, and reflected in the shift of congressional labor from policymaking to campaigning, has begun to devour its own. Any politician who dares suggest compromising with the other side can expect denunciation as a squish, disaffected campaign contributors, and a primary challenge from someone more willing to put partisanship over problem-solving.

The price of an all-out, nonstop effort to win by framing opponents as enemies of the people is that legislators are unable to govern once they're in office. Accuse your opponents often enough of being, per the GOPAC playbook "sick" and "bizarre," and your constituents won't forgive you for negotiating with terrorists. One step across the partisan line, and you might find yourself being labeled in the next primary a traitor, a liar, or an Establishment hack. There are plenty of enterprising political candidates happy to abandon a spirit of compromise with the other side in order to build a political base, and with the advent of direct mail and the internet, it's easier than ever to reach supporters directly. The consequence is a US Congress that is more polarized than at any time since before the Civil War.

Congressional scholar Kevin Kosar sums up what new members of Congress can now expect when they take their seats: "The newly arrived legislator is quickly confronted with a few basic demands: raise money for reelection; obey party leadership; and don't fraternize with members of the other party." Yuval Levin notes the conflict between this new posture and the purpose of Congress within our constitutional framework:

> It is Congress that is shaped to be representative. And more important still, Congress is shaped to enable the diverse interests and views of our society to be represented in a way that also enables them to negotiate and bargain, and ultimately to accommodate each other. This is a primary purpose of Congress as an institution—to enable and compel accommodation in a divided society. And the fact that accommodation now seems nearly impossible in our politics is a result of Congress's failure to recognize and serve its purpose more than it is the cause of that failure.

Or, as Alexander Hamilton explained in *Federalist No. 71*: "The republican principle demands that the deliberate sense of the community should govern the conduct of those to whom they intrust the management of their affairs." Our representatives are supposed to put their heads together, in other words, and sort out compromises that benefit our communities—not turn every decision into an ideological battle to the death.

An additional effect of greater party intransigence, as law professor David Schoenbrod has demonstrated, is that Congress writes vague laws, because otherwise its members can't agree. This gives federal agencies even greater ability to interpret the laws as they see fit, effectively undercutting American democracy. Conservatives were outraged in 2019, for example, by the Supreme Court decision in *Bostock v Clayton County*, which held that the extension of federal antidiscrimination protections to gay and transgendered employees was consistent with the law. They were doubly outraged that the author of the Court's majority opinion was Trump-appointee Neil Gorsuch. Gorsuch didn't base his opinion on penumbral fantasies, however—he faulted Congress for not only passing an antidiscrimination law that had failed to define what "sex discrimination" meant, but for broadening its applicability in a subsequent law. "When Congress chooses," he wrote, "not to include any exceptions to a broad rule, courts apply the broad rule." Many court cases the Right reads as proof of betrayal by Chief Justice Roberts and company bear a similar (and quite conservative) message: *it is not the function of the Supreme Court to make laws whenever Congress lacks the courage to do its job.*

Perhaps most maddening about vague laws that unleash unaccountable agencies on the people is that Congressmen get to play the role of rescuers, intervening on behalf of select constituents when federal agencies overreach. Whereas the Mafia would threaten to burn down your business unless you paid them protection money, our modern Congress lights the fire and then shows up with a bucket of water.

Even if we could transcend the trends that have driven congressional polarization, however, and attract more legislators who believe in governing rather than grandstanding, we'd still face an insurmountable obstacle to reining in a federal apparatus that renders American self-governance all but impossible. There's much to decry about some of the people we elect to represent us in Washington, DC. What we have to recognize, however, is that they're equipped with peashooters, and we're sending them into battle against a dragon. It's the nature of this beast that we have to reckon with if we're to have any hope of restoring American self-governance.

11

THE IMPERIAL CITY

I'm just a bill
Yes, I'm only a bill,
And I got as far as Capitol Hill.
Well, now I'm stuck in committee
And I'll sit here and wait
While a few key Congressmen discuss and debate
Whether they should let me be a law.
How I hope and pray that they will.
—Dave Frishberg, "I'm Just a Bill," *Schoolhouse Rock*

"GOVERNMENT IS A FRIEND"

Patch of Heaven, Nye County, NV
The relationship Victor Fuentes has with the United States government seems destined to be defined by water. Desperate to escape Castro's regime, the young Cuban slipped into the ocean off an unwatched beach in 1990, swam seven miles to the American naval base at Guantanamo Bay, and begged for political asylum. In early 1991 Victor came to America, where he became a Christian and then an ordained pastor. He made his way to Las Vegas, founded Solid Rock Ministries, and set about serving the many young people victimized by a culture that wears the moniker "Sin City" like a badge of honor.

Victor's church grew, and by 2006 they had raised the funds to buy and restore a forty-acre campground at the edge of the Ash Meadows National Wildlife Refuge outside Las Vegas. There, Victor and his team hosted church services and retreats, and provided shelter to youth and adults ravaged by addiction and abuse. The church ministered to the broken for four years, baptizing many of them in a stream that ran through the property. Victor Fuentes had realized his version of the American dream, serving the children of God in the oasis that the parishioners of Solid Rock Ministries called "the Patch of Heaven."

The US Fish and Wildlife Service (USFW), however, had other plans for that stream on the church's property—they intended to divert it for a wetlands restoration project. They justified their intention with a creative interpretation of federal law. In 1997, Congress passed the National Wildlife Refuge System Improvement Act, which was intended to unify the goals of 509 different federal wildlife refuges comprising 92 million acres across the US. As with many other such laws, Congress was clear that wildlife protection should be balanced with human uses and enjoyment. Congress also directed the USFW to "ensure effective coordination, interaction, and cooperation with owners of land adjoining refuges."

What Reverend Fuentes and the Solid Rock church received was something far less than "coordination, interaction, and cooperation." The law passed by Congress aimed to protect existing wildlife habitat, and to go beyond that maintenance baseline by restoring denuded or lost habitats "where appropriate." The neighboring Ash Meadows National Wildlife Refuge project—by its own admission—wasn't primarily to protect existing wildlife in its domain, but rather to "recover the listed species and their habitats through an ecosystem approach focusing on habitat restoration and the removal of threats." Congress had authorized habitat restoration "where appropriate," and Ash Meadows personnel interpreted "appropriate" to include stealing a stream and pond from a church.

If you read the thirty-eight-page environmental assessment

USFW's consultants prepared in concert with the Ash Meadows Refuge's director to justify their plans, you will find no mention of Solid Rock Ministries. No mention of the people the church served on their forty acres, or how they used the stream for baptisms, and used the pond it emptied into for the very kinds of recreation USFW is chartered to protect for all Americans. The report details potential effects on the pupfish and speckled dace, on migratory birds and ambient air quality, even on archeological sites—but it says nothing about the human beings experiencing life-changing transformations every year at the Patch of Heaven campground.

You will also not read that during public hearings about the intended project, agency officials shared plans that showed the stream continuing to flow through the church's property. An engineer later deposed by attorneys for the church said he simply decided to alter the plan to include taking the stream after public hearings were completed. Nor does the official USFW report reveal something else exposed during depositions, which is that while agency officials spoke to the public, a group of scientists was meeting in secret to plan the restoration effort. It doesn't explain, finally, what USFW even means by "restoration," because the stream taken from Solid Rock Ministries had run through its property since 1881. As with so many other federal environmental reclamation projects, the people in charge had arbitrarily chosen a nostalgic point in the distant past and declared that Science demanded the landscape clock be turned back to that date.

The year after the report, against the advice of a hydrologist associated with the project, and without permits required by state and local law, the Ash Meadows Refuge director not only had a dam built at the edge of the church's property, she had engineers reroute the stream *uphill*. Later that year, two days before Christmas, heavy rains caused the diversion channel to overflow, flooding the Patch of Heaven with water and mud that inflicted $90,000 in damage.

Greater outrages were to follow. When Reverend Fuentes notified USFW officials, he received no response whatsoever. Alarmed by this flagrant abuse of property rights and religious freedom by the federal government, the local Nevada Policy Research Institute provided legal assistance to Reverend Fuentes. Their letters went unanswered for months. Eventually Fuentes filed lawsuits seeking the return of his stolen water, and not in the form of muddy slurry that continued to wreck church buildings.

His legal odyssey continues to this day. The director of the Ash Meadows Refuge invoked qualified immunity, a doctrine manufactured by the Supreme Court in 1982 to shield government officials from lawsuits when they violate citizens' rights. USFW and Department of Justice attorneys likewise stonewalled, invoking a dizzying array of administrative rules that, when boiled down to layman's terms, meant this: when multiple federal agencies violate several of your constitutional rights at once, you have to choose which of your rights you want to sue to protect. This doctrine isn't the result of any congressional law, though I'm sure there's a Department of Justice attorney who can explain in excruciating detail how every jot and tittle is rooted in the rules that preceded it.

While federal agencies sent phalanxes of attorneys against Reverend Fuentes in every court hearing, the USFW's shoddy diversion apparatus flooded the camp at least three more times, the floods worsening as the erosion continued. Reverend Fuentes grew afraid the people his church ministered to would be in physical danger if they stayed on the property, so it lies unused. Damages to the church's property and buildings now stand at nearly a quarter million dollars.

Welcome to America, Victor Fuentes.

THE UGLY B-SIDE OF SCHOOLHOUSE ROCK

Let's talk about what happens after a federal law is created, once the little bill on Capitol Hill in the *Schoolhouse Rock* song has been approved by majorities in both chambers of Congress, and neither vetoed by the president nor struck down by federal courts. What a government textbook might say, if it bothered to address the question at all, would be something like this: *After a bill becomes a law, it is the responsibility of the Executive Branch to implement the law. Agency officials directed by the law to take action will develop the specific plans necessary to fulfill the law's requirements, and direct lower-level personnel accordingly.*

This is, more or less, correct most of the time, but with a catch: executive agency officials are not disinterested parties. To the contrary, they are very, very interested. To understand how what happened to Victor Fuentes and his church was not a fluke, but instead an inevitable result of what federal government power has become, let's look at a law that started out with very fine intentions, but became an absolute disaster nonetheless: the 1976 National Forest Management Act (NFMA).

The NFMA was intended, alongside previous legislation, to redirect the US Forest Service from its traditional mission, which focused on timber extraction, to ensuring multiple uses for our national forests. One of the chief provisions of the NFMA—at least so far as the Congress that created it was concerned—was to have the Forest Service be sure it was replacing the trees harvested from national forests. But the law also had a seemingly simple and innocuous provision which, by the time agency officials and a very active judge were through, would destroy thousands of livelihoods, set neighbor against neighbor, cause dozens of gruesome deaths, and cost thousands of people their homes.

This provision instructed the Forest Service to "provide for diversity of plant and animal communities based on the suitability and capability of the specific land area in order to meet overall multiple-use objectives." In plain English: "balance the protection of plants and animals with uses like logging and recreation." Not everyone would be happy with every decision to come out of such compromise, of course. The timber companies wouldn't like having to argue with environmentalists every time they wanted to open a new tract to logging. The dirt bikers and snowmobilers wouldn't want abandoned logging trails covered over. Some environmentalists, meanwhile, might tremble with rage on their condominium balconies in San Francisco and Manhattan at the thought of filthy humans setting foot anywhere on the 190 million acres comprising our (which is to say *their*) national forests. But that's how a deliberative democracy is supposed to work. You compromise with your neighbor.

But that assumes the agencies authorized by congressional laws will faithfully act within the letter and spirit of the laws passed by our representatives. The rest of this story illuminates just a few of the panoply of tactics extremists within and without government can use to reshape law in defiance of Congress. It also reveals how the machinery of our modern federal bureaucracy works, and the danger it poses to American self-governance.

Three years after Congress passed the NFMA, the US Forest Service issued a seventy-eight-page document based on input from scientists, members of Congress, and other interested parties, to guide the planning required by the new law. Buried in this documentation was a telling detail: more than a third of the recommendations came from *inside* the federal government, and nearly 25 percent from within the Forest Service itself. The agency had convened a Committee of Scientists (reverential capital letters in the original report), who had sagely determined that whereas Congress had said "provide for diversity of plant and animal communities" while enabling other land uses, what they really had meant was that "fish and wildlife habitat shall be managed to maintain viable populations of existing native and desired non-native vertebrate species in the planning area." The definition of *viable*, as well as what non-native animal species might need to be introduced into the habitat would be left, of course, up to a Committee of Scientists.

This alteration would serve as the cornerstone of additional agency rules, issued over the ensuing years in long compendia, and all overseen by distinguished Committees of Scientists. "The rule," observed environmental policy specialist George Hoberg in the *Natural Resources Journal*, "established ecological sustainability as the key objective guiding planning for the national forests." Since agency rules are treated as clarifications of the law, these statements by the Committee of Scientists could be used by environmental groups to challenge any activity in national forests that might threaten "ecological sustainability," which meant everything could be challenged. By 1991, a federal district judge named William Dwyer had halted logging in the Pacific Northwest until the Forest Service produced a plan to sustain the habitat of the northern spotted owl. When Forest Service experts came to him with a plan to set aside eight million acres where the spotted owl lived, Judge Dwyer said it wasn't good enough. The law (which is to say, hundreds of pages of regulations cooked up by Forest Service upstarts and their Committee of Scientists) required that the habitats of all creatures, great and small, be protected. As Hoberg explained: "From the time of his first injunction in 1989 to his approval of the Clinton forest plan in late 1994, Judge Dwyer essentially managed Region 6 of the Forest Service." The entire Pacific Northwest, in other words.

In an effort to break the impasse, Forest Service senior managers, who were still amenable to the old compromise of mixed use which included logging, brought in (you guessed it) another team of scientists. Nicknamed "the Gang of Four," they quickly shut out anyone who prioritized values aside from ecosystem protection. "It was an outlaw effort," reflected gang member Norman Johnson with glee during an interview by a scholar at Oregon State University. Referring to one of his academic partners in the effort, he said: "Franklin and I were in the university and they couldn't do a damn thing to us."

Following a pattern laid down by the earlier Committee of Scientists, the Gang of Four couched value judgments that were properly in the domain of citizens acting through their elected representatives—like weighing tradeoffs between ecosystem purity and jobs—as scientific matters about which there was only one right answer. The issues, described Hoberg, "were cast in technical terms to promote the social and political legitimacy of the outcomes."

And the Gang of Four succeeded. "I would challenge you," recounted Johnson, "to find any congressional criticism of this report. The Northwest delegation of Republicans and Democrats said, we asked you, and you told us, but the price is too high for us to allow legislation to pass on this." Shirking their responsibilities, most congressmen from the Northwest, wanting to oppose neither "science" nor jobs, called for more scientific study and waited on the incoming Clinton administration to fix the problem.

This had indeed been one of candidate Clinton's promises, so not long after taking office, he and Vice President Gore convened a "forest summit" in Oregon, along with several Cabinet secretaries. They spent a day listening to experts lay out the environmental imperatives. Johnson reports that one key slide, however, was withheld from that presentation: the one predicting that, based on the present state of USFS regulatory evolution, the timber harvest would fall "precipitously."

When a final plan was being hammered out months later, and Clinton's people saw those logging predictions, they pressed for "refinements" to the estimates, so their boss could announce technocratic victory: a solution that maintained high ecosystem protections yet at the same time protected jobs. USFS scientists dutifully produced a number, by simply adding to their yield calculations logging in old-growth forests. They did so because they knew environmental groups would stop it in court, using the very same Forest Service regulations they'd helped cook up. Hoberg summarized what agency activists accomplished in the twenty years that followed what once sounded like a reasonable law, as follows:

> An exceptionally vague statutory mandate to protect species diversity was clarified by a scientific committee and agency rule-making, and then transformed by a remarkable episode of judicial policy making into sharp cutbacks in logging in one region. The approach to planning in that region, which changed the agency's mission from multiple use to giving priority to ecosystem protection, then spilled over into other regions and filtered its way up to the agency leadership and finally was adopted as regulation.

The entire purpose of the US Forest Service was altered, in other words, without a single congressional vote.

The seeds were planted, meanwhile, for death and mayhem. A subsequent Forest Service rule, built on the accumulation of rules before it, not only restricted road-building on national forest lands, but required unused logging roads to be covered over with "vegetative growth." This became known as "the Roadless Rule." The Forest Service's own report mentioned objections from experts that roads were essential for removing dead and diseased trees before they become unquenchable kindling in wildfires. A subsequent General Accounting Office report warned the same. The Forest Service, however, was unfazed. Its latest rule was based, after all, on the "the law."

Not only had the agency eviscerated the 1976 law's expressed purpose of balancing land use with environmental protection, it had grown tentacles so far and wide that even subsequent efforts by the George W. Bush administration to rein it in were fruitless. Bush's people issued a ruling to replace the Roadless Rule, one that didn't change the preeminence of ecological protection, but which allowed states to pursue protection plans more suited to local conditions—like building roads to treat acres of diseased trees before they become deadly fuel. The layers of regulation enshrined as law in the decades preceding the Bush administration, however, were all that was needed by environmental groups in jurisdictions with sympathetic judges to stonewall this reform effort until President Obama took office and squashed it completely. Those regulatory layers, crafted in the shadows by activists, had taken on a life of their own, metastasizing beyond all democratic control.

So, the fuel built up, and eventually the wildfires came. 2020 was one of the worst wildfire years in American history. Several of the largest fires, fueled by tens of thousands of trees that had been killed in prior years by pine beetles, destroyed a half million acres across four western states, burning homes and taking human lives along the way. Scientists and politicians blamed global warming.

George Hoberg described how the environmentalists' victorious "strategy can be boiled down to two tactics: nationalization and judicialization." By keeping forestry decisions not just outside state authority, but even beyond the reach of locally-situated Forest Service officials, activists centralized their power. Then they extended it through careful, obscure, years-long rules revisions, each serving as a perch from which to craft the next one. Eventually, the entire edifice of law was far removed from anything the people's representatives had authorized, and so entrenched that even subsequent Forest Service officials, and the US presidents above them, had limited control.

DEEP AND WIDE

This is the real "deep state," a term that makes my liberal friends twitchy. They hear it wielded by conspiracy theorists who wear AR-15s into McDonald's and plaster "Don't Tread on Me" bumper stickers on their pickup trucks. It sounds like it belongs in a *Jason Bourne* reboot, not a thoughtful discussion of American politics. *Washington Post* writer Marc Ambinder was so fed up with deep-state claims from Trump administration officials and their supporters that he debunked the "myths" he felt they were disseminating. But then Ambinder made this damning admission: "the deep state contains multitudes, and they are often at odds with one another."

There's no singular deep state, there are *thousands* of deep states. I feel so much better now, don't you?

Armbinder's "debunking" is cold comfort for those of us who still believe in representative democracy. Though the specifics of the 1976 National Forest Management Act are unique, the machinations, the elite disdain for everyday Americans, the willingness to circumvent and subvert the law, are not. In one federal government agency after another, officials with strong convictions about how you and I should live our lives have been working their will for decades, amassing layers of rules and directions that the courts treat as if they were congressional laws.

Regulatory policy analyst Wayne Crews found that in recent years, for every law passed by Congress, federal agencies issue twenty-seven rules that have the force of law. Increasingly, they don't even worry about going through the cumbersome process of creating rules that allow for public comment, instead offering "guidance," "best practices," "fact sheets," and other breezily named instruments, "all of which is done," writes administrative law expert Philip Hamburger, "with the unmistakable hint that it is advisable to comply." Eventually, even our elected representatives, befuddled by reams of paper filled with technical legalese, take their proclamations at face value. *You're telling us the law we ourselves passed says we have to eliminate 90 percent of logging in national forests? Well, you're the experts!*

This unchartered, inexorably growing organism has been mangling congressional laws for decades, and as laws passed by a more polarized Congress become necessarily more vague, federal agencies gain even wider latitude to oversee American life. Instead of subjecting the inevitable tradeoffs of public policies to open debate, federal officials creatively interpret the laws as they see fit, laboring in the time they have before their overseers are cast from power to extrude enough regulatory sediment to prevent the next administration from undoing their work. The American Founders would consider it a criminal enterprise, just as they did when King George and his minions behaved similarly.

It's federal agencies, however, that are defining who the criminals are. If justice flows from the barrel of a gun, then our federal government is positioned to establish plenty of it, what with 132,000 full-time, law enforcement officers employed across eighty-three federal agencies excluding the military. It's understandable why they need all the firepower given that, as an American Bar Association task force on the federalization of crime noted, more than 40 percent of all federal crime laws enacted since the Civil War were passed after 1970. More alarming than congressional posturing to look tough on crime, which mostly creates federal penalties for what were already crimes well-covered and punishable by state laws, is the extent to which federal crimes are established not by elected representatives but by federal agencies interpreting congressional laws. "The number of federal criminal filings," writes law professor Julie Rose O'Sullivan, "more than doubled from 1964 through 2011 despite a significant overall decline in crime rates." O'Sullivan cites research estimating—because even its defenders can't quantify the number of agency-created criminal laws—that by the mid-1990s there were 300,000 regulations that carried criminal penalties. When the government can't even count how many ways it has to throw you in jail, you no longer live in a free society.

Aside from twisting and stretching laws beyond their original purpose, and then conjuring 300,000 ways to throw people in jail for not complying, federal agencies have birthed a hybrid creature that, according to Hamburger, has more in common with the Star Chamber under King James I than it does with American law. It combines the powers to make, adjudicate, and enforce the law, and places that power in the hands of officials who never have to face American voters and account for their actions. "The result," Hamburger writes, "is a state within the state—an administrative state within the Constitution's United States."

THE INEVITABLE DESTRUCTION OF THE REPUBLIC

There are some things that some agencies of the federal government can do well sometimes, like wage war, or quickly distribute funds to the bank accounts of citizens in dire straits during financial crises caused by other agencies of that same government. There are many more things that federal agencies can do well only in the sterile world of plans and paper, where their employees, contractors, and advisors are not themselves deeply invested in particular outcomes. I'm not saying that everyone who works for the federal government is more selfish or manipulative than any of the rest of us.[†] I am saying that the system in which they operate has metastasized to the point that it can no longer be effectively overseen or even reined in by our representatives in Congress even if they suddenly got a hankering to, which they almost certainly won't.

This isn't a polemical point, it's a mathematical point. Congressional scholar Philip Wallach has observed that the federal government has grown astronomically since the New Deal, rendering its operations too vast for any reasonably sized Congress to oversee. "Just 535 members of Congress," he writes, "with about 20,000 staff working to support them, must contend with their counterparts in the executive branch, whose numbers are several orders of magnitude greater than their own and whose permanence and institutional memories tend to be far superior."

Stretching all the way back to the 1940s, Congress has tried to restrain executive agencies with big reforms that required transparency, citizen input, and congressional approval. However, they can't overcome the sheer numerical superiority of the federal beast. It extrudes rules twenty-seven times faster than Congress passes laws. Many of those rules are intentionally crafted to bend the arc of government away from the will of We the People, and certainly not toward justice. This machinery is the antithesis of self-governance.

Congress, meanwhile—polarized and captive to the worst behaviors of the political class—shows little sign of wanting to change this dynamic. There certainly have been some shining lights, but they are few and far between and, so far, unable to rally

---

[†] I will say, however, that individuals in the political branches of the federal government *are* more likely to incline toward selfishness—among other bad qualities—because the game they've rigged drives away good people and attracts charlatans, manipulators, grifters, wind-testers, ass-kissers, and con artists.

enough support among their self-seeking colleagues to engage in the one kind of reform that has any promise of halting the mathematically inevitable destruction of the American republic. That reform is so radical that it would outrage most members of the political class, invite proclamations of doom from political scientists and the press, and frighten a great many regular people who can't envision a United States that doesn't have most of its political decisions made inside an imperial city. It's a reform, however, that's already happening, and it holds the promise to undo even binds like the one the Forest Service finds itself in, giving citizens authority once again to manage their lives, communities, and resources.

12

A RETURN TO THE UNITED STATES

"All societies think of themselves, once they begin to think of themselves at all, as representing a truth, a meaning, about the nature and destiny of man, and thus about that which, in the constitution of being, is above and beyond man."

—Willmoore Kendall, *The Basic Symbols
of the American Political Tradition*

WE THE PEOPLE OF THE UNITED STATES

Philadelphia, PA, 1787

To understand what we have to do, we must understand what we once were. What the Founders constructed during those sweltering summer weeks in Philadelphia was something unprecedented, even scandalous. Navigating between monarchy and mob rule, they crafted a republic rooted in deliberative democracy, accountable to the people, but with restraints on popular passions and factional abuses. Their vision was a system within which citizens governed themselves toward common ends.

Self-governance is the revolutionary concept at the heart of our distinctive experiment in liberty. It's the animating conviction behind neglected yet essential words that explain what the Founders intended by crafting our Constitution:

> We the People of the United States, in Order to form a more perfect Union, establish Justice, insure domestic Tranquility, provide for the common defense, promote the general Welfare, and secure

the Blessings of Liberty to ourselves and our Posterity, do ordain
and establish this Constitution for the United States of America.

The architects of our Constitution offered these words to
explain *what* they were doing, and *why* they were doing it. The
Preamble articulates a great aspiration about what America can
be. What's more, it offers a vision of what we Americans can be,
together. We know this is true because what follows the Preamble
isn't a document that appoints legions of government agents to
do the work of producing justice, tranquility, defense, welfare,
and the blessings of liberty for us. It doesn't consign We the
People to labor as loyal servants while leaving all that *common
good* business to our overseers.

Instead, the Constitution lays out a specific—and specifically
limited—set of responsibilities assigned to America's federal
government apparatus, with a clear intention that those functions be subject to oversight and approval by the representatives
we elect in our home states. To make the point crystal clear, the
Founders tacked on two amendments to the tail-end of the Bill
of Rights, noting that all the powers necessary for a people serious about pursuing justice, tranquility, welfare, and the rest of it
reside—unless they're specifically granted to federal officials in
the body of the Constitution—within the states and the people:

9th Amendment

The enumeration in the Constitution, of certain rights, shall not
be construed to deny or disparage others retained by the people.

10th Amendment

The powers not delegated to the United States by the Constitution, nor prohibited by it to the states, are reserved to the states
respectively, or to the people.

When we read the Preamble with these facts in mind, we hear the Founders calling all of us through the ages to participate in building up that "more perfect union," and to do so chiefly within our communities and our states. The common good was truly intended to be a pursuit that we citizens undertake together, not a Beltway scrum watched from afar. The Founders certainly meant for the federal government to have an essential role—indeed, their impetus for crafting the Constitution was the failure of states under a looser confederation to engage in the essential cooperation necessary to preserve the nation and allow their various citizens to engage in productive commerce. The purpose of the federal apparatus wasn't to pursue the common good, however, so much as enable *our* pursuit of it. Nor was it even to solve only those problems states can't solve well enough on their own, which is how its hyperactivity today is so often justified. It was created to "form a more perfect union," within which we citizens would establish justice, promote the general welfare, secure all those unspecified blessings of liberty, and so on.

Why did the Founders trust states more than their own creation?† Because state and local officials are closer to the people. We have greater ability to communicate with and hold them accountable than we do officials living in a distant city. James Madison explained it like this:

> The powers delegated by the proposed Constitution to the federal government are few and defined. Those which are to remain in the State governments are numerous and indefinite. The former will be exercised principally on external objects, as war, peace,

---

† It's worth noting that some Founders crafted state constitutions as well, and they gave those states greater powers than those enumerated for the federal government. In fact, they empowered states to do things clearly forbidden in the Bill of Rights, which is strong proof that they didn't intend those ten amendments to form a blanket prohibition on all governmental activity in America, just federal activity.

negotiation, and foreign commerce; with which last the power of taxation will, for the most part, be connected. The powers reserved to the several States will extend to all the objects which, in the ordinary course of affairs, concern the lives, liberties, and properties of the people, and the internal order, improvement, and prosperity of the State.

Taking all this alongside the documents and speeches swirling around that pivotal point in the history not just of America but of the world, it's abundantly clear that in our system of governance, We the People have the most important responsibility of all, because government officials are only allowed to do what we authorize them to do. They represent us, and they're supposed to be accountable to us. We citizens thus have a double role. We are invited into community with our neighbors, where we can pursue all manner of joint, voluntary endeavors. We are also called to appoint and hold accountable legislators who have specific, limited mandates to pursue *some* aspects of a common good.

This is self-governance. We select representatives to make the decisions about what our government does, and to rein in agents of the state who act contrary to the law and the people. We, through our authorized representatives, pursue portions of the common good through our government, which is limited to things that only governments can do well, and bounded by the Constitution's protections of minority rights. Being believers in freedom and free enterprise, moreover, the Founders knew most of our common-good pursuits would happen via our own hands, in our communities. They shared an understanding of democracy alien to us now, wherein voting is a last resort, after efforts to reason together and accommodate one another's views have failed to achieve consensus. From churches to social clubs to charitable endeavors to neighborhood-watch programs, Americans have traditionally enriched one another's lives not via the ministrations of government agents, nor by subjecting every decision to a vote, but cooperatively in our communities, with our own hands and labors.

Not that we're fussy about the distinction between what's public and private. Economists and ideologues fret over those things, whereas normal people just want what works. Public schools, libraries, and post offices can be community rallying points the same as barber shops, skating rinks, and local taverns. Whatever the root source of an institution's funds or the intentions of its creators, what ultimately gives or denies it vibrancy is whether people in the community where it sits choose to integrate it into their lives, and thereby let it integrate them into one another's lives.

The necessity of citizen action for all this to work reveals the centrality of two requirements for self-governance: freedom; and virtue. The first is a condition in which people must live, the second a quality they must possess. Numerous philosophical and theological tomes have explored the meanings of freedom and virtue. For our purposes here, common-sense definitions will do. Freedom is the absence of external constraint. Virtue, meanwhile, entails the presence of internal restraint. It encompasses many good things we choose to do, like helping our neighbor and working hard, as well as the good we accomplish by refraining from evil. John Adams put it this way:

> We have no government armed with power capable of contending with human passions unbridled by morality and religion. [...] Our Constitution was made only for a moral and religious people. It is wholly inadequate to the government of any other.

The Founders recognized freedom and virtue as counterbalancing forces in a healthy community. Freedom without virtue leads to license and ruin. It will manifest itself in what we see today, unfortunately, in parts of our country where norms and values have broken down, yielding consequences like neglected children, decaying buildings, and no trust among neighbors. Virtue without freedom likewise leads to the same sorry state. Absent freedoms like private property and free enterprise, communities remain desperately poor. They become subservient, and the state must step in to make their denizens behave. Good behavior that's forced rather than chosen ceases to be virtue.

Understanding these twin pillars of self-governance reveals the ultimate threat our unchecked federal behemoth poses. It undermines productive, cooperative endeavors in our communities. It seizes not only authority that originally resided in states and communities, but even that reserved for our elected representatives in Congress. Everything from where our sons and daughters are sent to die in undeclared wars, to whether local libraries can restrict access to pornography, has been taken out of the hands of we citizens and our elected representatives. This decades-long overrun of freedoms large and small has subtly and methodically undermined the virtues essential to a free citizenry, and has replaced them with subservience. The softly creeping tyranny of the political class impoverishes life and spirit.

None of this is new to students of the Constitution and American history. There's a reason I reiterate it here, however, in light of a metastasizing federal bureaucracy, a succession of US presidents who've overrun the Constitution in everything from trade to war powers, and courts that either (on the conservative side) regretfully apply the evolved agency understandings of vague laws, or (on the liberal side) happily invent progressive understandings of the law. American freedom, students of history know, began in the states. Now that the political class has turned Washington, DC, into an imperial city, *freedom can only be reclaimed by the states.*

The truth we must face is that we cannot allow the present level of power to reside in the federal government and still hold it accountable via the mechanisms woven into our Constitution. The American Founders designed a system to keep that kind of power *out* of the hands of federal politicians and agents, not make them behave nicely once they've grasped it. Perhaps there's no fixing things now. Perhaps America will go the way of other empires in decline. But we may as well face the reality we're in. Admitting it, as they say, is the first step.

A NEW REVOLUTION IN THE STATES

There is likely no restoring, in our lifetimes, the full authority our Founders intended for citizens to wield in our communities and state capitals. This doesn't mean we can't make great strides in that direction. Organizations like the New Civil Liberties Alliance, for example, are doing yeoman's work using the rules of the administrative state to beat it at its own game. They've filed lawsuit after lawsuit challenging the power of administrative courts, those dangerous hybrids that undermine law and justice by blending the roles of judge, jury, and executioner. They would say that we *can* make substantial progress, by waging relentless legal war against federal-agency practices that have no place in a constitutional republic of free people.

There's another organization working right now in your state, wherever you live, to pull power back into the hands of individuals and communities. It's your local affiliate of the State Policy Network (SPN), an organization I've served and supported for many years. State-based organizations devoted to restraining the power of government began popping up across the country in the 1990s, thanks to the work of SPN. Now they're active in all fifty states, challenging overreach by governors and state bureaucracies, but also working in concert to stop federal intrusion on our rights and self-governance.

Here's an example of how SPN groups work together to protect everyday Americans. In 1992, strategists with the Service Employees International Union (SEIU) and the American Federation of State, County and Municipal Employees (AFSCME), facing declining membership, launched a plan to bring tens of thousands of home caregivers into their ranks. Home caregivers look after the elderly, disabled adults, and children, allowing them to remain in their homes rather than live in institutions. Many caregivers are family members of the people they serve. They're paid either directly from state Medicaid agencies, or indirectly from healthcare providers who are paid in turn by states. For many people, this program is a way to give love and care to vulnerable family members without going bankrupt.

Union strategists saw home caregivers as cash cows who didn't need traditional union services, and whose pay "negotiation" would amount to a conversation with amenable government officials every few years. Using a variety of deceptive, coercive, and undemocratic practices, the unions pulled home caregivers into their fold, raking in an estimated $1.4 billion in dues from 2000-2017. Out of that sum, hundreds of millions of dollars were deployed in service to Democratic political campaigns from coast to coast.

Many caregivers, seeing the checks intended for their loved ones docked by union bosses, were understandably unhappy. Pam Harris was one such person. Harris relied on Medicaid to care for her disabled son in Illinois. Even though the Illinois Labor Relations Board had previously ruled that people like Harris were not state employees and therefore not subject to unionization, the SEIU-supported Illinois governor Rod Blagojevich—later imprisoned for trying to sell Barack Obama's vacated Senate seat—used an executive order to allow the state SEIU to enroll caregivers without a vote. Pam Harris reached out to a nearby organization, the Illinois Policy Institute, for help. That group in turn publicized the plight of Harris and others, and connected them to the National Right to Work Foundation, which offered legal representation in her effort to be freed from a union she hadn't asked to join. Harris's case went all the way to the Supreme Court, and laid the groundwork for subsequent victories in federal and state courts on behalf of people just like her, many of them assisted by other state-based litigation centers.

Opponents of the unions' practice, meanwhile, had begun to stress that rules established by Congress in the Social Security Act forbade third parties like unions from skimming funds intended for healthcare providers. To seal off this vulnerability, President Obama issued a rule that exempted unions from the law. It was pure abuse of power that prioritized the demands of an interest group over the well-being of vulnerable citizens. It's also the kind of insider DC baseball that most of us never read about. Unsurprisingly, then, when President Donald Trump took office, few people on his staff understood this rule. A coalition of State Policy Network affiliates and national partners laid out the facts for Trump's policy advisors. Within weeks, President Trump reversed the unjust rule, which otherwise might have stood in perpetuity, funding political campaigns at the expense of the elderly and disabled.

I tell this story to drive home my point: even if it were filled with work horses instead of show horses, Congress can't monitor and overturn everything federal agencies are doing to wreck individual rights and self-governance. Even presidential administrations have difficulty seeing what the people who supposedly work for them are up to. Given what the federal behemoth has become, only a nationwide network of watchdogs, policy analysts, independent journalists, and public-interest legal teams has a chance of evening the odds. And because most of what the federal government does is in (and to) our communities, state-based organizations are essential. Since the 1990s, state-based research centers, investigative journalists, and litigation groups have been the ones to shine a light on federal incursions into our communities, often drawing the attention of representatives and officials in Washington who still care about federalism and community autonomy, but who by themselves simply lack the research capabilities to discern what's going on.

Returning to the disastrous federal mismanagement of our forests, for example, there's new hope in the fact that organizations like the Goldwater Institute in Arizona and the Mackinac Center in Michigan have formulated viable paths state officials can take to navigate byzantine US Forest Service rules and protect forests within their borders. Taking a similar tack, the Washington Policy Center has documented how the Colville Indian nation in Washington State, exempted from USFS control, has managed forests on its lands to prevent the devastating conflagrations that are the backdrop to every summer in the western US. As the Forest Service itself grows increasingly desperate to find a way out of its self-created bind, it's these kinds of solutions, generated by people who live near the forests and want to protect them, that have the greatest chance of carrying the day. This is the kind of concerted action it will take to beat back federal agencies and their enablers, and it has to originate at the state level.

An often-overlooked challenge among states concerns not what federal agencies do directly, but how they bend states and communities to their will with funding that has strings attached. This is the poisoned carrot to complement the big sticks agencies wield against our communities. The average state now receives a third of its revenue from various federal agencies, and taking that money almost invariably means altering program goals and standards to suit DC bureaucrats. Some of the "shackles that come with the shekels" are better known, like the way Congress tied education funds to compliance with its byzantine No Child Left Behind Act, or highway dollars to a twenty-one-year-old drinking age. Others are so interwoven and subject to endless revision by federal agencies that teams of experts are needed to keep up with them. Browse through the Centers for Medicare and Medicaid Services' (CMS) website to see what I mean. It was CMS regulations during the COVID-19 pandemic that the governor in my state of North Carolina blamed for his draconian policy of keeping nursing-home residents isolated from their loved ones for months, until some were suicidal. His counterpart in New York, meanwhile, claimed CMS made him stuff COVID-positive residents *into* nursing homes. The most maddening part is that nobody could get a clear answer from CMS itself.

In a similar vein, federal agencies have showered funds on state and local law enforcement, hijacking them in service to federal priorities like the destructive drug war. The Department of Defense has dispensed military weapons that convert police units into assault squadrons. The Department of Justice operates a civil asset forfeiture program that turns local law enforcement into a crime ring that collectively seizes more personal property than all nationwide thefts combined. Federal dollars are subverting one of the most basic functions of local government, which is to protect citizens and preserve order.

There are thousands more strings than the few I've mentioned, and they're turning states and cities into mere administrative districts of Washington, DC. The Badger Institute found in 2016, for example, that large portions of Wisconsin state employees, including nearly half the administrators in its Department of Public Instruction, held positions created by federal funds. Many of them were devoted to bringing in more federal dollars, and ensuring compliance with the myriad regulations those dollars entail. Even more scandalous is that too many elected officials make it their business not to scrutinize these arrangements. The SPN-affiliated Oklahoma Council of Public Affairs uncovered, for example, that when Oklahoma legislators advanced a bill requiring state agencies to report the extent to which federal funds impinge on local autonomy, it was vetoed by their Republican governor. Nearly three-quarters of states have similar don't-ask-don't-tell postures, requiring no legislative approval for unelected officials in their state agencies to accept grants—and all their strings—from the feds. A third of states don't even require agencies to get approval from leaders in their own executive branch. One can see why, in his majority opinion in *NFIB v. Sebelius*, which concerned yet another instance of the federal government using monetary and regulatory strings to force state compliance with its will, Chief Justice Roberts wrote: "The States are separate and independent sovereigns. Sometimes they have to act like it."

Justice Roberts is right. A choice for independence over dependence is what has to animate us at the state level if we're going to take back from the political class our right of self-governance. It's the reason SPN and its allies have resisted the money DC dangled to induce states to join the Obamacare bandwagon, for example, at one point rallying 181 state legislators across twenty-seven states in just thirty-six hours to help stop a congressional Medicaid expansion bill. We know much of that supposedly free money will dry up, leaving state taxpayers saddled with enormous costs driven primarily by DC regulations over which we have no control. Programs like this take decisions about how to care for the most vulnerable among us out of our communities and place them in the Imperial City.

It's hard, at a point in history where it's second nature to let the feds handle all the big stuff, to imagine not wanting all those "free" DC dollars. What we have to remember is that it's far better to have less money and retain authority over how it's used, than to have more money but less authority as citizens. The federal treasure trove creates an enormous temptation for state and local government officials to take the cash, hand out goodies to constituents, and retire on their pensions long before the negative effects start creeping into our neighborhoods. That's why we need state-based organizations that hold local officials accountable for preserving self-governance and self-determination.

It may seem a contradiction to argue for local control given the weakness of some state and local representatives. Why should we trust them to make better decisions for our communities than experts in DC? The answer from a localist like me, when confronted with the enduring reality of fallen man, can only ever be the same: *we'll get more of the bastards, in the long run, if where they live is within a car ride of where we live.*

This really is the crux of the whole matter, as it always has been back to the days of our founding. Can citizens govern themselves without bringing about their own destruction? Often, when people prefer federal over state and local control, it's because the answer in their hearts is *No*. And, inevitably tied to that conviction is a darker one: *that power should be entrusted instead to people like me.*

This is the enduring conceit of the political class. It's buried in a document wherein the Forest Service justified its extensive alteration of laws governing national forests. Noting that legislators had debated for decades how to balance competing values with regards to logging, recreation, and environmental protection, USFS self-righteously declared: "Based on these factors, the agency decided that the best means to reduce this conflict is through a national level rule." Representative democracy, in other words, is too messy. The experts should be in charge.

Arrogant technocrats aside, there's another reason, given the toxicity of our political class and the destructive influence of their partisan foot soldiers, to be wary of pushing more authority back to citizens in our states. Won't that just spark Team Blue vs Team Red fights in our communities? Yes, the federal government is wasteful, abusive, and captive to ideologues, but at least it's, well, *over there*. Is self-governance really worth turning every state capital and townhall into a miniature version of DC?

If we were to apply the zero-sum thinking that dominates the Beltway, our answer may well be *No*. But restoring authority to states and communities isn't just about restaging DC battles closer to home. It's about doing government differently, deliberatively, with an aim toward greater understanding, consensus, and compassion. This is what the Founders intended and, despite their own bouts of acrimony, modeled. Readopting the deliberative mindset, however, demands we shake off partisan tribalism and rediscover the identities that should matter more. The encouraging news, as discussed in the next chapter, is that these nation-saving identities come more naturally to us. In fact, we've been carrying them inside us all along.

13

RECOVERING AMERICAN IDENTITY

"We are not enemies, but friends. We must not be enemies. Though passion may have strained, it must not break our bonds of affection. The mystic chords of memory, stretching from every battle-field and patriot grave to every living heart and hearthstone all over this broad land, will yet swell the chorus of the Union when again touched, as surely they will be, by the better angels of our nature."
—Abraham Lincoln, First Inaugural Address

"Somebody your age doesn't even remember what the country was like before. I do, and the country was a very good one. It had its problems, but the place worked. For one thing, we believed in the country more. Now nobody understands it. It isn't taught."
—Gore Vidal, interview in *The Progressive*, 1986

"A SEASON OF PEACE AND GOODWILL"

Neuve Chapelle, France, Christmas Day, 1914
The "extraordinary state of affairs," wrote Brigadier General Walter Congreve of Her Majesty's 18th Infantry Brigade, began when a German soldier shouted across no-man's land that they wanted a truce, and that he would come out if the British did. One of Congreve's men cautiously lifted his head from the trench and saw a German soldier across the torn and ruined landscape do the same. Before long the soldiers from both sides were mingling on the soil between their trenches, shaking hands, singing hymns, exchanging cigars, cigarettes, even helmets. Some, noted an article in *The Illustrated London News*, exchanged addresses. One Brit even gave a German a much-needed haircut. Several

soldiers buried the dead who'd been lying unattended among them. Elsewhere along the front, combatants played soccer games with whatever might serve as a ragtag ball.

This magnanimity was bounded by realism. General Congreve noted in his letter home that he declined to join the festivities, "as I thought they might not be able to resist a General." He also noted that one of his men, having enjoyed the company of the Germans' top sniper, a young man no older than eighteen, now knew where to aim when hostilities recommenced. "I hope we down him tomorrow," Congreve's informant told him. "I hope devoutly they will," Congreve wrote to his wife.

Elsewhere along the front, Captain Robert Miles of the King's Shropshire Light Infantry wrote of an "unarranged and quite unauthorized but perfectly understood and scrupulously observed truce [...] between us and our friends on the front." As in General Congreve's section, this began with a German soldier who, according to Captain Miles, shouted "Merry Christmas, Englishmen!" Miles reported the Germans were tired of the war, and that one asked, "what on earth we were doing here fighting them?"

Not everyone was as touched by these spontaneous displays of compassion; some commanders issued stern reprimands, and the French published a reminder that fraternizing with the enemy constituted treason. Corporal Adolf Hitler of the 16th Bavarian Reserve Infantry also strongly disapproved. There was deadly business to conduct, after all, and commanders feared what might happen if these human instincts spread throughout the ranks. Indeed, noted Captain Miles, the Germans in his sector were reluctant for the peace to end. "The beggars simply disregard all our warnings to get down from off their parapet," he wrote, "so things are at a deadlock. We can't shoot them in cold blood." The comity came to an end, as everyone surely knew it must, all too quickly. Captain Miles was himself killed in action just five days later, as were many of the others who'd enjoyed this brief spate of peace. Some of them likely died at one another's hands.

Killing is the norm in wartime, of course, which made this unauthorized peace all the more curious. Why did men who'd been fighting one another desperately for months lay down arms and greet one another as brothers? Perhaps because Christmas Day reminded them that they were more than soldiers; they were Christians. They were young men who missed their families. They had visited one another's countries in peacetime; many even had relatives across the border. Wartime patriotism can be a powerful motivator, but as the writer Alex Bellamy observes: "because we are all simultaneously members of different groups, we have multiple identities and sometimes this plurality comes to the fore, dampening bellicosity." For a brief time, at least, some of these soldiers remembered what they had in common, rather than what divided them.

LIFE: THE CHOOSE-YOUR-OWN-IDENTITY GAME

We all have multiple identities, and mostly not in the sense that demands clinical treatment. Quite to the contrary; they are essential to whole personhood. Researchers across a variety of disciplines call them *social identities*, with varied theories about how they function. In a nutshell, social identity is found where psychology intersects relationships. Our internal reasoning and perceptions deeply affect what we do, but so do relational factors like what's required of us in the social roles we play, our stake in various groups, and how we think people in other groups feel about us. Two of my social identities, for example, are Christian and father. They are roles I've taken on, they are facts that shape me, they are memberships in distinct groups with whom I share certain interests.

When our social identities remind us of the commonalities we share with others, they can indeed "dampen bellicosity." That's what happened for those soldiers on the Western Front; they were reminded that their enemies were men who also celebrated Christmas. I once heard a top martial artist recount how he had gotten into an altercation with another driver while driving with his training buddies. He and the other driver became so furious that they pulled over their cars and got out to confront one another. The martial artist was understandably thinking with the ego of a fighter, especially with his friends watching, so when the other driver rushed him, he swiftly put his violent talents to use.

What happened next, he said, was that as he was beating the other driver senseless, he glanced up at the man's car. Peering through the back window were two small children, tears streaming down their faces, screaming for their father. In that moment, the martial artist said, he thought of his own child. Thinking as a father rather than a fighter, he imagined what it would be like for his own little one to watch *him* being beaten in the street. His bloodlust and exultation immediately became the deepest shame.

The sight of those children activated, in other words, a powerful social identity that directly conflicted with his identity as a martial-arts gym bro. It broke the spell of his rage. The social identity we bring to bear in any situation profoundly shapes how we behave in that situation. How we respond can, in turn, deepen our commitment to certain identities over others. This martial artist, for example, was so affected by his experience that he developed a variety of de-escalation techniques that he now teaches to others, so they too can avoid, as he does, violence that isn't absolutely necessary. Whereas before he thought and reacted through the identity of a combatant, he became someone who works to engage his communities as a peacemaker. It's not that he abandoned his social identity as a combatant entirely—he still trains with other fighters and enters competitions. But that identity no longer governs his actions as it once did.

Cocky cage fighters have plenty of roadside altercations, parking lot shoving matches, and bar fights. We'll never see them, however, band together for widescale, coordinated nerd-bashing. Nor will all of us nerds and nerd allies rove our cities with torches, burning down every mixed martial-arts gym our noses can sniff out. Not only would that be weird, it's also the case that most of us have better things to do. The stakes just aren't that high in the jock-versus-nerd wars.[†] Neither side needs what the other side has. What's more, there are plenty of things connecting jocks with nerds. They're in the same families, go to the same churches, have their kids in the same schools, and live in the same neighborhoods.

Contrast that with competition in many parts of the world between ethnic, racial, and religious groups. Stuck in systems where those who control the government control everything from basic freedoms to scarce resources, and where loyalty to one's tribe is paramount, members of those groups have everything at stake in their competition. They have little to bind them to people in competing tribes. As a consequence, horrific violence sometimes erupts, metastasizing as more and more people are drawn in.

I worry America is headed in the same direction. One way we've mostly avoided such atrocities, despite deep religious and ethnic identities of our own, is with a Constitution that protects individual rights and limits government power. But stable societies depend at least as much, if not more, on norms of behavior, and on restraint, forgiveness, trust, goodwill, and many other virtues that can't be manufactured by a government. All of these qualities have diminished as our two major political parties have forced

---

† At least not in normal circumstances, though the film *Revenge of the Nerds* shows what can happen when nerds are pushed too far.

their followers to choose sides on issue after issue, erasing cross-cutting cleavages that once did so much to keep things collegial.

While most Americans remain pragmatic, not highly ideological, and cognizant of the many things that bind us to people who don't vote the way we do, that one-fifth of our nation who are strong partisans have come to resemble warring tribes. They hold few beliefs in common, they believe they have everything at stake, and as a consequence they feel little but disgust toward the other side. The people who lead them likewise sound like tribal chieftains whipping their warriors into a frenzy. The most outspoken among them portray their enemies as contemptible, as when Newt Gingrich labeled his opponents traitors, and Hillary Clinton wrote off her opponent's supporters as "deplorables."

In the age of fevered internet cliques and self-perpetuating partisan whirlpools, this acrimony has taken on a life of its own. Our political parties used to be more like rival sports teams. Cowboys and Redskins fans certainly enjoy seeing one another lose, and sometimes even have fistfights on Half-Price Beer Night, but they don't hate each other the way American partisans do. They don't end relationships with kin who root for the other team. They don't infest the comments sections online, turning each news item into proof that the other team's quarterback is a child molester, or an illegal alien. Even the most rabid among them has yet to open fire on the other team's training camp.

The political class doesn't want our partisan soldiers in their trenches to remember what they have in common. In healthy societies, political identity is a distant priority behind identities like parent, child, sibling, parishioner, neighbor, co-worker—hell, even bass fisherman. For too many of our fellow citizens, our political class has made political identity all-encompassing. They've divided family member from family member, neighbor from neighbor, co-worker from co-worker. They've energized their followers to get one another censored, shamed, and fired from their jobs. They've nurtured the most destructive elements of our nature in pursuit of the bare-minimum electoral margins needed to seize the reins of power.

We've got to find a way to restore the connections that cut across partisanship. We've got to find a way to activate within American partisans the same transformation of identity that occurred in that martial artist as he beat a man in front of his children. We've got to find a way to remind the enemies in their political trenches about Christmas.

THE DANGER IN US

The political scientist Robert Putnam is worried about America, too. Putnam's research revealed how deeply government behavior depends on something called *social capital*. If our social identities comprise relationships to individuals and groups, social capital is a quality of those relationships that makes fruitful cooperation possible. It allows children to buy eggs for their mother without getting ripped off by the grocer. It enables small businesses to transact without resorting to extensive contracts. It helps people secure housing and jobs. The absence of social capital, on the other hand, explains why some communities remain mired in poverty, crime, and social pathology despite truckloads of federal aid. Societies with ample social capital function better, and are happier places to live.

What Putnam found is that no matter how well-designed a government, the social capital of the society surrounding it will determine whether it's corrupt and abusive, or instead serves people's needs. This echoes what the American Founders understood, which is that "a dependence on the people is, no doubt, the primary control on the government." Constitutional scholar

Adam J. White elaborated on this idea further in *The Atlantic*: "the people themselves must have certain qualities of self-restraint, goodwill, and moderation." Citizens' qualities shape the qualities of their government. If the political class manages to twist the qualities of enough citizens so that they become distrustful enemies, then no constitution or law can save us.

Putnam next turned his attention to what he believed was a collapse of American social capital. In his popular book *Bowling Alone*, Putnam contended that Americans have disengaged from social life at a precipitous rate since the 1960s, which he said was indicated by declining membership in national organizations, as well as reduced engagement in communities and politics. In a newer book written with Shaylyn Garrett, *The Upswing*, he claimed that American civic-mindedness has been collapsing since 1960, displaced by selfishness and egotism. He identifies several causes, most of them rooted in individualism and free enterprise that the American Founders, among many others, considered a cornerstone of successful societies.

Putnam is enormously influential among disparate bands of communitarians, progressives, and conservative sectarians for whom his thesis is so grimly satisfying that they take it at face value. His work is, however, riddled with empirical errors and flimsy anecdotes. Several researchers have shown that when the data are properly examined, his claims about everything from dwindling group membership to reduced voter turnout are exaggerated. Other researchers show, meanwhile, that even where associations are dwindling, this may well be driven by social trends that have nothing to do with people becoming more selfish.

Despite these and many other analytical shortcomings, however, most scholars agree that Putnam has his finger on *something* that's wrong in America. Much of what he describes appears true of our most ardent partisans, who have indeed become less civic-minded, less trusting, and less tolerant of people who disagree with them. Putnam may be wrong about how far the cancer has spread, but he's not wrong about the disease. He and other scholars warn that as more citizens disconnect from one another and from the organizations that unify them, peaceful cooperation will be replaced by strife, lawbreaking, and violence. It may be worse than that, though; what we're seeing is not just the dissolution of social bonds, it's the formation of bellicose political tribes. The kind of social capital erosion we're witnessing can lead not just to chaos, but to civil war.

As we've seen over and over, this sickness among our nation's most ardent partisans doesn't describe most of us. Many Americans have plentiful connections with one another that Putnam's measures overlook. Likewise, as discussed a few chapters back, pundits' gloomy claims about American trust are also overblown. However, dysfunctions spawned by the political class aren't neatly contained. Even if not another one of us gets sucked into their machinery, escalating strife within the political class and their partisan foot soldiers has a destabilizing influence on the rest of American society. Since our media perpetuates the fiction that we're *all* in a red-state-versus-blue-state war, everyday Americans have less trust in the political judgments of their fellow citizens than they did even ten years ago. Too many of us believe that nearly everyone else is a committed member of Team Red or Team Blue. We don't realize how many normal, thoughtful, mentally healthy people are out there. This undermines, in turn, our willingness to trust the legitimacy of elections, of governmental decisions, of democracy itself. While it's healthy in a free society to be wary of government, when skepticism becomes cynicism, good people check out.

This suits the political class just fine. The less citizens participate in and trust the political process, the more our legislatures stay gridlocked, the more power gravitates to the Imperial City beyond the Potomac, and the more excuses political elites have to make decisions outside the legislative process. The only way to reverse the power of the identities they trigger in us—Democrat versus Republican, liberal versus conservative—is to strengthen better identities such as citizen, neighbor, co-worker, parishioner, friend. It's by seeing our communities and country through these eyes that we can begin to focus more on pragmatic solutions than partisan victory. This means we have a common goal with Robert Putnam, which is to strengthen social capital.

Unfortunately, Putnam believes that the best way to restore American social capital is by resurrecting the Progressive movement. Though I've mentioned progressivism a few times, I haven't explained the movement and its philosophy, mostly because that's the kind of cruelty that keeps people from buying one's next book. Suffice it to say that progressivism was a mostly well-intentioned but nebulous mixture of philosophy and political movement.† There are many conflicting accounts—from its admirers, no less—of progressivism's exact dimensions, so I offer instead this simple but reliable rule of thumb: if it protects experts from accountability and brings the common man to heel in the name of democracy and progress, it's probably progressivism.

The danger here is that the people who tend to agree about our need to build up connections between Americans that are rooted in healthier identities than partisanship are also partial to the kinds of policies and programs that flow from the progressive mindset. Putnam, to his partial credit, mostly calls for a rejuvenation

---

† The progressivism I'm talking about shouldn't be confused with the wheelbarrel full of grievance-besotted, crypto-Marxist, crybaby hatemongering carted around by college children and their adult enablers, who have resorted to calling themselves "progressives" because their predecessors appropriated and ruined the perfectly good descriptor "liberal."

of the progressive *spirit* rather than specific national programs, but this is like extolling the spirit of litigation, or leeching—the bloodsucking is implied. You can practically hear the vampires licking their lips as they read Putnam's call for "a retraining and retooling of average Americans for active citizenship."

At least Chairman Mao made that kind of thing sound fun. And who would place the American mind on a hydraulic lift, that it might be refitted with better ideas and convictions and—if Silicon Valley continues on its present Orwellian trajectory—a trust microchip? Who will foster the inevitable public-private partnerships, attend the conferences in Aspen and New York and Palo Alto, shake down the corporations, dole out the grant money, and hurl down the marbled hallways of byzantine federal buildings sunny but inscrutable annual reports on our Great American Retraining and Retooling?

Well, who do you think? They won't live in Tulsa or Tucson or Toledo, I can promise you that. They won't have experienced the stagnant wages afflicting a wide swath of the American working class. They almost certainly won't have seen combat, or raised foster children, or served on a town council. They *will* be able to tell you, however, which gastropubs in DC make a killer mojito.

At best, the leaders of the New Progressivism will be veterans from the ranks of America's Big Institution do-goodism. Academics, education specialists, managers from the nonprofit and even mushier public-private partnership domain, all of them with the best of intentions and not the slightest idea what many average American communities look, smell, and feel like.

At worst, wolves from the political class will oversee the flock, with all the perils that entails. Presidential commissions on citizenship. US Department of Education directives to revise curricula. Funding from the usual laundry list of federal agencies and their allies in the foundation and corporate world, every grant bearing pleasant-sounding but vague objectives, and each dollar aimed at strengthening political allies, weakening enemies, and raising up new cadres of acolytes. Undergirding all this would be the usual efforts to revise what words mean and what therefore may not be said, to redraw boundaries so opponents are beyond the pale, and to softly clarify for the lower ranks in organizations ranging from schools to government-contract recipients that challenges to the new orthodoxy will not be tolerated.

The last thing we should do is give the political class more power to conjure plans for national "unity," but our social capital continues to wane, and it's bound up with the danger of polarized partisan identities. The nature of our connections and the strength of our bonds substantially affect which social identities come to the surface. The animosity between Team Red and Team Blue goes up as partisan identities crowd out our commonalities as parents, workers, neighbors. This process was dangerously accelerated in the 1990s, as interest and social groups sorted themselves more thoroughly into one party or the other. Gun owners to the right; abortion-choice advocates to the left; white evangelicals to the right; black city dwellers to the left, and so on. In her book *Uncivil Agreement: How Politics Became Our Identity*, political scientist Lilliana Mason wrote that before this sorting, even people with firm partisan convictions were likely to "welcome the opposing team into their lives and to consider them as fellow citizens." Now, however, this bundling of interests and partisanship means "partisans have grown more intolerant of their political opponents. The new prejudice and distrust did not come simply from more extreme and intense policy disagreements. It comes out of the simple power of two or more social identities lining up together." If polarization is a threat, but we can't trust political elites to concoct remedies for it, what can be done?

FORGING AN AMERICAN IDENTITY

Though it received little news coverage because it was something stupid that Dan Quayle didn't say, conservative pundits certainly noticed when soon-to-be-sworn-in Vice President Al Gore reversed the meaning of the informal US motto, *E Pluribus Unum*, in his 1994 speech to the Institute of World Affairs, declaring that it meant: "out of one, many." We're wont to take our opponents' misstatements as proof of what they *really* think, so Mr. Gore's flub was judged by some to reveal disdain for American unity. America's strength, they grumbled, comes not from turning itself into a multicultural fair, but from tossing all those diverse flavors into the melting pot. Anyone who's enjoyed a good cheese fondue can attest that it's the marriage of flavors—along with a little heat—that makes the mélange superior to gnawing on a hunk of cheese and washing it down with a jug of wine.

It's reasonable therefore, in the face of rising, orchestrated animosity between members of Team Blue and Team Red, to believe that a fruitful way to rejuvenate nonpartisan identities would be to resist Mr. Gore's revision and stoke more appreciation for the Great Melting Pot. We are all of us, after all, Americans. Shouldn't this command greater allegiance than a political party, or an ideology? And if so, doesn't it require that we elevate our chief identity as Americans? More Pledge of Allegiance recitations, flags in front yards, reinvigorated history curricula, all that sort of thing? The danger in stoking up social identity rooted in mass collectives like race or nation, however, is that it's more abstract, and thereby more manipulable by demagogues. It evokes what Tocqueville described among French citizens as "an instinctive patriotism," which was "a sort of joy in surrendering themselves irrevocably to the arbitrary will of the monarch."

Little wonder, then, that American identity has been dragged into the political class's culture war. Even now they battle to simplify and polarize the meaning of the American Founding; (you may pick one and only one: *freedom*, or *slavery*), and to force their perspectives on the rest of the country via Department of Education edicts, textbook revisions, and propping up Howard Zinn's corpse in the passenger seat of Matt Damon's Tesla Roadster for another lap around the pedagogy circuit. The political class has no more interest in popularizing a truly inclusive American identity than a skunk wants to stand still when the wind shifts. As a consequence, our nation's partisans—the ones most in need of de-escalating conflict—eye any proclamation about the American Founding, or what it means to be an American, with great suspicion, and await directions from their party leaders.

All isn't hopeless, however, and maybe we can even thank Al Gore for inadvertently pointing the way forward. *E pluribus unum*, we must recall, was never a statement about rainbow coalitions and multicultural understanding. It referred primarily to the creation of a political union among thirteen independent, self-governing colonies. That understanding of *e pluribus unum* is, no doubt, discomfiting to a political class that would sooner we forget that we're citizens of towns and states governed by distinct institutions. Citizens of self-governing communities, after all, might start to question why everything now gets decided by a singular and metastasizing behemoth in Washington, DC.

Ex unum pluribus, to render Gore's phrase back unto Caesar, can return our thoughts to what it means to be citizens of states, cities, and communities. All these hold the promise of more significant social-capital cultivation than any abstract appeal to our common Americanness. We are American, the Founders would remind us, precisely because we are Virginians and New Yorkers and Minnesotans. "A commitment to localism," wrote Jay Ruckelshaus in *Governing* magazine, "promises ready-made practices, institutions and narrative resources to lower the partisan temperature and reorient American politics for the better."

Tocqueville would have agreed. He observed the ability of local associations to strengthen democracy by promoting what he called "enlightened self-interest." People who work alongside one another in particular associations—be they official organizations or a spontaneous crew of neighbors clearing out a tree that's fallen across the road—realize they share commonalities that extend beyond the immediate cause of their working together. The more they engage in side-by-side work, the more they experience a sense of the common good, a shared identity, and corporate (as in collections of people, not legal creations designed to protect individuals from the consequences of their actions) responsibility.

A closer look at the large-scale voluntary organizations esteemed by Putnam and others reveals that many of them grew in exactly the manner described by Tocqueville. A host of nation-spanning associations like the Independent Order of Odd Fellows, the Ancient Order of United Workmen, and others with names now lost to all but a few historians, were homegrown federations of local and state chapters that maintained considerable say over national operations. They mirrored what the American Founders intended for the relationship between the federal government and the states.

Most of these associations weren't political, wrote social movement historian Theda Skocpol in *Civic Engagement in American Democracy*, "but all celebrated 'American' identity, republican governance, and service to the nation." They also carried within them immense reservoirs of trust and compassion. We would do well to remember that the Odd Fellows kept empty chairs, during the Civil War years, for their southern brethren, and welcomed them back with open arms afterward. Compare this generosity to Pennsylvania congressman Thaddeus Stevens, who demanded that "just as a tribe of savages are treated with more rigor than civilized foes," Southerners should be stripped of their property in order to see "the criminals reduced to poverty." Little wonder that private groups of everyday Americans effected greater and swifter community-level reconciliation after the Civil War than the federal government. Again, the power of peaceful identities that are evoked within contexts beyond elite control can overcome the starkest partisanship and help people who have literally been shooting at each other to come together again as equal citizens.

This is a deeper kind of patriotism than what political leaders evoke on their stages with focus-group tested speeches and flag-draped pageantry. In contrast with the "instinctive patriotism" afflicting his countrymen, Tocqueville said Americans possessed a patriotism "more rational than that; less generous, perhaps less ardent, but more creative and lasting [...] mingled with personal interest." Observing that the French drew on centuries of attachment to land and country, yet suffered from citizen disinterest in daily affairs, Tocqueville asked:

> How is it that in the United States, where the inhabitants arrived but yesterday [...] where, to say it in one word, the instinct of country can hardly exist—how does it come about that each man is as interested in the affairs of his township, of his canton, and of the whole state as he is in his own affairs? It is because each man in his sphere takes an active part in the government of society.

Tocqueville saw that durable patriotism and civic engagement arose not from appeals by national leaders, but as a consequence of thousands of individuals and small groups cooperating in tangible work and self-governance within their communities. It was their engagement with one another that knitted bonds between people in communities, and those commonalities lifted their eyes nation-ward. As Putnam argued: "If we are to make our political system more responsive, especially to those who lack connections at the top, we must nourish grassroots organization." But if we can't trust Washington, DC, to cultivate networks of citizen relationships, what are we to do? The answer lies in understanding where a "we" originates. As in so many other areas of life, it's children who point the way.

THE MYTH OF ROBBERS CAVE

Robbers Cave, OK, 1954

The official story went something like this: several well-meaning social psychologists gathered twenty-two middle-class boys at the Robbers Cave State Park in eastern Oklahoma, and set them up in what might have been a fun summer camp. They transported the boys in two separate groups, so that neither knew about the other, and placed them in cabins on opposite sides of the campground. Before long, each group had given itself a name—one called themselves the Rattlers, the others were the Eagles. After a week of activities designed to bond the two separate groups, the experimenters allowed the two cabins of boys to discover one another.

Next came a series of competitions between the cabins, like baseball and tug-of-war. Before long, the two groups began behaving like rival street gangs, mercilessly mocking one another, getting in fistfights, and ransacking one another's cabins. The violence escalated until the experimenters faked an emergency that required the entire camp's cooperation. They followed this with other challenges aimed at the common good. Before long, the boys were behaving as one community, their animosities forgotten.

202 ■ I, CITIZEN

Billed as "the real-life Lord of the Flies" when it was published, Muzafer Sherif's study is now considered a classic of social psychology, and cited in thousands of academic papers. It's taught to students as proof that even among subjects with no underlying social or ethnic differences, strife ultimately emerges when they compete for resources. The only path to world peace, therefore, is to set aside competition, share resources, and work alongside one another for the common good.

The true story of what Sherif and his associates did to those boys was unearthed in 2018 by psychologist Gina Perry, after she happened upon notes detailing a failed experiment Sherif had conducted the year before his famous study. She used those notes to track down some of his subjects, and hear their stories. Prior to that aborted effort, Sherif had lied to the boys' parents by claiming he was offering their children "scholarships" to a Yale University-affiliated camp where they would enjoy a "wholesome cooperative living experience." Once he and his associates had the boys at the isolated campsite, they divided them into two groups, giving them names—Panthers and Pythons—and structuring competitions. The problem was that they failed to keep the boys separated from the beginning. The boys had grown to like each other, and didn't want to be separated. The experimenters had to work to keep them apart.

Worse still for Sherif, his planned competitions didn't generate the ugliness he was hoping for. He instructed his staff to stir up animosity between the two groups. Experimenters stole things from the boys' cabins, destroyed their personal belongings, and convinced them the rival group had done it. They pushed the boys into confrontations, encouraging them to fight. All along, Sherif stayed in the shadows, pretending to be a camp custodian as he took detailed notes.

Eventually the boys had a confrontation after the Panthers'

flag was found cut down. Something happened amidst their arguing, however, that the academics didn't expect: the boys listened to each other. The Pythons pointed out that none of them had knives, and the Panthers realized that if one of the Pythons had cut down the flag, he wouldn't have been able to keep from gloating. Someone brought out a Bible, and one after another, each boy from the Python cabin swore on it. The feud was over.

A frustrated Sherif, inclined to drunken anger, ordered his staff to step up the manipulation. He wanted those boys fighting, not reconciling. Eventually, the boys caught on to what his staff was doing, and despite their young age, they banded together. They refused to cooperate with Sherif's commands. This threw a monkey wrench in Sherif's grand finale, which was to reunite the groups around common projects, thereby proving his thesis about the power of community goals to overcome selfishness. Furious, he shut the experiment down, and sent the boys—some of them traumatized for years afterward—home to their parents.

The following year, with a new batch of boys at Robbers Cave, Sherif was ready. He and his staff took extra care to keep the boys absolutely separated except during times of orchestrated conflict, and manipulated the boys' emotions more subtly. They also made sure not to reveal any of this in their official reports. Thus, the "real-life Lord of the Flies" became standard wisdom among academics. Muzafer Sherif, manipulator of children and dedicated Marxist, finally had his proof that centralized societal goals in a communist regime were the only way to ward off the inevitable violence that comes from capitalist competition.

What lesson are we to draw from this, other than never to entrust our children to social psychologists offering lollipops and summer-camp scholarships? Academics still cite Sherif's research because it validates their belief that people—especially toxic males—are so inherently predisposed to tribalism that all manner of social interventions are justified. Even though researchers before Gina Perry's investigation had noted that Sherif's oversight of the camp likely polluted some of his findings, scholars remain reluctant to abandon his conclusions. We've all read *Lord of the Flies*, after all. We know what boys do when left to their own devices.

Except that those of us with children—including boys—know no such thing. Children cooperate far more than they fight. Visit any playground, and you'll see children making friends with one another much faster than adults do, and sharing the equipment far more often than they fight over it. Anyone who's attended a youth sporting event can tell you it's usually a few parents—not the children—who cause any problems. Similarly, it is rare to see students destroying one another's homework, or stealing much-needed library books to sabotage their classmates' research.[†]

Though Dr. Sherif, his colleagues, and the many academics who based their theories on his work all believed his research revealed insights about the children, what it really revealed was insights into the hearts of the kinds of people who would do such a thing: people whose pursuit of vainglory gave them no pause in manipulating and harming children. One of their subjects, years later, described what it felt like to gradually realize what Sheriff and his researchers were up to. They wanted the boys to believe they were at odds with each other, "but there was no way," Sherif's subject recalled, "that the fighting between us was 'natural.' It was crazy—a crazy situation run by crazy people!"

Perhaps not crazy, but certainly not well. One of Dr. Sherif's co-conspirators, Herbert Kelman, went on to become a highly

---

† Law students constitute, I am told, the occasional exception, but this can be explained by the fact that law students are generally the kind of people who go on to become lawyers.

influential scholar, ending his career as Professor of Social Ethics at Harvard. Several years after assisting Dr. Sherif, Kelman wrote a widely cited paper arguing against the practice of deceiving experimental subjects. Gina Perry recounted asking him whether his work with Dr. Sherif crossed his mind as an example of unethical deception. Kelman said it had never occurred to him, and added that if he were still under the care of a psychologist this oversight would be something he'd like to bring up in therapy. Dr. Sherif, meanwhile, was diagnosed with manic depression, and attempted suicide before finally dying of a heart attack in 1988.

The lesson from Robbers Cave is not that competition breeds violence or that small communities which are not centrally directed devolve into tribalism. The lesson is that manipulative authorities can evoke our worst identities. More encouraging still is this lesson: even eleven-year-olds can stand up to authority when that authority is dead wrong. If those children summoned the fortitude to say *No* to the adults pulling their strings, then so can we.

A GRAMMAR OF HOPE

We can find a final lesson from this sad tale, in the words Sherif's subjects used to describe their experience under his brief reign of terror. "They were testing us all the time," one said later, "as to whether we could be better than the others." Another reported:

> The point was to try to have us lose sight of what we'd been taught since we were little boys, and that was sportsmanship. You might want to fight tooth and nail over your ability to win a ballgame over another group, but you would not fight physically with them afterwards because that would have made you a lesser person.

Notice the battle for identity, to determine whether the boys could be transformed into the lesser people Sherif needed them to become, or instead hold on to the virtues their parents had instilled in them. When the boys finally began to catch on to what Sherif and his comrades were up to, one of them said: "You want to make us fight the others."

What underlies all of these statements is a point of grammar. The boys refer to themselves in the object form: *us*. The object of a sentence has things happen to it. The boys' use of the word *us* makes sense, because they were the recipients of cruel torments at the hands of Dr. Sherif and his co-conspirators.

But then the boys began to think for themselves and exercise volition. They banded together to resist the pressuring and hectoring from Sherif's crew. They broke the experiment, and Dr. Sherif's team came apart. Sherif blamed individuals on his research team for failing to follow his protocols. The graduate students who'd been assisting him gave up any pretense of being camp counselors and spent their time clustered together, worrying over what would become of their dissertations. Sherif retreated to lick his wounds and strategize how to salvage what remained of his Rockefeller Foundation grant.

"When it came down to it," one of the subjects said years later, "we stuck together, didn't we?" They certainly did. The passive *us* had become an active *we*.

This is where we stand now, as citizens of the United States of America. For too long, we have allowed a divisive, manipulative political class to foment discord in our communities while they concentrate power for themselves. It's time we resist their machinations, and take back the power granted to us in our Constitution. That begins by recalling that we are not a powerless *us*, but instead are *We the People*. As individual members of *We the People*, furthermore, each of us can rightly say, *I, Citizen*. The question then becomes: what are we going to do next, you and I?

14

A MANUAL FOR AMERICAN SELF-GOVERNANCE

"Five decades? Six? Seven? How long should it take to understand that the life of a community cannot be reduced to politics or wholly encompassed by government?"
—Aleksandr Solzhenitsyn, *November 1916*

"Hate and war are the *modus operandi* of the ruling class and its shills. But at the end of all our exploring, love wins. Doesn't it?"
—Bill Kauffman, *America First! Its History, Culture, and Politics*

It's no easy thing, saving a country. Some of us have all we can handle just saving ourselves. Many of us have families, businesses, churches, friends. We can't just grab a pitchfork and march on Washington. Which is good, because this isn't a march-on-Washington kind of book. Much of the problem is *in* DC, but that's precisely why DC must come last. You don't fix that place by marching on it. You might irritate a few people by clogging up the Metro, but the Metro doesn't work half the time anyway. The partisans in DC won't pause their nation-devouring work to reflect on the purpose of your march. They'll just take aerial photos and compare the size of your crowd to previous crowds. In typical KC Shuffle fashion, they'll turn the specifics of your cause into an argument about whose crowd-size estimates are better. They'll draw you into complaining that this or that news outlet ignored you, or slighted your crowd's magnitude. No, we don't fix DC by marching on it. We fix DC bit by bit, every time we make it irrelevant to one more decision in our communities.

As for your part in that, well, it depends on what you've got the time and stomach for. I've structured the remainder of this book, which I think of as the first draft of a citizen's manual, with an image of concentric circles in mind. I'll start at the innermost one, closest to home, and work outward. Hopefully you'll find more than a few things you can fit into your life. Maybe you'll even find some things into which your life can fit.

LOVE

When one of the boys victimized by Muzafer Sherif's failed experiment departed the camp, a researcher, fishing for a quote that indicated fanatic in-group loyalty, asked him how he felt about his group, the Panthers. "They're all good guys," the boy replied, "every one of them, even in the other group, I love them all."

That was not the answer the researcher was hoping for. Nothing is more threatening to divisive people than love. So maybe that's where we start, with loving our neighbors. Loving one another is always a good idea, but true love is an *action*, not a *feeling*.[†] Loving our neighbors means *doing* things. I don't offer this lightly, so I hope that you don't take it lightly. Loving our neighbors is hard work. I mean, you have to get to know them and spend time with them, and put up with stories they think are interesting but which don't interest you, and be around their children who are maybe a little annoying or even downright terrible. Harder still is suspecting, in the back of your mind, that

---

† I was going to say that this isn't a "relationship" book, but I suppose that actually it is. In which case allow me to suggest that a relationship can be transformed once each partner stops obsessing over how much love he *feels*, and focuses instead on how much love he *practices*.

they are likely thinking all of the same things about you and your stories and your children.

People are exhausting, and as a dedicated introvert, I'd rather they stay on their side of the fence. But here's the thing, and there's just no getting around it: we can't heal a nation if we can't love our own neighbors. We can't govern ourselves if we can't find a way to get along with the people next door.

Alexis de Tocqueville, alongside many scholars of democracy, would say that learning to love our neighbors is good training for people who govern their communities together. Loving your neighbor entails resolving problems together, like what to do about a dog that keeps getting loose, or how to approach a homeowner whose pine tree has begun to lean too far over the street. It entails working alongside one another to build a wheelchair ramp for an incapacitated neighbor, or bringing meals to a grieving home, or looking after the kids of a drunk down the street. All these efforts at working out problems in our communities orient us toward an older form of democracy, in which, according to chronicler of local governance Jane Mansbridge, "people who disagree do not vote; they reason together until they agree on the best answer."

Loving our neighbors will help counteract our tendency—made easier in an atomized, customized, earbuds-in, eyes-on-the-screen, insulated society—to avoid face-to-face conversations with people who don't communicate the way we do, or want what we want, or even agree with us about what the actual problems are. It may surprise you to read this after my castigation of our polarizing political class, but face-to-face conflict among people who share common ends is the sign of a healthy community. The philosopher John Courtney Murray wrote that civilization doesn't even exist, in fact, unless its members are "locked together in argument." That's because we know then that citizens share enough in common to have an argument, and they are bound closely enough together to seek a widely acceptable resolution.

Contrast that with partisans and our political class, who shout past and try to discredit, outmaneuver, disempower, and silence one another. It's tempting, watching their antics, to believe our goal should be nationwide consensus, if only to shut them up. "It is not true," Willmoore Kendall counters, "as we are often told nowadays, that argument ends when agreement is reached; it is, rather, when agreement is reached that argument *begins*, becomes *possible*." What Kendall describes is a community that agrees on ends, which is the case for most everyday Americans even now, though certainly not for the political class.

COMMUNITY

I've always liked reading about coffeehouses and taverns where great ideas and movements take hold. Introvert that I am, there's still something deeply appealing about the notion of coming together with people who want to talk about things that matter, quaffing beverages that either stimulate our synapses or lower our inhibitions or both at once, and having great and small meetings of the mind. No orthodoxies, no sacred cows, no tender feelings to tiptoe around, just adults in conversation and deliberation.

Ray Oldenburg has written eloquently about what the disappearance of these "third places," as he calls them, has cost society. They used to function as democratic meeting places where people of varied social stripes would congregate, knitting together communities in "a good-hearted atmosphere in which honest expression triumphs over sophistication." Think of them as extensions of loving our neighbors. Instead of just being with people on our block, we can mingle with people from several surrounding blocks, and others besides.

Or rather, we *could*. Our cultural collision of suburbanization, zoning, and a highly-scheduled, two-income-family economy has all but eliminated the neighborhood bar or coffeehouse within walking distance. Other establishments have filled portions of that void, here and there. If your local McDonald's is like mine, for example, you'll probably find there are certain hours of the day when all the old-timers congregate to eat value meals, sip coffee, and banter. When I lived in Wichita, there was a particular Starbucks where a lot of divorced and hurting men would gather every morning. Nobody planned it, they just learned that was the place to go and not be alone.

What does any of this have to do with saving America? Well, you can start your own version of a gathering place. Earlier, I mentioned an ecumenical, monthly gathering of men with which I'm involved. My wife hosts one for women. In both groups we talk about various notable figures in the Christian faith, though my men's group invariably strays into politics and culture. I don't know what happens in the women's group, but my home office is above the room where they gather, and for church-going women, they sure can get rowdy. Both gatherings are based on a similar group that I was part of in Wichita, which grew into the Eighth Day Institute.

My point isn't that you should start a same-sex, Christian-oriented discussion group. Start a coed gardening co-op, or a fantasy-novel book club. Just join with some people you trust, turn off the TVs and smartphones, and start being together in community. Harkening back to my point that we don't need to argue less as a society but to argue better, the aptly named Better Arguments Project offers a host of free resources you can use if you want to spark these kinds of group discussions in your community.

There are three essential ingredients, however, to which you must hold fast. The first is open dialogue. Our groups have twenty-to-thirty-minute presentations sandwiched between ample periods of group and one-on-one conversation. The second ingredient is an open door. Every person in my group is urged to invite people he thinks will fit in. Nobody does this lightly, because none of us wants to be stuck in the room with a knucklehead. The third ingredient is open dialogue. People say what they have to say, and if other people don't like it they say so.

Perhaps you're still wondering how any of this saves America. Well, as we've seen, one of the reasons that power drifted to DC, and from there into the hands of an unaccountable federal bureaucracy, is because our political leaders and their partisan foot soldiers became polarized. The political class polarized because ideological victory became more important to them than governing. A fifth of our population dutifully followed suit in part because the bonds that ought to be more important to them than partisanship were weak. To pull them out of their ideological whirlpools, we have to reinvigorate those nonpolitical bonds. My group is just twenty or so guys, and maybe yours won't be any bigger. But imagine what could happen if more and more of us citizens started groups like that, pulling in neighbors, colleagues, and friends. We can emulate those "third places" and all the beneficial democratic flora they cultivated, along with the inoculations they provided against isolation, demagoguery, and the elevation of political identities over identities that are far more important to a community seeking its own way.

MEMBERSHIP

Given Robert Putnam's work on how associations once knitted together citizens from all walks of life, you won't be surprised to see me recommend, as we expand outward from our neighborhoods, that you get engaged in some, if you aren't already. From F3 Nation, a network of local groups for men focused on fitness, faith, and friendship, to 4H, which is still one of the best places you can go if you want your children to learn gun safety and marksmanship, there's plenty out there that will do more to advance self-government than scoring political points on Facebook.

Even if you're not religious, you might be interested to learn that churches have proven to be prime generators of social engagement in communities. Churches of all stripes bring people out into their communities, fueling arts, cultural associations, and humanitarian efforts. One urban study found that while every other nonprofit that claimed to serve the needy had moved out of poor neighborhoods, it was church-affiliated groups that remained. Interestingly, that study also found that church groups were the only ones shut out of funding by grant makers like the United Way, which didn't want to be associated with religion. This finding fits other research indicating that many large foundations, rather than empowering local communities, have bankrolled lofty efforts—often in conjunction with federal endeavors—to steamroll communities in pursuit of goals held by the political class. So even if you're not part of a church, if you care about increasing community ties that cut across partisanship and remind citizens of their more enduring identities, you might consider supporting one.

CONSUMPTION

There's plenty of reasons to support local businesses that don't have DC lobbyists working to sell out your community and subvert your values. One product that frequently gets overlooked among those of us who try to buy local, however, is journalism. We've already talked about the grimly distorted picture national news corporations paint for Americans. A distressing corollary is that most of us now get far less state and local news than we once did. Public policy scholar Philip Napoli and his research team found that only 17 percent of news delivered into communities is about local issues, problems, and governance. Many news organizations that we think of as "local" have mirrored the transformation in political parties, turning their eyes from their communities to (at least where politics is concerned) Washington, DC.

When citizens don't have reliable news about their towns and counties, their capacity for self-governance is diminished. Summarizing research showing that the decline in local reporting has led to lower voter turnout, less responsive officials, and increased government corruption, Joshua Benton wrote in the *Nieman Journalism Lab* that insufficient journalism directly undermined citizen control over local government: "With fewer resources [...] reporters are more likely to report on an issue only when it reaches a public state of prominence—by which time the city's plans may have already been shaped without much public input."

Perhaps just as damaging, by displacing local focus with conflict-oriented national political coverage, it drives up partisan animosity in communities. Rather than engage in local problems that have the critical side benefit of yielding communication and compromise across party lines, citizens sit in their homes, raging at congressmen, presidents, and the buffoons in the Other Party who elect them.

In my neck of the woods, I receive three print publications focused on state and local news. One is an ad-supported weekly that covers my town and the two adjacent towns. Its handful of writers reports on every town-council meeting, as well as county matters. The other two are weeklies that cover state politics. I also subscribe to the Substack feed of a state-focused independent journalist who is deeply knowledgeable about North Carolina and how state and local politics work in general.

If you want to follow suit, you needn't spend months comparing local news sources, but I urge you to look into their ownership. An underreported story following the political defeat of a natural gas pipeline planned by Virginia-based Dominion Power, for example, was that associates of Warren Buffett bankrolled the opposition, including key legislators. Buffett's Berkshire Hathaway empire, meanwhile, had quietly bought up most of the newspapers in central and western Virginia. Perhaps unsurprisingly, their reporting about the pipeline was uniformly skeptical. After the pipeline was defeated, Dominion Power exited gas-transmission altogether, and sold those assets to a company owned by—you probably guessed it—Berkshire Hathaway, which now controls the largest stake in the mid-Atlantic's only liquid natural gas storage exporting facility. Knowing who makes the products we consume is important, and not just when it comes to food.

After investigating who owns what news sources, I urge you to pick a few and pay attention to what they cover. Browse the website of your State Policy Network-affiliated think tank to see what they're concerned about, and see if your local paper reports on it. If not, find one that does, even if it disagrees with that think tank. *Especially* if it disagrees. Just support people who are still trying to tell you what's happening in your back yard. Maybe they're too liberal for your tastes, or too conservative, or too dull. At least their eyes are focused in the right place. That's an important start.

STATE POLICY ORGANIZATIONS

Moving beyond your neighborhood and local community, I encourage you to find and support organizations affiliated with

State Policy Network. Not only have they banded together to stop egregious federal encroachments on self-governance, they battle the same kind of executive overreach within state borders. The COVID-19 pandemic put into sharp relief just how dictatorial some state governors can be when given the chance, and it was state policy watchdogs that pushed back. As I write this book, for example, federal investigators and state legislators are waking up to the likelihood that New York governor Andrew Cuomo not only exercised unilateral authority to pull thousands of elderly COVID patients out of hospitals and push them back into their nursing homes, but covered up the subsequent death count as the disease raged through those vulnerable populations, taking more than 12,000 lives. While the governor's staff has denied that his decision contributed to the death toll, statistical analysis from the Empire Center for Public Policy, whose legal team helped force the state to reveal data it had been obscuring, has indicated otherwise. Every nursing home in otherwise low-incidence areas that Governor Cuomo forced to take in a COVID-positive patient, Empire's researchers found, was correlated with just over nine additional deaths in that facility.

It's likely Cuomo isn't the only governor whose dictatorial behavior, unchecked by legislators who shirked their responsibilities, cost lives. The Mackinac Center for Public Policy in Michigan has sued the state Department of Health and Human Services for data it has refused to disclose related to Governor Gretchen Whitmer's policy, similar to Cuomo's, of shunting COVID-positive patients into nursing homes.

Beyond nursing homes, Whitmer, Cuomo, and a host of other governors shut down their economies, often with byzantine rulings about what constituted "essential" businesses (liquor stores, *yes*; churches, *no*). Governor Tom Wolf of Pennsylvania closed payroll companies, without which essential medical personnel couldn't be paid, and shuttered turnpike rest-stop bathrooms even as he called on truckers to keep delivering products throughout the Keystone state. SPN's affiliate in Pennsylvania, the Commonwealth Foundation, has steadily kept these and other arbitrary exercises of state power in front of the press and lawmakers.

The Wisconsin Institute for Law and Liberty, likewise, has hammered away at its governor's tyrannical behavior in lawsuit after lawsuit, permanently altering the power of the state executive branch to rule citizens without input from their elected representatives. Dozens of state legislatures have now begun to rein in governors' creative interpretations of emergency-powers statutes, in no small part because state policy organizations were shining a light on them. We have no hope of restraining the feds so long as we allow our state governments to mimic them, so supporting state-based policy organizations that keep government accountable is essential.

Beyond groups focused on public policy, there are opportunities to emulate programs emerging across the US which bring together people from divergent political viewpoints to give them the experience of discussing divisive issues in a respectful manner. The conservative John William Pope Foundation in North Carolina, for example, partners with the liberal Z. Smith Reynolds Foundation to sponsor the NC Leadership Forum, based at Duke University, which convenes gatherings of business, civic, and political leaders. They discuss issues central to the state's future, like job growth and education policy. The goal isn't to reach consensus, it's to build camaraderie and respect and to help people understand why political opponents disagree with them.

The social psychologist Jonathan Haidt has identified failure to cultivate such understanding as a key impediment to collegial politics—the contending sides literally can't imagine anything motivating their opponents beyond stupidity or hatred. This only reinforces the cycle of conflict, because when we view our opponents that way, we see no point in a conversation. Programs like the NC Leadership Forum reverse that dynamic, making it harder to dislike someone solely because of his views, because you've spent time in genuine conversation with him. One state legislator who participated in the forum noted that prior to that, he'd never even had lunch with a legislator from the other party.

The Pope Foundation and several centrist and left-of-center partners also sponsor the NC Institute of Political Leadership, which prepares leaders for public service, regardless of political party. Participants learn everything from how to run a campaign to strategies for building consensus once in office. Restoring decency to public service begins by attracting and training decent citizens to throw their hats in the ring. This program is a way to open the door not just to better politics, but to more representative government, as citizens who otherwise wouldn't know the first thing about how to get into public service receive soup-to-nuts training.

These initiatives by far-thinking foundations in North Carolina, Aspen Institute programs like the Better Arguments Project and Devil's Advocacy Initiative, learning exchanges sponsored by the Kettering Foundation, and many other local initiatives by politically diverse thinkers who care about restoring American representative democracy, are the philanthropic equivalent of the small discussion-group formation I'm urging every reader to consider. No one program by itself will reshape the political landscape, but thousands of them, well, that's a different matter. Just as American polarization was an intentional strategy by members of the political class, healing our divisions will require the same deliberate, long-term work. The more charitable foundations that emulate these programs in other states, the better for all of us.

Finally, even if no organizations in your area do this kind of work, and you haven't the wherewithal to get such a thing started, you can still do your small part to attract and sustain better people in public service by simply getting to know some of your local public officials. Many of them are well-meaning people, but if they only ever hear from hardcore ideologues and representatives from narrow interest groups, they're vulnerable to tunnel vision, disillusionment, or both. Your act to restore democratic accountability can be as simple as meeting your town councilman for coffee.

CONGRESSIONAL REFORMS

Just as there are numerous books about how Congress does and does not work, there are dozens on how to fix Congress. I won't summarize them here, and I won't list my favorites, because most of them require a willingness among congressional leaders to cooperatively change their behavior. If such willingness existed, Congress wouldn't be nearly so dysfunctional in the first place. I do want to mention one reform that I believe does have a chance of enactment, because it would give neither party an advantage over the other. It would, however, give them more leverage when dealing with runaway federal agencies. As discussed earlier, a key reason agencies have run roughshod over congressional laws is the overwhelming decision-making and information advantages they've built up over Congress. Quite simply, members of Congress who are serious about reclaiming their traditional oversight and legislative roles need to beef up their independent research organizations. "By shortchanging its own internal resources for decades," argued a politically diverse team of congressional scholars in a volume of studies titled *Congress Overwhelmed*, "Congress has effectively outsourced policymaking to the executive branch and to the thousands of lobbyists who have become the true keepers of expertise and policy know-how in Washington."

Some Republicans (I used to be one of them) denounce legislative support entities like the Congressional Budget Office (CBO) as unimaginative bean-counters sold out to old Keynesian models of political economy. However, organizations like the CBO, the Government Accountability Office, and the now defunct Advisory Commission on Intergovernmental Relations, which used to keep watch over federal incursions on state and local authority, can play a valuable role in counterbalancing reams of data from deceptive federal agencies and breezy, ill-supported claims from lobbyists and interest groups.

TRAINING CITIZENS INSTEAD OF FOLLOWERS

The final step I'll mention is, I believe, the most important. Many of us have been entrusted not just with the privileges of citizenship, but the responsibility of training up future citizens. This is too sacred a trust to be handed over mindlessly to any organization, and in particular to any school. Too much of our education system, driven by exactly the kinds of federal meddling and manipulation that undermine American self-governance in so many other areas, has been bent towards churning out obedient, standardized test-takers, not whole individuals interested in the world and capable of logical, civil discourse.

This is not a brief for private schools. I have six living children, and we've run the gamut from homeschooling to Classical Conversations to charter schools to plain-vanilla public school. What I am arguing is that we all need to be *engaged* in our children's schooling. My experience is that in public and charter schools, the engagement we need is going to be very different than what administrators want, which is booster clubs and dance chaperones (I've happily done both). It means asking a lot of questions about curricula and standards, and how the school is run. It means being an ally to competent teachers and a burr under the saddles of the incompetent ones. It means making sure teachers and principals and school boards know we're watching, we care, and we're not intimidated.

None of that is possible without a point of view, and so I recommend further that you read *The Making of Americans*, written by the progressive yet radically antiestablishment scholar E.D. Hirsch. If you're connected with an SPN affiliate in your state, you'll probably find that they're working on education reform, which is a central focus of our network from coast to coast. From school choice to learning pods to homeschooling, to charters and improved public-school curricula, our organizations are engaged in the critical work of putting children's interests over those of teacher unions, government educrats, Big Tech, Big Agriculture, the college-loan cartel, the military-industrial complex, and anyone else who treats our children like so many cogs in their machinery.

Engaging in the systems that purport to educate our children is, of course, its own education. It's also beneficial; one of the key findings of the seminal Coleman report on school performance was that private and Catholic schools outperform public schools not because of better teachers or more money, but due to significantly greater parental involvement. When we engage, our kids do better. That's probably true about more things in life than just school.

THE END OF THE BEGINNING

History, as everyone says someone said, is written by the victors. This is why most citizens never learn that there was a time before newspapers feigned objectivity, before presidential debates were buzzword exhibitions tightly managed by national journalists, before nearly every politician was an attorney with no record of accomplishment beyond "public service," before so much power was concentrated in the Imperial City, and before our leaders deliberately fomented animosity among the citizens they claim to serve. We're inclined to believe what the political class does is legitimate because they tell us it is. Because they write the rules, and they write the history.

But they're not the victors yet, are they?

I've mentioned above just a few things to get us started on the path to the fuller citizenship our Founders intended. I hope to hear more ideas from readers who care to reach out. Lord knows there's plenty that needs to be done. If nothing else, we all need to start repeating the truth to our families and neighbors: *we* are not broken, the political class is. *We* are not at war, they are. *We the People can still make this country work.*

But We the People have to get it together while there's still time. As I mentioned at the start of this book, we're all citizens, which means we're all responsible. I also said this is a story of hope. The hope is that when we look deep enough into our communities, we see a population unlike that which the political scientists and pundits describe. We may not be the best educated, we may be uncouth, distracted, tired, and occasionally confused. But most of us have similar goals for our families and communities. Most of us are willing to listen, to compromise, and to help one another along. We're still a pretty good country, all in all. If nothing else, we know this is true by the characters of the people who despise us.

And if history, even after the professionals have warped and sanitized it, has taught us anything, it's that you can't count Americans out. We're innovative. We're scrappy. We're stubborn.

Don't count yourself out, because those qualities ran through your ancestors, and now they run through you. You're a citizen of a country established in blood and faith and freedom. It's not perfect, and neither are you, and neither, certainly, are its critics. But it's your country, and you are its citizen, and that can mean something again.

ACKNOWLEDGMENTS

Many thanks to the following people for reading early drafts and giving me unvarnished feedback: Veronica Burchard, Carrie Conko, Todd Davidson, Carl Helstrom, John Hood, Brooke Medina, Kathleen O'Hearn, Rebecca Painter, Madison Ray, Tracie Sharp, and Jon Sink. For their research assistance and valuable insights along the way, I thank Jacob Meckler and Nate Wilbert.

Finally, I give thanks to and for Maggie Woodlief, who managed our home and children and a thousand things I neglected while writing this book, all while working her own full-time, stressful job. Thank you, Maggie. You make my life work.

NOTES

INTRODUCTION

2 "Whenever you find yourself..." Twain, *The Complete Works of Mark Twain: Mark Twain's Notebook*, 1935, p. 393.

3 "...the latter's podcast." Klein, *Vox Conversations* podcast, 2020.

CHAPTER 1: THE GREAT AMERICAN CON

19 "believe that citizen..." If you want a solid grounding in what citizenship once entailed, I recommend Victor Davis Hanson's *The Dying Citizen*, 2021.

CHAPTER 2: THE AMERICAN SPHINX

23 "background checks..." FBI, "NICS Firearm Checks: Month/Year," 2021.

23 "40 percent of sales..." Firearm Industry Trade Association, "First-Time Gun Buyers Grow to Nearly 5 Million in 2020."

24 "...even his race." Pew Research Center, "The Partisan Divide on Political Values Grows Even Wider," 2017.

24 "violence is justified..." Diamond et al., "Americans Increasingly Believe Violence is Justified if the Other Side Wins," 2020.

24 "...injured or die." Kalmoe and Mason, "Lethal Mass Partisanship," 2019.

25 "vapor of duplicity..." This is a theme of historian Joseph Ellis's biography of Jefferson, from which I borrow the title of this chapter, *American Sphinx*, 1996.

25 "people do not think..." Feldman, "Structure and Consistency in Public Opinion," 1988.

25 "fill a book..." The academic literature on American public opinion is so voluminous that you could spend months reading only the most interesting and credible research, and many months more trying to make sense of it. Or you could get a PhD in political science, as I did, at that flagship of public opinion, the University of Michigan. Neither path is pleasant. As an alternative, I recommend a handful of relatively recent books that do an outstanding job of summarizing the work that's gone before: the aforementioned *Democracy for Realists*, by Christopher Achen and Larry Bartels, *Unstable Majorities*, by Morris

Fiorina, *Neither Liberal Nor Conservative*, by Donald Kinder and Nathan Kalmoe, and *The Nature and Origins of Mass Opinion*, by John Zaller. I don't agree with every conclusion in these books (nor do their authors completely agree with each other), but they're fair and reasonable efforts by smart people to uncover truths about the American mind.

26 **"things they can't control…"** These and other examples of voter irrationality can be found in the aforementioned *Democracy for Realists*, by Achen and Bartels, in which they offer statistical analysis indicating that voters on New Jersey's shoreline voted against President Woodrow Wilson in retaliation for a spate of shark attacks in 1916. No need to feel sympathy for Wilson, though; two years later he ran a series of political attacks to unseat Republican senator Albert Fall of New Mexico, even as Fall grieved the recent deaths of two children from the Spanish Flu. It appears that voters, no matter what we think of their rationality, demonstrated compassion in this case; the data indicates their vote to re-elect Fall was in part a rebuke of Wilson's callousness.

26 **"rational decision…"** Anthony Downs coined the term "rational ignorance" to describe this phenomenon in *An Economic Theory of Democracy*. Given the very low odds his vote will affect the outcome, a self-interested person needn't waste his time keeping up with information that he can't put to practical use.

26 **"live in Wyoming…"** Gelman, "What Are the Chances Your Vote Matters?" 2016. This perspective suggests that voting in a large election is an irrational act, but if you assume that average Americans care not just about themselves, but about their country and everyone in it, then it *is* rational to vote, because even though the odds your vote will decide the outcome are nearly zero, the impact of the election is vastly important to all those living and future citizens whose well-being you care about. See: Gelman et al., "Voting as a Rational Choice," 2017.

26 **"consider the mystification…"** See Paul Krugman's tweet: "The more I look at this election, the less I imagine I understand. Florida was a surprise Trump triumph — and also voted to increase the minimum wage to $15. CA is very liberal — and voted to let Uber and Lyft keep treating their employees as independent contractors, with no benefits. According to Fox exits, majorities favor a government health-care plan and a larger role for government in general. Yet they seem to have voted for Senate Republicans who want to drown government in the bathtub." @paulkrugman: Nov. 4, 2020. 11:26—11:28 AM.

27 **"in panel surveys…"** Researchers who run the American National Election Studies (ANES) make much of their data, including various permutations of questions asked over the decades, accessible by academics and the interested public here: https://electionstudies.org/resources/anes-guide/. A word to the wise, however: if you're not downloading their data to a statistics program, be sure to doublecheck charts against their associated codebooks, because they occasionally fail to account for the fact that questions in some survey years were only presented to a portion of the total survey sample, which throws off their percentages.

27 **"800 percent higher…"** Zaller, "What *Nature and Origins* Leaves Out," 2012.

27 **"replace democracy…"** Brennan, *Against Democracy*, 2017.

28 **"morally and intellectually inadequate…"** Croly, *The Promise of American Life*, 1909.

30 **"orderly, predictable patterns…"** Kinder and Kalmoe, *Neither Liberal Nor Conservative*, 2017, p. 13.

31 **"spotted and inconstant…"** Shakespeare, *A Midsummer Night's Dream*, 1600.

32 **"about 5-7 percent…"** Bowman and Hunter, *The State of Disunion: The 1996 Survey of American Political Culture*, 1996. A more recent study of American political beliefs likewise found little difference between residents of "red" and "blue" congressional districts. See Program for Public Consultation, "A Not So Divided America: Is the Public as Polarized as Congress, or Are Red and Blue Districts Pretty Much the Same?" 2014.

32 **"self-consciously antagonistic…"** Hunter and Wolfe, *Is There a Culture War?* 2006, p. 26.

32 **"remotely ideological…"** Campbell et al., *The American Voter*, 1960; and Lewis-Beck et al., *The American Voter Revisited*, 2008.

33 **"…nor fervidly partisan."** For a dissenting opinion about polarization among average Americans, see Abramowitz, *The Disappearing Center*, 2010. He has interesting insights, but his eagerness to detect a broad ideological streak in America leads him to exaggerate the extent to which regular citizens are truly politically active, to rely on discredited hypotheses like the "Big Sort" (Bishop, 2008), to confuse Independent leaners with true partisans (while the vote choices of leaners and partisans are very similar in any single election, leaners jump back and forth between parties far more frequently than true partisans), and to generally get excited because Americans are marginally more ideologically minded than they were in the 1950s, which is like saying a snail who departed Miami for Chicago two days ago has covered twice the distance he'd traveled by the end of day one.

33 **"vast and growing…"** French, *Divided We Fall*, 2020, p. 39.

CHAPTER 3: AMERICAN PARTISANS

35 **"I plead guilty…"** Agnew's quote is attributed to a 1971 *Washington Post* article cited by James Sundquist in *The Dynamics of the Party System*, 1973.

36 **"are not Americans…"** Ellmers, "'Conservatism' is No Longer Enough," 2021.

36 **"magically disappeared…"** On Twitter: @Judson4Congress, May 31, 2021. 11:12 AM.

36 **"ideologues are not alone…"** Pew Research Center, "Partisan Antipathy: More Intense, More Personal," 2019.

37 **"definition of the political class…"** Fiorina, et al., *Culture War? The Myth of a Polarized America*, 2011, p. 16.

37 **"wisdom of Frodo…"** Tolkien, *The Fellowship of the Ring*, 1954.

38 **"horrified Ezra…"** Klein, *Why We're Polarized*, 2020.

38 **"locus of distrust…"** Pew Research Center, "Few See Adequate Limits on NSA Surveillance Program," 2013.

39 **"assassinate American citizens…"** Friedersdorf, "Obama's Weak Defense of His Record on Drone Killings," 2016.

39 **"flip-flopped harder…"** Hudson, "How Nancy Pelosi Saved the NSA Surveillance Program," 2013.

40 **"…Two Minutes Hate."** Orwell, *Nineteen Eighty-Four*, 1949.

40 **"ideology in mind…," "in ideological terms…"** Kinder and Kalmoe, *Neither Liberal Nor Conservative*, 2017, p. 12-13.

41 **"judgments of politicians…"** Hetherington and Rudolph, *Why Washington Won't Work: Polarization, Political Trust, and the Governing Crisis*, 2015.

42 **"*subjects with strong worldviews…*"** Kahan, et al., "'They Saw a Protest': Cognitive Illiberalism and the Speech-Conduct Distinction," 2012.

43 **"public relations misfires…"** Korecki, "Biden Has Fought a Pandemic Before. It Did Not Go Smoothly," 2020.

43 **"vaccination more aggressively…"** Parmet, "Pandemics, Populism and the Role of Law in the H1N1 Vaccine Campaign," 2010.

43 **"going to mutate…"** Shah et al., "Beck, Limbaugh Fomenting Fear About H1N1 Vaccine," 2009.

43 **"14 million people…"** Farhi, "No Rush to Measure Limbaugh's Ratings," 2009.

43 **"Screw you, Ms. Sebelius…"** Rush, "Heated Debate Over Swine Flu Vaccine Efforts Divides Some on Capitol Hill," 2009.

44 **"didn't think H1N1…"** Parker-Pope, "Bill Maher vs. the Flu Vaccine," 2009.

44 **"Americans diverged substantially…"** Baum, "Red State, Blue State, Flu State: Media Self-Selection and Partisan Gaps in Swine Flu Vaccinations," 2011.

44 **"dangerous to children…"** Roos, "CDC Sharply Raises H1N1 Case Estimates; Kids Hit Hard," 2009; and Swedish, et al., "First Season of 2009 H1N1 Influenza," 2010.

44 **"on par with previous…"** Osterholm et al., "Efficacy and Effectiveness of Influenza Vaccines: A Systematic Review and Meta-Analysis," 2012.

44 **"similarly low incidences…"** US Centers for Disease Control and Prevention, *H1N1 Vaccine Safety*, 2010.

45 **"actual fatality data…"** Desai, "They Blinded Us from Science," 2020.

45 **"…visiting the hospital."** Alpert, "Mortality from Fear," 2021.

46 **"evolving views…"** Layman and Carsey, "Party Polarization and 'Conflict Extension' in the American Electorate," 2002.

CHAPTER 4: THE PRAGMATIC AMERICAN

49 **"rather be governed…"** Wakefield, "William F. Buckley, Jr.: Portrait of a Complainer," 1961.

50 **"thoughtfully constructed…"** Achen and Bartels, *Democracy for Realists*, 2016, p. 32-3.

50 **"consistent beliefs *within*…"** See Feldman and Johnston, "Understanding the Determinants of Political Ideology: Implications of Structural Complexity," 2014; and Carmines et al., "Who Fits the Left-Right Divide? Partisan Polarization in the American Electorate," 2012.

52 **"demonstration of availability…"** Tversky and Kahneman, "Availability: A Heuristic for Judging Frequency and Probability," 1973.

53 **"one's own behaviors…"** See Jones and Nisbett, *The Actor and the Observer*, 1971; Malle et al., "Actor-observer asymmetries in explanations of behavior," 2007; and Malle, *How the Mind Explains Behavior*, 2004.

55 **"Nixon repeatedly mangled…"** Gibson, "Problems with Open-Ended ANES Questions Measuring Factual Knowledge about Politics," 2018.

55 **"72 percent of responses…"** Gibson and Caldeira, "Knowing the Supreme Court? A Reconsideration of Public Ignorance of the High Court," 2009.

58 **"generous or stingy…"** Pollsters at the Pew Research Center seem similarly inclined to avoid investigating the actual beliefs of average Americans. They reported in 2020, for example, that overwhelming majorities of Americans across demographic groups agreed with the statement: "There should be a way for them [undocumented immigrants now living in the U.S.] to stay in the country legally, *if certain requirements are met*" (emphasis added), but evidenced no curiosity about what respondents believed those requirements ought to be. Perhaps they'd just as soon not have the stern but welcoming attitudes of everyday Americans intrude on elites' debates about immigration policy. See Pew Research Center, "Americans Broadly Support Legal Status for Immigrants Brought to the U.S. Illegally as Children," 2020.

61 **"It is a cultural war…"** While far more widely covered, Buchanan was not the first person to reintroduce the concept of culture war into American intellectual discussion after a long dormancy following tumultuous conflicts between urban and rural America, not to mention anxiety over immigration, in the 1920s. That honor belongs to James Davison Hunter, who a year before Buchanan's speech published *Culture Wars: The Struggle to Define America*. In it, Hunter laid out a more nuanced and troubling conceptualization of culture war, in which elites spanning news media, universities, entertainment, and other overruling institutions subtly but definitively shape American tastes and values, leading to slow-moving but revolutionary changes that permanently alter the moral and cultural landscape. In this model, there is no widescale, coast-to-coast culture war, only local skirmishes as elite outsiders foist their will on locals in areas like education policy, moral codes, treatment of the vulnerable, and so on. For an excellent debate between Hunter and other thinkers about his thesis, see Hunter and Wolfe, *Is There a Culture War? A Dialogue on Values and American Public Life*, 2006.

62 **"backed this up…"** 1994 General Social Survey.

65 **"opportunities for women…"** Yankelovich, *New Rules: Searching for Self-Fulfillment in a World Turned Upside Down*, 1981.

66 **"values that unites us…"** Garfinkle and Yankelovich, *Uniting America: Restoring the Vital Center to American Democracy*, 2005.

66 **"ambivalent, moderate, and pragmatic…"** Fiorina et al., *Culture War? The Myth of a Polarized America*, 2011. See also Hawkins, et al., *Hidden Tribes: A Study of America's Polarized Landscape*, 2018.

66 **"rejection of ideological extremes…"** Fiorina, *Unstable Majorities*, 2017.

67 **"Independent leaners…"** Fiorina, *Unstable Majorities*, 2017, p. 115-120.

67 "particular corridor..." Lawler and Reinsch, *A Constitution in Full*, 2019.

68 "catastrophic decline..." Brooks, "America is Having a Moral Convulsion," 2020.

68 "trust is declining..." Vallier, "Why Are Americans So Distrustful of Each Other?" 2020.

68 "can't be too careful..." The American National Election Studies survey uses the same question about trust, to which the following critiques apply.

69 "62 percent of them..." Wuthnow, *Loose Connections*, 1998.

69 "indicates declining trust..." Interestingly, the decline occurred entirely among non-partisans. Strong Republicans and Democrats showed almost exactly the same proportions (41 percent said most people could be trusted; 55 percent said you couldn't be too careful) in 2018 than they did in 1972. Forty-four percent of Independents, on the other hand, said "you can't be too careful" in 1972, while 73 percent said so in 2018. Independents who reported leaning toward the Democratic or Republican parties had similar shifts over the same period, with the percentage of D-leaners who said "you can't be too careful" going from 44 to 63 percent, and a corresponding shift from 35 to 66 percent among R-leaners. It would take more analysis to understand why, and whether it had any connection to rising distrust among Independents of political parties and partisans.

69 "some of the time..." The trust-in-government question also captures a few "never" responses, but this has to be volunteered by respondents, which almost certainly reduces its incidence.

70 "35 percent in 1997..." Dimock, "How Americans View Trust, Facts, and Democracy Today," 2020. Similarly, no doubt influenced by narratives from partisans and pundits, American voters tend to perceive voters for the opposing party to be far more extreme in ideology and lifestyle than is in fact the case. See Ahler and Sood, "The Parties in Our Heads: Misperceptions About Party Composition and Their Consequences," 2018.

71 "sorted ourselves geographically..." For the original claims regarding a "big sort," see Bishop, *The Big Sort*, 2008. For the corrective, see Abrams and Fiorina, "The Myth of the Big Sort," 2012, and Abrams, "Do People Decide Where to Live Based on Their Politics?" 2021. In a nutshell, while Bishop relied on presidential election returns to make his case, in many instances the majority in a supposedly deep red or blue state will vote for one party in the presidential race, but the other party in statewide races. What's more, county-level party registration reveals a reduction in one-party dominance, not the increase implied by Bishop's claims.

71 "see politicians compromise..." Wolak, *Compromise in an Age of Party Polarization*, 2020.

72 "found in 2019..." Pew Research Center, "Partisan Antipathy: More Intense, More Personal," 2019.

72 "not live near..." The study I cited on the prior page to refute the hypothesis of a "big sort" also carries evidence that a minority of partisans *do* express a desire

not to live near people with whom they disagree. This reflects a pattern in the public-opinion literature: attitudes of small, ideologically animated minorities get projected by pundits onto the entirety of the US voting public. See Abrams, "Do People Decide Where to Live Based on Their Politics?" 2021.

72 **"not self-conscious partisans..."** Hunter and Wolfe, *Is There a Culture War?* 2006, p. 33.

CHAPTER 5: SCIENTISTS, MAD AND POLITICAL

77 **"mostly neglected report..."** American Political Science Association, 'Toward a More Responsible Two-Party System': A Report of the Committee on Political Parties, 1950.

78 **"democracy does not exist..."** Kirkpatrick, "'Toward a More Responsible Two-Party System': Political Science, Policy Science, or Pseudo-Science?" 1971, p. 966.

78 **"policy the central..."**, **"prize goes to..."** Kirkpatrick, "'Toward a More Responsible Two-Party System': Political Science, Policy Science, or Pseudo-Science?" 1971, p. 968-70.

79 **"deliberate sense..."** Hamilton, *Federalist* No. 71, 1788.

80 **"goal of national socialism..."** "Republican Party Platform of 1952," *The American Presidency Project*.

81 **"are weak agents...,"** **"softened the rough edges..."** Rossiter, *Parties and Politics in America*, 1960, p. 54-9.

82 **"...find common ground."** Cohen, et al., *The Party Decides*, 2008.

82 **"civil-war potential..."** Rossiter, *Parties and Politics in America*, 1960, p. 59, who references for his phrasing here Ranney and Kendall, *Democracy and the American Party System*, 1956.

82 **"completely nuts..."** Klein, *The Natural*, 2002, p. 91.

82 **"develop intraparty consensus..."** For a succinct history of American party polarization, see Rosenfeld, *The Polarizers*, 2018.

83 **"rug on the floor..."** Goodwin, *Lyndon Johnson and the American Dream*, 1976, cited in Rosenfeld, *The Polarizers*, 2018, p. 44.

83 **"obsessively to maximize..."**, **"tableau of establishment..."** Rosenfeld, *The Polarizers*, 2018, pp. 42, 105.

84 **"Government is a friend..."** Eisenhower presidential news conference, January 27, 1954.

84 **"collectivism at home..."** Meyer, "Where is Eisenhower Going?" 1954.

84 **"kinder, gentler statement..."** "Republican Party Platform of 1956," *The American Presidency Project*.

85 **"elaborate pretense..."** Kendall, "Basic Issues Between Conservatives and Liberals," 1971.

86 **"inherently destructive..."** Klein, *Why We're Polarized*, 2020; and French, *Divided We Fall*, 2020.

86 **"loyal opposition..."** We got this wonderful idea, like so many others, from

our British cousins, in this case the particular cousin named Sir John Hobhouse, who is credited as the first to employ the phrase "loyal opposition" during a House of Commons address in 1826. See Foord, *His Majesty's Opposition, 1714-1830*, 1964.

87 **"Twain's protagonist..."** Twain, *A Connecticut Yankee in King Arthur's Court*, 1889.

87 **"polarization is not..."** The National Conference of State Legislatures (NCSL) found, for example, that even though state legislatures are just as polarized as Congress, they are far more functional, reaching compromise on budgets and laws, and in many instances maintaining cross-party collegiality. They do so in part via mechanisms Congress abandoned, like empowered committees and adequate nonpartisan staffing, and through informal agreements to apply rules consistently and avoid duplicitous grandstanding. The same harmful behaviors that infest Congress, of course, threaten state legislatures, especially on the part of "show horse" legislators who have their sights set on higher office. See NCSL, "State Legislative Policymaking in an Age of Political Polarization," 2018.

CHAPTER 6: THE MONSTER COMES TO LIFE

91 **"Dionne described..."** Dionne, *Why Americans Hate Politics*, 1991, p. 118.

92 **"infamous political advertisement..."** Mann, "How the 'Daisy' Ad Changed Everything About Political Advertising," 2016.

93 **"secretly tagged him..."** Noah, "'Acid, Amnesty, and Abortion': The Unlikely Source of a Legendary Smear," 2012.

93 **"firmly to the right..."** Lehrer, "1972 Campaign Reveals How Much Modern Democrats Have Changed," 2019.

94 **"open to capture..."** cited in Rosenfeld, *The Polarizers*, 2018, p. 169.

94 **"differential application..."** Shafer and Wagner, *The Long War over Party Structure: Democratic Representation and Policy Responsiveness in American Politics*, 2019.

94 **"...elected to purify."** Lawrence, "How the 'Watergate Babies' Broke American Politics," 2018.

94 **"transformative period of reform..."** Rosenfeld, *The Polarizers*, 2018, p. 158.

95 **"show horses..."** Matthews, *U.S. Senators and Their World*, 1960.

95 **"ushered in the new age..."** Both chambers of Congress had allowed television coverage during special circumstances in the past, like during the Senate Watergate investigation, and the House Judiciary Committee's hearing on Nixon's impeachment. The temporary bump in public approval following these broadcasts was a reason some put forward for full-time TV coverage, arguing that it would help restore a balance of public persuasion power tilted toward presidents with ready access to TV audiences. See Wolfensberger, *Congress and the People*, 2001, and Mansky, "How Watching Congressional Hearings Became an American Pastime," 2017.

95 **"speaker gaveled him..."** C-SPAN, "First Televised Session of the House of Representatives," 1979. The third congressman to speak in this session, Rep. Harold "Roadrunner" Volkmer, offered a vivid picture of how much Congress

had been transformed by ideological polarization. A Democrat from Missouri, he used his time to rail against inflation and government waste, sounding very much like a modern-day Republican. A staunch gun-rights advocate and opponent of abortion, Volkmer also supported an Equal Rights Amendment, civil rights, and strong environmental protections. He was instrumental in leading one of the last great bipartisan efforts in Congress, a bill to rein in the Bureau of Alcohol, Tobacco, and Firearms, and protect gun-owner rights. By the mid-1990s he was too conservative for Democrats, and too liberal for Republicans. His nickname, incidentally, came from Missouri Senator Thomas Eagleton, the very same person who tagged George McGovern with "acid, amnesty, and abortion."

95 **"predicted the outcome…"** Madden, "Congress Report Asks TV Coverage," 1974. "The real harm in the merging of politics and cable news," observed journalist Matt Bai, "isn't necessarily that we elevate the natural-born entertainers and the bullies among our politicians. It's that we begin to undervalue everyone else, confusing the theater of politics with the indispensable real thing." Bai, "Cable Guise," 2009.

96 **"described the effect…"** Lawrence, "How the 'Watergate Babies' Broke American Politics," 2018.

96 **"this rights language…"** For a richer discussion of this trend see MacLeod, *The Age of Selfies*, 2020.

97 **"sit at long tables…"**, **"Democrats were arrogant…"** Klein, "The Town That Ate Itself, 1998"

97 **"Before an empty house…"** C-SPAN, "House Session, May 15, 1984." In fairness to Newt, delivering a speech to an empty room was pretty show-horsey, but he was careful in his remarks to avoid direct claims about his opponents' patriotism. His dust-up with O'Neill was precipitated by Republican anger that O'Neill violated a rule mandating that C-SPAN cameras would remain stationary, which is what late-night speechifiers counted on in order to appear to viewers that they were lambasting a full House. The immediate victim of O'Neill's mischief was Robert Walker (R-PA). See C-SPAN, "First Panning of House Chamber," 1984.

98 **"nice-guy Republican…"** Dionne, *Why Americans Hate Politics*, 1991, p. 296.

98 **"further centralized power…"** Drutman and LaPira, "Capacity for What? Legislative Capacity Regimes in Congress and the Possibilities for Reform," 2020.

99 **"money primaries…"** Brownstein, "The Money Machine," 1987.

99 **"… invisible primary."** Cohen, et al., *The Party Decides*, 2008.

99 **"icing on the cake…"** Diamond and King, "Let's Have an Honest Debate on the Debates," 2015.

99 **"informal party organizations…"** Masket, *No Middle Ground*, 2014.

100 **"These zealots…"**, **"based in blue-collar…"** Shafer, *Quiet Revolution*, pp. 361, 8. For a fascinating account of how the national party's insistence on gender and race quotas among presidential convention delegates balkanized California Democrats, see Cavala, "Changing the Rules Changes the Game," 1974.

101 **"made subservient..."** Sam Rosenfeld notes that this process began under presidents Kennedy and Johnson, who consolidated national party power by prioritizing large, national issues-oriented donors over others. Neither president cared for the ideological sharpening agenda of party reformers, but their own agendas were inherently ideological in that they empowered the nation-state over American states. The emaciation of small-donor influence and local party authority, therefore, began long before the party reformers came to power. See Rosenfeld, *The Polarizers*, 2018.

101 **"concentrated the stakes..."** As a consequence, observed Abigail Hall and Alexander Salter, partisans have become desperately vicious. "While the blow from losing a policy contest at the state level can be softened in many ways, losing Washington could be disastrous. Defeat at the national level means not only forfeiting control over federal policy, but over state policies as well." See Hall and Salter, "To 'Lower the Temperature' Raise Commitments to Federalism," 2021.

101 **"transitioning from organizations..."** Hopkins, *The Increasingly United States: How and Why American Political Behavior Nationalized*, 2018. See also Shafer, "Anti-Party Politics," 1981, and *Quiet Revolution*, 1983.

101 **"movement-minded politicians..."** Shafer and Wagner observed that "different incentives plus different structures pitted the old formal organizations of long-serving party officials against the new social networks of issue activists," which means as a result that voters get stark choices between uncompromising candidates, and all the rancor and gridlock that come with them. See Shafer and Wagner, "The Trump Presidency and the Structure of Modern American Politics," 2019.

102 **"deeply and tangibly..."** Rosenfeld, *The Polarizers*, 2018, p. 284.

102 **"access, transparency, and democracy..."** There's also evidence that reforms enacted in the name of transparency made legislative deliberations vulnerable to lobbyists and other powerful influencers. See Ranalli, et al., "The 1970s Sunshine Reforms and the Transformation of Congressional Lobbying," 2018.

102 **"summed up the result...", "polarizing style of attack..."** Rosenfeld, *The Polarizers*, 2018, pp. 288-90 and 182-3.

CHAPTER 7: THE AMERICAN PANOPTICON

105 **"evening on October 27..."** Facts for this section are drawn primarily from Allen, "The Applause-O-Meter Still Thrives in Politics," 1996, and Grove, "Candidates Experiment with Instant Feedback," 1987.

108 **"Newt-like vernacular..."** GOPAC, "Language: A Key Mechanism of Control," 1990, and Page, "Talk Like a Newt with the Gingrich Diatribe Dictionary," 1990.

109 **"*us specifically...*"** Edsall, "Let the Nanotargeting Begin," 2012.

109 **"hyper-targeting of users..."** LaFrance, "Facebook is a Doomsday Machine, 2020."

112 **"most politically homogenous..."** Cox, et al., "Socially Distant: How Our Divided Social Networks Explain Our Politics," 2020.

113 **"little direct accountability…"** Klonick, "The New Governors: The People, Rules, and Processes Governing Online Speech," 2018.

113 **"altered its focus…"** Askonas and Schulman, "Why Speech Platforms Can Never Escape Politics," 2021.

114 **"yields greater misperceptions…"** Pew Research Center, "Americans Who Mainly Get Their News on Social Media Are Less Engaged, Less Knowledgeable," 2020.

114 **"social media for their news…"** Morris Fiorina tempers claims about increasing reliance on social media for news by noting that Pew counts news about sports, weather, traffic, entertainment, and other topics, leaving unclear the extent to which Americans truly rely on social media for *political* news. See Fiorina, *Unstable Majorities*, 2017.

114 **"tweaked environments…"** LaFrance, "Facebook is a Doomsday Machine," 2020.

115 **"effects partisan news…"** Levendusky, "Why Do Partisan Media Polarize Voters?" 2013.

115 **"legal scholar Cass…"** Sunstein, *Going to Extremes*, 2009.

116 **"similar dynamic within…"** Connors, "The Social Dimension of Political Values," 2020.

117 **"immunized to facts…"** Druckman et al., "How Elite Partisan Polarization Affects Public Opinion Formation," 2013.

CHAPTER 8: THROUGH A GLASS DARKLY

123 **"two-thirds of Americans…"** Swift, "Six in 10 in U.S. See Partisan Bias in News Media," 2017.

123 **"surveys of journalists…"** Silver, "There Really Was a Liberal Media Bubble."

123 **"identify as Democrats…"** Gold, "Survey: 7 Percent of Reporters Identify as Republican," 2014, and LaTour, "Fact Check: Do 97 Percent of Journalist Donations Go to Democrats?" 2017.

123 **"right of Alexandria…"** Hassell, et al., "There is No Liberal Media Bias in Which News Stories Political Journalists Choose to Cover," 2020. Though the title is provocative, the researchers' test for bias misses the mark. Their "proof" is that journalists are just as likely to cover the campaign announcements of Republicans as they are Democrats, which is like saying that the quantity of Donald Trump coverage proves that journalists are honest dealers rather than conflict-seeking ghouls.

123 **"coverage of transgenderism…"** The text of the Arkansas law can be found here: https://www.arkleg.state.ar.us/Acts/FTPDocument?path=%2FACTS%2F 2021R%2FPublic%2F&file=626.pdf&ddBienniumSession=2021%2F2021R. An example of the *Post's* hysterical coverage is Wax-Thibodeaux, "After Arkansas Passes its Trans Ban, Parents and Teens Wonder: Should We Stay?" 2021.

124 **"journalistic embarrassments…"** The *New York Times* and *Washington Post* average between them roughly 7 million unique website visitors per day, most of whom read just a fraction of their content, and *60 Minutes* boasts 9-10 million

viewers per week. For perspective, keep in mind that 209 million adults live in the US.

125 **"media polarize viewers…"** Levendusky, "Why Do Partisan Media Polarize Voters?" 2013.

125 **"…very limited audiences."** The authors remind those shaken by right-wing media influence of this calming reality as well. "If every one of Fox's viewers," they write, "was an eligible voter and voted for George W. Bush, they would make up about 5 percent of his total. In light of such numbers, liberal Democrats' preoccupation with Fox seems a touch paranoid." Fiorina et al., *Culture War?* 2011, p. 21.

125 **"on the rise…"** Pew Research Center, "Many Americans Get News on YouTube, Where News Organizations and Independent Producers Thrive Side by Side," 2020.

125 **"affecting the judgments…"** Dimock, "How Americans View Trust, Facts, and Democracy Today," 2020.

126 **"power of culture…"** Hunter and Wolfe, *Is There a Culture War?* 2006, p. 33.

127 **"profit-oriented business…"** There's also an indication that economic incentives drive news stations—especially local ones—to favor fluff over substance. See for example Hamilton, *All the News That's Fit to Sell*, 2003.

127 **"positive and negative…"** Leetaru, "Culturenomics 2.0: Forecasting large-scale human behavior using global news media tone in time and space," 2011.

128 **"plunge towards negativity…"** Leetaru, "Sentiment Mining 500 Years of History: Is the World Really Darkening?" 2019.

129 **"an American obsession…"** The novelist Ron Hansen, in *The Assassination of Jesse James by the Coward Robert Ford*, quotes a letter Oscar Wilde wrote after witnessing people raid the house of the freshly killed outlaw: "The Americans are certainly great hero worshippers, and always take their heroes from the criminal classes."

129 **"fallen to 3.9…"** FBI, "Crime in the United States, 2019." This trend was halted in some urban areas as a consequence of riots and associated violence in the wake of protests during the summer of 2020.

129 **"affect public fears…"** See Baranauskas and Drakulich, "Media Construction of Crime Revisited," 2018, and Callanan, "Media Consumption, Perceptions of Crime Risk and Fear of Crime," 2012.

129 **"20 percent of shows…"** Porter, "TV Long View: How Much Network TV Depends on Cop Shows," 2020.

129 **"between reality and perception…"** Gallup, "Crime," 2021.

129 **"hate crimes per agency…"** FBI, "Hate Crime Statistics, 2019" and "Hate Crime Statistics, 1996."

130 **"evidence of rising intolerance…"** See for example the *AP News* (Basalmo, "Hate Crimes in the U.S. Reach Highest Level in More Than a Decade," 2020), *National Public Radio* (Allam, "FBI Report: Bias-Motivated Killings at Record High Amid Nationwide Rise in Hate Crime." 2020), and not to be outdone, the ever prune-faced *New York Times* (Arango, "Hate Crimes in U.S. Rose to Highest

Level in More Than a Decade in 2019." 2020). The Poynter Institute's *PolitiFact* website (Xu, "Explaining the Numbers Behind the Rise in Reported Hate Crimes." 2019) gets partial credit for at least noting that the apparent increase is driven in substantial part by a greater propensity for victims to come forward than in years past, but *PolitiFact* still failed to check the fact that hate-crime rates have fallen.

130 **"77 million fewer tons…"** Tech Environmental, Inc., "Progress in Reducing National Air Pollutant Emissions, 1970-2015," 1999, and US Environmental Protection Agency, *National Air Pollutant Emission Trends, 1900-1994*, 1995.

130 **"two-thirds of Americans…"** International Communications Research, "Survey of Air Pollution Perceptions: Final Report," 1999.

130 **"32 percent stating…"** General Social Survey, 1993 and 1994.

133 **"like free enterprise…"** Pew Research Center, "The Partisan Divide on Political Values Grows Even Wider," 2017; Jones and Saad, "U.S. Support for More Government Inches Up, but Not for Socialism," 2019; and Pew Research Center, "Partisans in the U.S. Increasingly Divided on Whether Offensive Content Online is Taken Seriously Enough," 2020.

134 **"millions of gun-owning…"** French, *Divided We Fall*, 2020, pp. 97-8. French's claim that "millions of gun-owning Americans" watched the town hall is a bit of a stretch; the show had approximately 2.9 million viewers (Otterson, "CNN Gun Control Town Hall Draws 2.9 Million Viewers," 2018), so given that an estimated 32 percent of Americans own a gun (Saad, "What Percentage of Americans Own Guns?" 2019), and assuming the CNN viewership was a representative sample of America (also a stretch), that equates to roughly 930,000 gun-owning viewers out of a gun-owning population of roughly 90 million Americans. The reason I point this out is because pundits tend to assume that their political spats are widely seen by Americans, when the truth is that most of us are usually paying attention to other things.

134 **"Americans are genuinely indifferent…"** Haque, "Everyone's Dying and No One Cares," 2020.

135 **"exposed the darkness…"** See Twitter: @DavidAFrench, March 5, 2021, 12:50 AM.

135 **"personal is political…"** Firestone and Koedt, *Notes from the Second Year*, 1970.

CHAPTER 9: THE SPOILS OF WAR

138 **"respond to incentives…"** Landsburg, *The Armchair Economist: Economics and Everyday Life*, 1993.

138 **"raking in revenue…"** Sheingate, "The Political Consultant Racket," 2015, and Sheingate, *Building a Business of Politics*, 2016.

138 **"pocketed over $50 million…"** Peoples and Slodysko; "How a Leading Anti-Trump Group Ignored a Crisis in its Ranks," 2021, and McArdle, "FBI Investigating Allegations Against Lincoln Project Co-Founder John Weaver: Report," 2021.

138 **"people in DC had known…"** Girdusky, "The Lincoln Project's Predator," 2021.

138 "millions in advertising..." Kassel, "Election Boom," 2020.

138 "net worth of 15 percent..." Rosier, "Changes in Net Worth of U.S. Senators and Representatives," 2014.

138 "most Americans suffered..." Pew Research Center, "Trends in Income and Wealth Inequality," 2020.

139 "voters grown cynical..." Political scientist Logan Dancey found that voters exposed to allegations of scandal—which is increasingly a standard element of political campaigns—become more inclined to believe future allegations. Dancey, "The Consequences of Political Cynicism: How Cynicism Shapes Citizens' Reactions to Political Scandals," 2012.

140 "pessimistic one-third..." Pew Research Center, "Partisan Shifts in Views of the Nation, But Overall Opinions Remain Negative," 2017.

140 "left and right tails..." Fiorina, *Unstable Majorities*, 2017.

141 "Without the loyal opposition..." Stroud, *Niche News*, 2011, p. 177.

141 "emphasizing the *threat*..." Valentino, et al., "Election Night's Alright for Fighting: The Role of Emotions in Political Participation," 2011. Likewise has journalist Aaron Maté observed that it is "party elites, Democrats and Republicans alike, who have turned to deranged, xenophobic fantasies rather than taking responsibility for their own election failures." Maté, "The Rise and Fall of the 'Steele Dossier,'" 2021.

142 "parties seek to claim..." Garfinkle and Yankelovich, *Uniting America: Restoring the Vital Center to American Democracy*, 2005.

142 "training the public..." Funk, "Process Performance: Public Reaction to Legislative Policy Debate," 2001.

142 "little say in politics..." See General Social Survey, Pew Research Center, "Pew Values Update: American Social Beliefs 1997-1987," 1998, and, for a summary of how dramatically public trust in government changed from the 1960s to the 1980s, Lipset and Schneider, "The Decline of Confidence in American Institutions," 1983.

142 "preferences of the vast majority..." Gilens, *Affluence and Influence*, 2012.

144 "responsible for two-thirds..." Himmelstein, et al., "Medical Bankruptcy: Still Common Despite the Affordable Care Act," 2019.

144 "chief concerns of average Americans..." American National Election Studies, Time Series Cumulative Data File (1948-2016).

145 "literal slogan..." Keith, "Wielding a Pen and a Phone, Obama Goes it Alone," 2014.

145 "my own without Congress..." Thomas, "Obama: I Won't 'Wait for Congress' on Economic Fixes," 2014.

145 "reallocating military budget..." Allyn, "Appeals Court Allows Trump to Divert $3.6 Billion in Military Funds for Border Wall," 2020.

CHAPTER 10: THE INCREDIBLE SHRINKING LEGISLATURE

148 "representative of the will..." The election of senators by state legislatures

notwithstanding, the intention behind this rule was to hold senators accountable for representing the entirety of a state's interests, which is another way of saying that its aim was to ensure senatorial representation for all citizens of a state. For a thoughtful discussion of how the 17th Amendment, which established direct election of senators, undermined both federalism and democracy, see Zywicki and Somin, "Federalism and Separation of Powers: Ramifications of Repealing the 17th Amendment," 2012.

148 **"in its own diminution…"** Levin, "Congress's Day," 2021. See also Schoenbrod, *DC Confidential: Inside the Five Tricks of Washington*, 2017, which is replete with examples of how Congress has avoided responsibility for tradeoffs and costs such that we now face an estimated $100 trillion gap between projected future spending and revenue.

149 **"legislature is impotent…"** Opening Statement, Brett Kavanaugh SCOTUS Hearing, 2018.

149 **"the Great Abdication…"** King, press release, 2020.

149 **"reasons for congressional shirking…"** Former congressman Keith Rothfus offered a robust set of causes and solutions in Rothfus, "How to Fix the House of Representatives," 2021.

150 **"parity has yielded gridlock…"** Lee, *Insecure Majorities*, 2016.

150 **"built my staff…"** Vesoulis, "'He's Saying One Thing and Then He's Doing Another.' Rep. Madison Cawthorn Peddles a Different Kind of Trumpism in a Post-Trump World," 2021.

151 **"newly arrived legislator…"** Kosar, "New Lawmakers' Rude Awakening to the Realities of Congress," 2021. Similarly, a House aide speaking about the decline of congressional oversight described another informal rule: "This is the default mode of Congress, don't do your homework and see what happens." See Dayen, "Investigating Oversight," 2021.

151 **"Congress that is shaped…"** Levin, "Congress's Day," 2021.

152 **"Congress writes vague laws…"** Shoenbrod, *Power Without Responsibility: How Congress Abuses the People Through Delegation*, 1993.

CHAPTER 11: THE IMPERIAL CITY

156 **"National Wildlife Refuge…"** Public Law 105-57, https://www.govinfo.gov/content/pkg/PLAW-105publ57/pdf/PLAW-105publ57.pdf.

156 **"passed by Congress…"** US Fish and Wildlife Service, National Wildlife Refuge System Mission and Goals.

156 **"recover the listed species…"** BIO-WEST, Inc., "Environmental Assessment for Fairbanks Spring and Soda Spring Restoration," 2009.

157 **"chartered to protect…"** BIO-WEST, Inc., "Environmental Assessment for Fairbanks Spring and Soda Spring Restoration," 2009.

157 **"stream continuing to flow…"** This fact and several others in my account are based on publicly available depositions and court records. See for example the initial filing against USFS: https://mslegal.org/wp-content/uploads/2019/02/complaint_ministerio-roca-solida-1.pdf.

158 **"qualified immunity…"** Divito, "Refuge Manager Exits Baptismal Stream Fight," 2016.

158 **"the floods worsening…"** Another nonprofit, the Mountain States Legal Foundation, stepped in to help Reverend Fuentes in subsequent years. You can find related court documents on their website: https://mslegal.org/cases/ministerio-roca-solida-v-united-states/.

159 **"NFMA was intended…"** Public Law 94-588: https://www.congress.gov/bill/94th-congress/senate-bill/3091/text.

160 **"third of the recommendations…"** US Forest Service, "National Forest System Land and Resources Management Planning," 1979.

161 **"established ecological sustainability…"** Hoberg, "Science, Politics, and U.S. Forest Service Law: The Battle over the Forest Service Planning Rule," 2004.

162 **"an outlaw effort…"** Johnson, "Norman Johnson Oral History Interview," 2016.

162 **"couldn't do a damn thing…"** A subsequent lawsuit charged that giving non-federal employees so much authority over agency decision-making constituted a violation of the Federal Advisory Committee Act. The same judge who had used creatively evolved Forest Service regulations to halt logging ruled that the law had been technically violated, but that this didn't substantially change the outcome. Because Science. See Seattle *Audubon Society et al. v. Lyons*, 871 F. Supp. 1291 (W.D. Wash. 1994).

163 **"restricted road-building…"** US Forest Service, "Special Areas; Roadless Area Conservation," 2001.

164 **"…warned the same."** US General Accounting Office, "Forest Service Roadless Areas: Potential Impact of Proposed Regulations on Ecological Sustainability," 2000.

164 **"taking human lives…"** Hageman, "Bad Regulations Destroy Our Environment," 2020.

165 **"entire edifice of law…"** Robert Nelson points out how the intertwined USFS rules, subsequent court interpretations, and environmental groups empowered by USFS's shift from multiple-use to ecological management have created a web that even it can't get out of now, leaving it paralyzed and incapable even of taking the necessary steps to prevent massive fires. See Nelson, "Fire in the National Forest System," 2008.

165 **"deep state contains multitudes…"** Ambinder, "Five Myths About the Deep State," 2017.

166 **"twenty-seven rules…"** Crews, "What's the Difference between 'Major,' 'Significant,' and All Those Other Federal Rule Categories?" 2017.

166 **"unmistakable hint…"** Hamburger, *Is Administrative Law Unlawful?* 2014.

166 **"132,000 full-time…"** US Department of Justice, "Federal Law Enforcement Officers, 2016."

166 **"more than 40 percent…"** Strazzella, *The Federalization of Criminal Law,* 1998.

167 **"doubled from 1964…"** O'Sullivan, "The Federal Criminal 'Code': Return of Overfederalization," 2013.

167 **"state within the state…"** Hamburger, *The Administrative Threat*, 2017.

168 **"Just 535 members…"** Wallach, "How Congress Fell Behind the Executive Branch," 2020.

CHAPTER 12: A RETURN TO THE UNITED STATES

173 **"Beltway scrum…"** In contrast with the Founders' vision of common good, the writer Adam Smith (no, not that one) argues that today, the "common good is now understood by most people as the business of experts and the stuff of procedures, to which they have nothing to contribute but acquiescence." Smith, "Where is Our Freedom to Exercise Sympathy?" 2020.

173 **"powers delegated…"** Madison, *Federalist* No. 45, 1788.

175 **"no government armed…"** Adams, "From John Adams to Massachusetts Militia," 1798.

178 **"estimated $1.4 billion…"** The policy analyst Maxford Nelson explains how unions and their allies expanded their hold over home caregivers in "Getting Organized at Home," 2018.

179 **"to the Supreme Court…"** *Harris v. Quinn*, 573 U.S. 616, 2014.

180 **"Colville Indian nation…"** You can see an interview with the tribal natural resources director here: https://www.youtube.com/watch?v=6D8aVhNnTf4.

180 **"kind of concerted action…"** Worth noting as well is how environmentalists and loggers in eastern Oregon began talking to one another off the record until they reached an agreement that preserves logging jobs and reduces forest fire risks. See Kristof, "They Overcame Mutual Loathing, and Saved a Town," 2021.

180 **"third of its revenue…"** Stauffer et al., "Federal Funds Hover at a Third of State Revenue," 2019.

181 **"suit DC bureaucrats…"** See for example Husock, "The Coming Invasion by the Federal Government," 2021. DC rules and money also empower bad local actors, as in the case of Indiana county hospitals, which exploited Medicaid rules to draw in extra cash that they used to buy up over 90 percent of the state's nursing homes. See Cook, et al., "Here Are Five Takeaways From IndyStar's 18-Month Nursing Home Investigation," 2020.

181 **"half the administrators…"** Nichols, *Federal Grant$tanding*, 2016.

182 **"separate and independent…"** *National Federation of Independent Business v. Sebelius*, 567 U.S. 519, 2012.

183 **"the agency decided…"** US Forest Service, "Special Areas; Roadless Area Conservation," 36 CFR Part 294, *Federal Register* 66 (9) January 12, 2001.

CHAPTER 13: RECOVERING AMERICAN IDENTITY

185 **"Somebody your age…"** This Gore Vidal quote comes courtesy of Bill Kauffman's delightful book, *America First! Its History, Culture, and Politics*.

185 **"wanted a truce…"** BBC, "WWI Christmas Truce Letter Found in Staffordshire," 2014.

185 **"…exchanged addresses."** Michael, "Saxons and Anglo-Saxons Fraternising on the Field of Battle at the Season of Peace and Goodwill," 1915.

185 "much-needed haircut." Bairnsfather, *Bullets & Billets*, 1916.

186 "unarranged and quite unauthorized..." Neal, 2014 "Seasons Over the Decades, 1914," 2014.

186 "Corporal Adolf Hitler..." Vinciguerra, "The Truce of Christmas, 1914," 2005.

187 "lay down arms..." For excellent accounts of the WWI Christmas Truce, see Weintraub, *Silent Night: The Story of the World War I Christmas Truce*, 2001, and the fantastic 2005 film, *Joyeux Noel*.

187 "...dampening bellicosity." Bellamy, "Peace and the Promise of Christmas: 1914," 2019.

187 "variety of disciplines..." For a helpful synthesis of what these varied approaches mean for politics, see Brewer, "The Many Faces of Social Identity: Implications for Political Psychology," 2001.

190 "labeled his opponents..." Corn and Murphy, "A Very Long List of Dumb and Awful Things Newt Gingrich Has Said and Done," 2016.

190 "wrote off her opponent's supporters..." Montanaro, "Hillary Clinton's 'Basket of Deplorables,' in Full Context of this Ugly Campaign," 2016.

190 "most rabid among them..." Gaudiano, "Alleged Gunman James Hodgkinson Volunteered on Bernie Sanders' Campaign," 2017.

191 "Putnam's research revealed..." Putnam, *Making Democracy Work*, 1993.

191 "fruitful cooperation..." Coleman, "Social Capital in the Creation of Human Capital," 1988.

191 "remain mired in poverty..." Putnam, "The Prosperous Community: Social Capital and Public Life," 2001.

191 "dependence on the people..." Madison, *Federalist* No. 51, 1788.

192 "certain qualities..." White, "A Republic, If We Can Keep It," 2020.

192 "disengaged from social life..." Putnam, *Bowling Alone*, 2000.

192 "collapsing since 1960..." Putnam and Garrett, *The Upswing*, 2020.

192 "researchers have shown..." For a helpful summary of numerous critiques of Putnam's data, see Stolle and Hooghe, "Inaccurate, Exceptional, One-Sided, or Irrelevant? The Debate About the Alleged Decline of Social Capital and Civic Engagement in Western Societies," 2005. See also Ladd, "The Data Just Don't Show Erosion of America's 'Social Capital,'" 1996.

192 "associations are dwindling..." Durlauf, "Bowling Alone: A Review Essay," 2001.

194 "progressivism's exact dimensions..." For an interesting look at how the history of Progressivism has been dolled up by its admirers, I recommend Watson, *Progressivism: The Strange History of a Radical Idea*, 2020.

195 "retraining and retooling," Putnam and Garrett, *The Upswing*, 2020, p. 332.

196 "welcome the opposing team..." Mason, *Uncivil Agreement: How Politics Became Our Identity*, 2018, p. 19-23.

197 *"E Pluribus Unum..."* The US didn't have an official motto until 1956, when "In God We Trust" was advanced, as is often the case with such promulgations, in

response to the fear that it was no longer true. *E pluribus unum*, approved for the Great Seal by Congress in 1782, had been widely acknowledged until then as our *de facto* motto. See Bittker et al., *Religion and the State in American Law*, 2015.

197 "... out of one, many." Kamen, "For Gore, it's All in the Translation," 1994.

197 "joy in surrendering..." Tocqueville, *Democracy in America*, 1835-40, p. 234.

198 "Howard Zinn's corpse..." I'm only partly kidding. See the Zinn Education Project's website: https://www.zinnedproject.org/.

198 "commitment to localism..." Ruckelshaus, "A Way to Tamp Down the Toxic Politics of National Identity," 2021.

199 "nation-spanning associations...", "community-level reconciliation..." Skocpol, "How Americans Became Civic," 1999.

200 "tribe of savages..." Stevens, Thaddeus. "Speech of Hon. T. Stevens, of Pennsylvania, On the Bill (H.R. No. 20) Relative to the Damages to Loyal Men, and for Other Purposes," 1867.

200 "arrived but yesterday..." Tocqueville, *Democracy in America*, 1835-40, p. 236-7.

201 "nourish grassroots..." Putnam, "The Prosperous Community: Social Capital and Public Life," 2001.

202 "true story of..." Perry, *The Lost Boys*, 2018.

204 "cooperate far more..." As it turns out, there *was* a group of boys shipwrecked in real life, and they behaved quite well. See Bregman, "The Real *Lord of the Flies*: What Happened When Six Boys Were Shipwrecked for 15 Months," 2020.

CHAPTER 14: A MANUAL FOR AMERICAN SELF-GOVERNANCE

209 "working alongside one another..." The policy analyst Andy Smarick observed that solving problems together helps defuse partisanship: "Since self-rule makes us masters of our own fates, our energies are directed to real problems and practical solutions instead of abstract concepts and conspiracy theories about distant, invisible forces." See Smarick, "Amy Coney Barrett and the Virtue of Self-Government," 2020.

209 "people who disagree..." Mansbridge, *Beyond Adversary Democracy*, (1980).

209 "face-to-face conflict..." As the historian James Kloppenberg noted, "Democracy in America is suffering in 2016 because it lacks precisely what the experience of participating in town meetings was long thought to provide: experience in the hard, frustrating work of resolving conflicts through deliberation." See Bryan, et al., "Collective Interview on the History of Town Meetings," 2019.

209 "locked together..." Murray, *We Hold These Truths*, 1960.

210 "is not true..." Kendall, "The True Sage of Woodstock," 1971, p. 77.

210 "third places..." Oldenburg, *The Great Good Place*, 1989. They're called "third places" because our homes are generally the most important to us, and our workplaces second most important. Third places offer dynamics very different from those more structured environments.

211 "...Eighth Day Institute." Eighth Day is rooted in the Eastern Orthodox

Christian tradition, but it welcomes people from all Christian denominations: https://www.eighthdayinstitute.org/.

211 **"Better Arguments Project…"** See https://betterarguments.org/.

213 **"prime generators of…"** Wuthnow, "Mobilizing Civic Engagement: The Changing Impact of Religious Involvement," 1999.

213 **"church-affiliated groups…"** Hall, "Civic Engagement in New Haven," 1999.

214 **"17 percent of news…"** An encouraging point of resistance to these trends, according to Napoli's research, can be found in small local newspapers, many of which persist in focusing on what matters in their communities, despite economic pressures to rely on news wire services that prioritize national stories. Napoli found that while these small newspapers accounted for 25 percent of news organizations, they produced 47 percent of original news reporting, and 60 percent of local stories. For accessible summaries of these studies, see Napoli, "Newspapers Still the Best Bet for Local News," 2019.

214 **"time the city's plans…"** Benton, "Damaged Newspapers, Damaged Civic Life," 2019.

214 **"up partisan animosity…"** Darr et al., "Newspaper Closures Polarize Voting Behavior," 2018.

215 **"Warren Buffett bankrolled…"** Bloom, "The Great Virginia Pipeline Swindle," 2020.

215 **"liquid natural gas…"** Blunt, "Companies Cancel Atlantic Coast Pipeline After Years of Delays," 2020.

216 **"subsequent death count…"** McKinley and Ferré-Sadurni, "N.Y. Severely Undercounted Virus Deaths in Nursing Homes, Report Says," 2021.

216 **"to reveal data…"** For periodically updated links to articles covering the Cuomo investigations, see "New York's Nursing Home Nightmare," https://www.empirecenter.org/nursinghomes/.

216 **"nine additional deaths…"** Hammond and Kingsbury, "COVID-Positive Admissions Were Correlated with Higher Death Rates in New York Nursing Homes," 2021.

216 **"Gretchen Whitmer's policy…"** Delie and LeDuff, "Did Michigan Cover Up Nursing Home COVID Deaths Like New York?" 2021. The Detroit journalist James David Dickson wrote about another disastrous Whitmer policy, which directed local police to ticket people for defying her COVID curfew order. Her policy not only exposed thousands of police to the disease, it was ultimately overturned by a Michigan court. See Dickson, "There Should Be a Law? Be Careful What You Wish For," 2021.

216 **"constituted 'essential' businesses…"** McConchie, "Limit Governors' Emergency Powers," 2020.

216 **"closed payroll companies…"** Mitchell, "Wolf's Secretive Ways on Business Waivers a Flagrant Dismissal of Transparency," 2020.

217 **"rule citizens without input…"** For articles covering WILL's defeat of the Wisconsin governor's unlawful use of veto powers, see: https://will-law.org/tag/partial-veto/.

217 "NC Leadership Forum..." See https://sites.duke.edu/nclf/.

217 "failure to cultivate..." Haidt, *The Righteous Mind*, 2012.

218 "Institute of Political Leadership..." See https://iopl.org/about/.

218 "Devil's Advocacy..." See https://www.aspeninstitute.org/programs/citizenship-and-american-identity-program/the-devils-advocacy-initiative/.

218 "Kettering Foundation..." See https://www.kettering.org/.

218 "shortchanging its own..." LaPira et al., *Congress Overwhelmed: The Decline in Congressional Capacity and Prospects for Reform*, 2020, p. 2.

220 "Commission on Intergovernmental..." If you want to sample the wealth of data ACIR provided about all the ways federal action impinges on local resources and self-governance, which in turn illuminates why members of Congress from both major parties were willing to let it die, the University of North Texas has helpfully archived its reports here: https://digital.library.unt.edu/explore/collections/ACIR/.

220 "Classical Conversations..." See https://www.classicalconversations.com/.

221 "Making of Americans..." Hirsch, *The Making of Americans: Democracy and Our Schools*, 2010.

221 "seminal Coleman report..." Coleman et al., "Cognitive Outcomes in Public and Private Schools," 1982.

BIBLIOGRAPHY

Abramowitz, Alan, *The Disappearing Center: Engaged Citizens, Polarization, & American Democracy* (New Haven: Yale University Press, 2010).

Abrams, Samuel, "Do People Decide Where to Live Based on Their Politics?" *RealClear Policy*, February 3, 2021, https://www.realclearpolicy.com/articles/2021/02/03/do_people_decide_where_to_live_based_on_their_politics_658884.html.

Abrams, Samuel, and Morris Fiorina, "The Myth of the 'Big Sort'," *Hoover Digest*, August 13, 2012, https://www.hoover.org/research/myth-big-sort.

Achen, Christopher, and Lawrence Bartels, *Democracy for Realists* (Princeton: Princeton University Press, 2016).

Adams, John, "From John Adams to Massachusetts Militia, 11 October, 1798," *Founders Online*, National Archives, https://founders.archives.gov/documents/Adams/99-02-02-3102.

Ahler, Douglas, and Gaurav Sood, "The Parties in Our Heads: Misperceptions About Party Composition and Their Consequences," *Journal of Politics*, 80, no. 3 (2018): 964–981.

Allam, Hannah, "FBI Report: Bias-Motivated Killings at Record High Amid Nationwide Rise in Hate Crime," *National Public Radio*, November 16, 2020, https://www.npr.org/2020/11/16/935439777/fbi-report-bias-motivated-killings-at-record-high-amid-nationwide-rise-in-hate-c.

Allen, Mike, "The Applause-O-Meter Still Thrives in Politics," *New York Times*, August 26, 1996.

Allyn, Bobby, "Appeals Court Allows Trump to Divert $3.6 Billion in Military Funds for Border Wall," *National Public Radio*, January 9, 2020, https://www.npr.org/2020/01/09/794969121/appeals-court-allows-trump-to-divert-3-6-billion-in-military-funds-for-border-wa.

Alpert, Joseph, "Mortality from Fear," *American Journal of Medicine*, 134, no. 5 (2021): 557–58.

Ambinder, Marc, "Five Myths About the Deep State," *Washington Post*, March 10, 2017.

American National Election Studies, "Time Series Cumulative Data File (1948–2016)," https://electionstudies.org/data-center/anes-time-series-cumulative-data-file/.

American Political Science Association, "Toward a More Responsible Two-Party System: A Report of the Committee on Political Parties," *American Political Science Review* 44, no. 3, Part 2, Supplement (1950): i–99.

Arango, Tim, "Hate Crimes in U.S. Rose to Highest Level in More Than a Decade in 2019," *New York Times*, November 16, 2020.

Askonas, Jon, and Ari Schulman, "Why Speech Platforms Can Never Escape Politics," *National Affairs* 46 (2021), https://www.nationalaffairs.com/why-speech-platforms-can-never-escape-politics.

Bai, Matt, "Cable Guise," *New York Times Magazine*, December 2, 2009.

Bairnsfather, Bruce, *Bullets & Billets* (London: Grant Richards Ltd., 1916).

Baranauskas, Andrew, and Kevin Drakulich, "Media Construction of Crime Revisited: Media Types, Consumer Contexts, and Frames of Crime and Justice," *Criminology* 56, no. 4 (2018): 679–714.

Basalmo, Michael, "Hate Crimes in the U.S. Reach Highest Level in More Than a Decade," *Associated Press News*, November 16, 2020, https://apnews.com/article/hate-crimes-rise-fbi-data-ebbcadca8458aba96575da905650120d.

Baum, Matthew, "Red State, Blue State, Flu State: Media Self-Selection and Partisan Gaps in Swine Flu Vaccinations," *Journal of Health Politics, Policy and Law* 36, no. 6 (2011): 1021–59.

Bellamy, Alex, "Peace and the Promise of Christmas: 1914," *alexjbellamy.com*, December 16, 2019, https://www.alexjbellamy.com/post/peace-and-the-promise-of-christmas-1914.

Benton, Joshua, "Damaged Newspapers, Damaged Civic Life: How the Gutting of Local Newsrooms Has Led to a Less Informed Public," *Nieman Journalism Lab*, November 22, 2019, https://www.niemanlab.org/2019/11/damaged-newspapers-damaged-civic-life-how-the-gutting-of-local-newsrooms-has-led-to-a-less-informed-public/.

BIO-WEST, Inc., "Environmental Assessment for Fairbanks Spring and Soda Spring Restoration," report submitted to US Fish and Wildlife Service, September 2009. https://www.USFW.gov/uploadedFiles/springs_restoration_ea.pdf.

Bishop, Bill, *The Big Sort: Why the Clustering of Like-Minded America is Tearing Us Apart* (Boston: Houghton Mifflin Harcourt, 2008).

Bittker, Boris, Scott Idleman, and Frank Ravitch, *Religion and the State in American Law* (Cambridge: Cambridge University Press, 2015).

Bloom, Arthur, "The Great Virginia Pipeline Swindle," *American Conservative*, July 8, 2020, https://www.theamericanconservative.com/articles/virginia-pipeline-swindle/.

Blunt, Katherine, "Companies Cancel Atlantic Coast Pipeline After Years of Delays," *Wall Street Journal*, July 5, 2020.

Bowman, Carl, and James Davison Hunter, *The State of Disunion: The 1996 Survey of American Political Culture* (Charlottesville: Institute for Advanced Studies in Culture, 1996).

Bregman, Rutger, "The Real *Lord of the Flies*: What Happened When Six Boys Were Shipwrecked for 15 Months," *The Guardian*, May 9, 2020, https://www. theguardian.com/books/2020/may/09/the-real-lord-of-the-flies-what-happened-when-six-boys-were-shipwrecked-for-15-months.

Brennan, Jason, *Against Democracy* (Princeton: Princeton University Press, 2017).

Brewer, Marilynn, "The Many Faces of Social Identity: Implications for Political Psychology," *Political Psychology* 22, no. 1 (2001): 115–125.

British Broadcasting Corporation, "WWI Christmas Truce Letter Found in Staffordshire," *BBC News*, December 4, 2014, https://www.bbc.com/news/uk-england-stoke-staffordshire-30296660.

Brooks, David, "America is Having a Moral Convulsion," *The Atlantic*, October 5, 2020.

Brownstein, Ronald, "The Money Machine," *Los Angeles Times*, November 15, 1987.

Bryan, Frank, William Keith, James Kloppenberg, Jane Mansbridge, Michael Morrell, and Graham Smith, "Collective Interview on the History of Town Meetings," *Journal of Public Deliberation* 15, no. 2 (2019).

Callanan, Valerie, "Media Consumption, Perceptions of Crime Risk and Fear of Crime: Examining Race/Ethnic Differences," *Sociological Perspectives* 55, no. 1 (2012): 93–115.

Campbell, Angus, Philip Converse, Warren Miller, and Donald Stokes, *The American Voter* (Chicago: University of Chicago Press, 1960).

Carion, Christian, *Joyeux Noel* (Sony Pictures Classics, 2005).

Carmines, Edward, Michael Ensley, and Michael Wagner, "Who Fits the Left-Right Divide? Partisan Polarization in the American Electorate," *American Behavioral Scientist* 56, no. 12 (2012): 1651–53.

Cavala, William, "Changing the Rules Changes the Game: Party Reform and the 1972 California Delegation to the Democratic National Convention," *American Political Science Review* 68, no. 1 (1974): 27–42.

Cohen, Marty, David Karol, Hans Noel, and John Zaller, *The Party Decides: Presidential Nominations Before and After Reform* (Chicago: University of Chicago Press, 2008).

Coleman, James, Thomas Hoffer, and Sally Kilgore, "Cognitive Outcomes in Public and Private Schools," *Sociology of Education* 55, no. 2 (1982): 65–76.

Coleman, James, "Social Capital in the Creation of Human Capital," *American Journal of Sociology* 94 (1988): 95–120.

Connors, Elizabeth, "The Social Dimension of Political Values," *Political Behavior* 42 (2020): 961–982.

Cook, Tony, Emily Hopkins, and Tim Evans, "Here Are Five Takeaways From IndyStar's 18-Month Nursing Home Investigation," *IndyStar*, December 31, 2020, https://www.indystar.com/story/news/investigations/2020/12/31/indiana-nursing-homes-takeaways-indystars-investigation/6545944002/.

Corn, David, and Tim Murphy, "A Very Long List of Dumb and Awful Things Newt Gingrich Has Said and Done," *Mother Jones*, November 15, 2016, https://

www.motherjones.com/politics/2016/11/very-long-list-dumb-and-awful-things-newt-gingrich-has-said-and-done/.

Cox, Daniel, Ryan Streeter, Samuel Abrams, and Jacqueline Clemence, "Socially Distant: How Our Divided Social Networks Explain Our Politics," *Survey Center on American Life*, 2020, https://www.aei.org/wp-content/uploads/2020/10/Socially-Distant.pdf.

Crews, Clyde Wayne, "What's the Difference between 'Major,' 'Significant,' and All Those Other Federal Rule Categories? A Case for Streamlining Regulatory Impact Classification," *Issue Analysis* 8, Competitive Enterprise Institute, 2017, https://www.cei.org/wp-content/uploads/2017/09/Wayne-Crews-What-is-the-Difference-Between-Major-and-Significant-Rules.pdf.

Croly, Herbert, *The Promise of American Life* (New York: Macmillan, 1909).

C-SPAN, "First Televised Session of the House of Representatives," March 19, 1979, https://www.c-span.org/video/?318387-1/televised-session-house-representatives.

C-SPAN, "First Panning of House Chamber," May 10, 1984, https://www.c-span.org/video/?93701-1/panning-house-chamber.

C-SPAN, "House Session, May 15, 1984," https://www.c-span.org/video/?171083-1/house-session#.

Dancey, Logan, "The Consequences of Political Cynicism: How Cynicism Shapes Citizens' Reactions to Political Scandals," *Political Behavior* 34, no. 3 (2012): 411–423.

Darr, Joshua, Matthew Hitt, and Johanna Dunaway, "Newspaper Closures Polarize Voting Behavior," *Journal of Communication* 68, no. 6 (2018): 1007–1028.

Dayen, David, "Investigating Oversight," *American Prospect*, May 27, 2021, https://prospect.org/politics/investigating-oversight-why-congressional-hearings-are-bad/.

Delie, Steve and Charlie LeDuff, "Did Michigan Cover Up Nursing Home COVID Deaths Like New York?" *USA Today*, March 19, 2021.

Desai, Sonal, "They Blinded Us from Science," *Franklin Templeton*, July 28, 2020, https://us.beyondbullsandbears.com/2020/07/28/on-my-mind-they-blinded-us-from-science/

Diamond, Larry, Lee Drutman, Tod Lindberg, Nathan Kalmoe, and Lilliana Mason, "Americans Increasingly Believe Violence is Justified if the Other Side Wins," *Politico*, October 1, 2020, https://www.politico.com/news/magazine/2020/10/01/political-violence-424157.

Diamond, Larry and David King, "Let's Have an Honest Debate on the Debates," *The Hill*, June 17, 2015, https://thehill.com/blogs/congress-blog/presidential-campaign/245135-lets-have-an-honest-debate-on-the-debates.

Dickson, James David, "There Should Be a Law? Be Careful What You Wish For," *Stories About Stories*, February 5, 2021, https://storiesaboutstories.com/f/there-should-be-a-law-be-careful-what-you-wish-for.

Dimock, Michael, "How Americans View Trust, Facts, and Democracy Today," Pew Research Center, February 19, 2020, https://www.pewtrusts.org/en/trust/archive/winter-2020/how-americans-view-trust-facts-and-democracy-today.

Dionne, E.J., *Why Americans Hate Politics* (New York: Simon & Schuster, 1991).

Divito, Nick, "Refuge Manager Exits Baptismal Stream Fight," Courthouse News Service, May 5, 2016, https://www.courthousenews.com/refuge-manager-exits-baptismal-stream-fight/.

Downs, Anthony, *An Economic Theory of Democracy* (New York: Harper, 1957).

Druckman, James, Erik Peterson, and Rune Slothuus, "How Elite Partisan Polarization Affects Public Opinion Formation," *American Political Science Review* 107, no. 1 (2013): 57–79.

Drutman, Lee, and Timothy LaPira, "Capacity for What? Legislative Capacity Regimes in Congress and the Possibilities for Reform," in *Congress Overwhelmed: The Decline in Congressional Capacity and Prospects for Reform*, Ed. Timothy LaPira, Lee Drutman, and Kevin Kosar (Chicago: University of Chicago Press, 2020).

Durlauf, Steven, "Bowling Alone: A Review Essay," *Journal of Economic Behavior & Organization* 47 (2001): 259–73.

Edsall, Thomas, "Let the Nanotargeting Begin," *New York Times*, April 15, 2012.

Eisenhower, Dwight, "The President's News Conference, January 27, 1954," *American Presidency Project*, https://www.presidency.ucsb.edu/documents/the-presidents-news-conference-469.

Ellis, Joseph, *American Sphinx* (New York: Alfred A. Knopf, 1996).

Ellmers, Glenn, "'Conservatism' is No Longer Enough," *The American Mind*, March 24, 2021, https://americanmind.org/salvo/why-the-claremont-institute-is-not-conservative-and-you-shouldnt-be-either/.

Farhi, Paul, "No Rush to Measure Limbaugh's Ratings," *Los Angeles Times*, March 9, 2009.

Feldman, Stanley, "Structure and Consistency in Public Opinion: The Role of Core Beliefs and Values," *American Journal of Political Science* 32, no. 2 (1988): 416–440.

Feldman, Stanley, and Christopher Johnston, "Understanding the Determinants of Political Ideology: Implications of Structural Complexity," *Political Psychology* 35, no. 3 (2014): 337–58.

Fiorina, Morris, "The Decline of Collective Responsibility in American Politics," *Daedalus* 109 (1980): 25–45.

Fiorina, Morris, *Retrospective Voting in American Elections* (New Haven: Yale University Press, 1981).

Fiorina, Morris, "Extreme Voices: A Dark Side of Civic Engagement," in *Civic Engagement in American Democracy*, Eds: Theda Skocpol and Morris Fiorina, (Washington, DC: Brookings Institution Press, and New York: Russell Sage Foundation, 1999).

Fiorina, Morris, Samuel Abrams, and Jeremy Pope, *Culture War? The Myth of a Polarized America* (London: Longman Publishing, 2011).

Fiorina, Morris, *Unstable Majorities* (Chicago: Hoover Institution Press, 2017).

Firearm Industry Trade Association, "First-Time Gun Buyers Grow to Nearly 5 Million in 2020," August 24, 2020, https://www.nssf.org/first-time-gun-buyers-grow-to-nearly-5-million-in-2020/.

Firestone, Shulamith, and Anne Koedt, *Notes from the Second Year: Women's Liberation: Major Writings of the Radical Feminists* (New York: Radical Feminism Press, 1970).

Foord, Archibald, *His Majesty's Opposition, 1714–1830* (Oxford: Oxford University Press, 1964).

Foucault, Michel, *Discipline and Punish*, (London: Pantheon Books, 1977).

French, David, *Divided We Fall: America's Secession Threat and How to Restore Our Nation* (New York: St. Martin's Press, 2020).

Friedersdorf, Conor, "Obama's Weak Defense of His Record on Drone Killings," *The Atlantic*, December 23, 2016.

Funk, Carolyn, "Process Performance: Public Reaction to Legislative Policy Debate," in *What is It About Government That Americans Dislike?* Eds: John Hibbing and Elizabeth Thiess-Morse (Cambridge: Cambridge University Press, 2001).

Gallup, "Crime," *In Depth: Topics A to Z*, 2021, https://news.gallup.com/poll/1603/crime.aspx.

Garfinkle, Norton, and Daniel Yankelovich, eds. *Uniting America: Restoring the Vital Center to American Democracy* (New Haven: Yale University Press, 2005).

Gaudiano, Nicole, "Alleged Gunman James Hodgkinson Volunteered on Bernie Sanders' Campaign," *USA Today*, June 14, 2017.

General Social Survey, National Opinion Research Center at the University of Chicago, https://gss.norc.org/.

Gelman, Andrew, "What Are the Chances Your Vote Matters?" *Slate*, November 7, 2016, https://slate.com/news-and-politics/2016/11/here-are-the-chances-your-vote-matters.html.

Gelman, Andrew, Aaron Edlin, and Noah Kaplan, "Voting as a Rational Choice: Why and How People Vote to Improve the Well-Being of Others," *Rationality and Society* 19, no. 3 (2007): 293–314.

Gibson, James, and Gregory Caldeira, "Knowing the Supreme Court? A Reconsideration of Public Ignorance of the High Court," *Journal of Politics* 71, no. 2 (2009): 429–41.

Gibson, James, "Problems with Open-Ended ANES Questions Measuring Factual Knowledge about Politics," *American National Election Studies*, 2018. https://electionstudies.org/wp-content/uploads/2018/03/Gibson_transcript.pdf.

Gilens, Martin, *Affluence and Influence: Economic Inequality and Political Power in America* (Princeton: Princeton University Press, 2012).

Girdusky, Ryan, "The Lincoln Project's Predator," *American Conservative*, January 11, 2021, https://www.theamericanconservative.com/articles/the-lincoln-projects-predator/.

Gold, Hadas, "Survey: 7 Percent of Reporters Identify as Republican," *Politico*, May 6, 2014, https://www.politico.com/blogs/media/2014/05/survey-7-percent-of-reporters-identify-as-republican-188053.

Goodwin, Doris Kearns, *Lyndon Johnson and the American Dream* (New York: Harper & Row, 1976).

GOPAC, "Language: A Key Mechanism of Control," 1990.

Grove, Lloyd, "Candidates Experiment with Instant Feedback," *Washington Post*, November 13, 1987.

Hageman, Harriet, "Bad Regulations Destroy Our Environment," New Civil Liberties Alliance, October 30, 2020, https://nclalegal.org/2020/10/bad-regulations-destroy-our-environment/.

Haidt, Jonathan, *The Righteous Mind: Why Good People Are Divided By Politics and Religion* (New York: Random House, 2012).

Hall, Peter Dobkin, "Civic Engagement in New Haven," in *Civic Engagement in American Democracy*, Eds: Theda Skocpol and Morris Fiorina, (Washington, DC: Brookings Institution Press, and New York: Russell Sage Foundation, 1999).

Hall, Abigail, and Alexander William Salter, "To 'Lower the Temperature' Raise Commitments to Federalism," *The Hill*, January 25, 2021, https://thehill.com/opinion/white-house/535454-to-lower-the-temperature-raise-commitments-to-federalism.

Hamburger, Philip, *Is Administrative Law Unlawful?* (Chicago: University of Chicago Press, 2014).

Hamburger, Philip, *The Administrative Threat* (New York: Encounter, 2017).

Hamilton, Alexander, John Jay, and James Madison, *The Federalist: A Collection of Essays*, 1788, Eds: George Carey and James McClellan (Indianapolis: Liberty Fund, 2001).

Hamilton, James, *All the News That's Fit to Sell: How the Market Transforms Information Into News* (Princeton: Princeton University Press, 2003).

Hammond, Bill, and Ian Kingsbury, "COVID-Positive Admissions Were Correlated with Higher Death Rates in New York Nursing Homes," Empire Center for Public Policy, February 18, 2021, https://www.empirecenter.org/publications/covid-positive-admissions-higher-death-rates/.

Hansen, Ron, *The Assassination of Jesse James by the Coward Robert Ford* (New York: Knopf, 1983).

Hanson, Victor Davis, *The Dying Citizen: How Progressive Elites, Tribalism, and Globalization Are Destroying the Idea of America* (New York, Encounter, 2021).

Harper's Magazine, Editorial Staff, "Accentuate the Negative," *Harper's Magazine*, November 1990.

Haque, Umair, "Everyone's Dying and No One Cares," *Eudaimonia & Co.*, April 22, 2020, https://eand.co/everyones-dying-and-no-one-cares-d05d97f2b43f.

Hassell, Hans, John Holbein, and Matthew Miles, "There is No Liberal Media Bias in Which News Stories Political Journalists Choose to Cover," *Science Advances* 6, no. 14 (2020), https://advances.sciencemag.org/content/6/14/eaay9344.

Hawkins, Stephen, Daniel Yudkin, Miriam Juan-Torres, and Tim Dixon, *Hidden Tribes: A Study of America's Polarized Landscape* (New York: More in Common, 2018).

Hetherington, Marc, and Thomas Rudolph, *Why Washington Won't Work: Polarization, Political Trust, and the Governing Crisis* (Chicago: University of Chicago Press, 2015).

Himmelstein, David, Robert Lawless, Deborah Thorne, Pamela Foohey, and Steffie Woolhandler, "Medical Bankruptcy: Still Common Despite the Affordable Care Act," *American Journal of Public Health* 104, no. 3 (2019): 431–33.

Hirsch, E.D., *The Making of Americans: Democracy and Our Schools* (New Haven: Yale University Press, 2010).

Hoberg, George, "Science, Politics, and U.S. Forest Service Law: The Battle over the Forest Service Planning Rule," *Natural Resources Journal* 44, no. 1 (2004).

Hofstadter, Richard, "The Paranoid Style in American Politics," *Harper's Magazine*, November, 1964.

Hopkins, Daniel, *The Increasingly United States: How and Why American Political Behavior Nationalized* (Chicago: University of Chicago Press, 2018).

Hudson, John, "How Nancy Pelosi Saved the NSA Surveillance Program," *Foreign Policy*, July 25, 2013, https://foreignpolicy.com/2013/07/25/how-nancy-pelosi-saved-the-nsa-surveillance-program/.

Hunter, James Davison, *Culture Wars: The Struggle to Define America* (New York: Basic Books, 1991).

Hunter, James Davison, and Alan Wolfe, *Is There a Culture War? A Dialogue on Values and American Public Life* (Washington, DC: Brookings Institution Press, 2006).

Husock, Howard, "The Coming Invasion by the Federal Government," *Washington Examiner*, May 13, 2021, https://www.washingtonexaminer.com/politics/the-coming-invasion-by-the-federal-government.

International Communications Research, "Survey of Air Pollution Perceptions: Final Report," Prepared for the Foundation for Clean Air Progress, June 1999.

Johnson, Norman, "Norman Johnson Oral History Interview," *Northwest Forest Plan Oral History Collection*, Oregon State University Libraries, November 29, 2016, http://scarc.library.oregonstate.edu/omeka/items/show/34826.

Jones, Edward, and Richard Nisbett, *The Actor and the Observer: Divergent Perceptions of the Causes of Behavior* (New York: General Learning Press, 1971).

Jones, Jeffrey, and Lydia Saad, "U.S. Support for More Government Inches Up, but Not for Socialism," *Gallup*, November 18, 2019, https://news.gallup.com/poll/268295/support-government-inches-not-socialism.aspx.

Kahan, Dan, David Hoffman, Donald Braman, Danieli Evans, and Jeffrey Rachlinski, "'They Saw a Protest': Cognitive Illiberalism and the Speech-Conduct Distinction," *Stanford Law Review* 64, no. 4 (2012).

Kalmoe, Nathan, and Lilliana Mason, "Lethal Mass Partisanship: Prevalence, Correlates, and Electoral Contingencies," (National Capital Area Political Science Association, American Politics Meeting, 2019).

Kamen, Al, "For Gore, it's All in the Translation," *Washington Post*, January 10, 1994.

Kassel, Matthew, "Election Boom: Here's How Much Ad Money CNN, Fox News and MSNBC Are Expected to Make in 2020," *Mediate*, January 8, 2020, https://www.mediaite.com/tv/election-boom-heres-how-much-ad-money-cnn-fox-news-and-msnbc-are-expected-to-make-in-2020/.

Kauffman, Bill, *America First! Its History, Culture, and Politics* (Amherst: Prometheus Books, 2016).

Keith, Tamara, "Wielding a Pen and a Phone, Obama Goes it Alone," National Public Radio, *Morning Edition*, January 20, 2014, https://www.npr.org/2014/01/20/263766043/wielding-a-pen-and-a-phone-obama-goes-it-alone.

Kelman, Herbert, "Human Use of Subjects: The Problem of Deception in Social Psychological Experiments," *Psychological Bulletin* 67 (1967): 1–11.

Kendall, Willmoore, "Basic Issues Between Conservatives and Liberals," in *Contra Mundum*, Ed: Nellie Kendall, (New Rochelle: Arlington House, 1971).

Kendall, Willmoore, "The True Sage of Woodstock," in *Contra Mundum*, Ed: Nellie Kendall, (New Rochelle: Arlington House, 1971).

Kinder, Donald, and Nathan Kalmoe, *Neither Liberal Nor Conservative* (Chicago: University of Chicago Press, 2017).

King, Angus, "The Great Abdication" – King Condemns Congress Surrendering Power of the Purse, Ignoring Constitutional Responsibilities," news release, January 16, 2020, https://www.king.senate.gov/newsroom/press-releases/the-great-abdication_king-condemns-congress-surrendering-power-of-the-purse-ignoring-constitutional-responsibilities.

Kirkpatrick, Evron, "'Toward a More Responsible Two-Party System': Political Science, Policy Science, or Pseudo-Science?" *American Political Science Review* 65, no. 4 (1971): 965–990.

Klein, Ezra, *Why We're Polarized* (New York: Simon & Schuster, 2020).

Klein, Ezra, *Vox Conversations* Podcast, September 22, 2020.

Klein, Joe, "The Town That Ate Itself," *New Yorker*, November 23, 1998.

Klein, Joe, *The Natural: The Misunderstood Presidency of Bill Clinton* (New York: Penguin Random House, 2002).

Klonick, Kate, "The New Governors: The People, Rules, and Processes Governing Online Speech," *Harvard Law Review* 131 (2018): 1598–1670.

Korecki, Natasha, "Biden Has Fought a Pandemic Before. It Did Not Go Smoothly," *Politico*, May 4, 2020, https://www.politico.com/news/2020/05/04/joe-biden-contain-h1n1-virus-232992.

Kosar, Kevin, "New Lawmakers' Rude Awakening to the Realities of Congress," *RealClearPolitics*, February 19, 2021, https://www.realclearpolitics.com/articles/2021/02/19/new_lawmakers_rude_awakening_to_the_realities_of_congress_145270.html.

Kristof, Nicholas, "They Overcame Mutual Loathing, and Saved a Town," *New York Times*, April 10, 2021.

Ladd, Everett Carll, "The Data Just Don't Show Erosion of America's 'Social Capital,'" *Public Perspective* 7, no. 4 (1996): 5–22.

LaFrance, Adrienne, "Facebook is a Doomsday Machine," *The Atlantic*, December 15, 2020.

Landsburg, Steven, *The Armchair Economist: Economics and Everyday Life* (New York: Free Press, 1993).

LaPira, Timothy, Lee Drutman, and Kevin Kosar, eds., *Congress Overwhelmed: The Decline in Congressional Capacity and Prospects for Reform* (Chicago: University of Chicago Press, 2020).

LaTour, Amée, "Fact Check: Do 97 Percent of Journalist Donations Go to Democrats?" *Ballotpedia*, August 16, 2017, https://ballotpedia.org/Fact_check/Do_97_percent_of_journalist_donations_go_to_Democrats.

Lawler, Peter Augustine, and Richard Reinsch, *A Constitution in Full: Recovering the Unwritten Foundation of American Liberty* (Lawrence: University of Kansas Press, 2019).

Lawrence, John, "How the 'Watergate Babies' Broke American Politics," *Politico*, May 26, 2018, https://www.politico.com/magazine/story/2018/05/26/congress-broke-american-politics-218544/.

Layman, Geoffrey, and Thomas Carsey, "Party Polarization and 'Conflict Extension' in the American Electorate," *American Journal of Political Science* 46, no. 4 (2002): 786–802.

Lee, Frances, *Insecure Majorities: Congress and the Perpetual Campaign* (Chicago: University of Chicago Press, 2016).

Leetaru, Kalev, "Culturenomics 2.0: Forecasting large-scale human behavior using global news media tone in time and space," *First Monday* 16, no. 9 (2011), https://firstmonday.org/ojs/index.php/fm/article/view/3663.

Leetaru, Kalev, "Sentiment Mining 500 Years of History: Is the World Really Darkening?" *Forbes*, May 14, 2019.

Lehrer, Eli, "1972 Campaign Reveals How Much Modern Democrats Have Changed," *The Hill*, February 5, 2019.

Levendusky, Matthew, "Why Do Partisan Media Polarize Voters?" *American Journal of Political Science* 57, no. 3 (2013): 611–623.

Levin, Yuval, "Congress's Day," *National Review*, February 14, 2021, https://www.nationalreview.com/corner/congresss-day/.

Lewis-Beck, Michael, William Jacoby, Helmut Norporth, and Herbert Weisberg, *The American Voter Revisited* (Ann Arbor: University of Michigan Press, 2008).

Lipset, Seymour Martin, and William Schneider, "The Decline of Confidence in American Institutions," *Political Science Quarterly* 98, no. 3 (1983): 379–402.

MacLeod, Adam, *The Age of Selfies: Reasoning About Rights When the Stakes Are Personal* (Lanham: Rowman & Littlefield, 2020).

Madden, Richard, "Congress Report Asks TV Coverage," *New York Times*, October 20, 1974.

Malle, Bertram, *How the Mind Explains Behavior: Folk Explanations, Meaning, and Social Interaction* (Cambridge: M.I.T. Press, 2004).

Malle, Bertram, J.M. Knobe, and S.E. Nelson, "Actor-Observer Asymmetries in Explanations of Behavior: New Answers to an Old Question," *Journal of Personality and Social Psychology* 93, no. 4 (2007): 491–514.

Mann, Robert, "How the 'Daisy' Ad Changed Everything About Political Advertising," *Smithsonian Magazine*, April 13, 2016.

Mansbridge, Jane, *Beyond Adversary Democracy* (Chicago: University of Chicago Press, 1980).

Mansky, Jackie, "How Watching Congressional Hearings Became an American Pastime," *Smithsonian Magazine*, June 8, 2017, https://www.smithsonianmag.com/history/how-watching-congressional-hearings-became-american-pastime-180963614/.

Masket, Seth, *No Middle Ground: How Informal Party Organizations Control Nominations and Polarize Legislatures* (Ann Arbor: University of Michigan Press, 2014).

Mason, Lilliana, *Uncivil Agreement: How Politics Became Our Identity* (Chicago: University of Chicago Press, 2018).

Maté, Aaron, "The Rise and Fall of the 'Steele Dossier,'" *The Nation*, January 11, 2021, https://www.thenation.com/article/politics/trump-russiagate-steele-dossier/.

Matthews, Donald, *U.S. Senators and Their World* (Chapel Hill: University of North Carolina Press, 1960).

McArdle, Mairead, "FBI Investigating Allegations Against Lincoln Project Co-Founder John Weaver: Report," *National Review*, February 12, 2021, https://www.nationalreview.com/news/fbi-investigating-allegations-against-lincoln-project-co-founder-john-weaver-report/.

McConchie, Dan, "Limit Governors' Emergency Powers," *Wall Street Journal*, April 30, 2020.

McKay, Steven, *Diggstown* (Metro-Goldwyn-Mayer, 1992).

McKinley, Jesse, and Luis Ferré-Sadurní, "N.Y. Severely Undercounted Virus Deaths in Nursing Homes, Report Says," *New York Times*, January 28, 2021.

Meyer, Frank, "Where is Eisenhower Going?" *American Mercury* 78 (1954): 123–126.

Michael, A.C., "Saxons and Anglo-Saxons Fraternising on the Field of Battle at the Season of Peace and Goodwill," *Illustrated London News*, January 9, 1915.

Mitchell, Charles, "Wolf's Secretive Ways on Business Waivers a Flagrant Dismissal of Transparency," *Pennsylvania Press & Journal*, April 16, 2020, https://www.pressandjournal.com/stories/gov-wolfs-secretive-ways-on-business-closures-and-waivers-a-flagrant-dismissal-of-transparency,90274.

Montanaro, Domenico, "Hillary Clinton's 'Basket of Deplorables,' in Full Context of this Ugly Campaign," National Public Radio, September 10, 2016.

Murray, John Courtney, *We Hold These Truths* (New York: Sheed and Ward, 1960).

Napoli, Philip, "Newspapers Still the Best Bet for Local News," Interview with Sanford School of Public Policy, Duke University, September 12, 2019.

National Conference of State Legislatures, "State Legislative Policymaking in an Age of Political Polarization," February 2018, https://www.ncsl.org/Portals/1/Documents/About_State_Legislatures/Partisanship_030818.pdf.

Neal, Toby, "Seasons Over the Decades, 1914," *Shropshire Star*, December 26, 2014.

Nelson, Maxford, "Getting Organized at Home," Washington Freedom Foundation, July, 2018, https://www.freedomfoundation.com/wp-content/uploads/2018/07/Getting-Organized-at-Home.pdf.

Nelson, Robert, "Fire in the National Forest System: California Solutions for a California Problem," *Mercatus on Policy* 16 (2008): 1–4, https://www.mercatus.org/system/files/Fire_in_the_National_System_-_California_Solutions_for_a_California_Problem.pdf.

Nichols, Mike, *Federal Grant$tanding: How Federal Grants are Depriving Us of Our Money, Liberty and Trust in Government—and What We Can Do about It* (Milwaukee: Badger Institute, 2016).

Noah, Timothy, "'Acid, Amnesty, and Abortion:' The Unlikely Source of a Legendary Smear," *New Republic*, October 22, 2012.

Oldenburg, Ray, *The Great Good Place: Cafés, Coffee Shops, Bookstores, Bars, Hair Salons and Other Hangouts at the Heart of a Community* (New York: Marlowe & Company, 1989).

Orwell, George, *Nineteen Eighty-Four: A Novel*, 1948, (New York: Knopf, 1987).

O'Sullivan, Julie Rose, "The Federal Criminal 'Code': Return of Overfederalization," Essay adapted from remarks delivered at Federalist Society Annual Student Symposium, March 2, 2013, https://www.harvard-jlpp.com/wp-content/uploads/sites/21/2014/01/37_1_57_OSullivan.pdf.

Osterholm, Michael, Nicholas Kelley, Alfred Sommer, and Edward Belongia, "Efficacy and Effectiveness of Influenza Vaccines: A Systematic Review and Meta-Analysis," *Lancet* 12, no. 1 (2012): 36–44.

Otterson, Joe, "CNN Gun Control Town Hall Draws 2.9 Million Viewers," *Variety*, February 22, 2018.

Page, Clarence, "Talk Like a Newt with the Gingrich Diatribe Dictionary," *Chicago Tribune*, September 19, 1990.

Parker-Pope, Tara, "Bill Maher vs. the Flu Vaccine," *Well Blog, New York Times*, October 13, 2009, https://well.blogs.nytimes.com/2009/10/13/bill-maher-vs-the-flu-vaccine/.

Parmet, Wendy, "Pandemics, Populism and the Role of Law in the H1N1 Vaccine Campaign," *Saint Louis University Journal of Health Law & Policy* 4 (2010): 113–53.

Peoples, Steve, and Brian Slodysko, "How a Leading Anti-Trump Group Ignored a Crisis in its Ranks," *Associated Press News*, February 11, 2021, https://apnews.com/article/john-weaver-lincoln-project-crisis-b14be5f06588b8f1d78125d4141394cb.

Perry, Gina, *The Lost Boys: Inside Muzafer Sherif's Robbers Cave Experiment* (Melbourne: Scribe Publications, 2018).

Pew Research Center, "Pew Values Update: American Social Beliefs 1997-1987,"

April 20, 1998, https://www.pewresearch.org/politics/1998/04/20/pew-values-update-american-social-beliefs-1997-1987/.

Pew Research Center, "On the Eve of '92: Fault Lines in the Electorate," December 4, 1991, https://www.pewresearch.org/politics/1991/12/04/on-the-eve-of-92-fault-lines-in-the-electorate/.

Pew Research Center, "Partisan Shifts in Views of the Nation, But Overall Opinions Remain Negative," August 4, 2017, https://www.pewresearch.org/politics/2017/08/04/partisan-shifts-in-views-of-the-nation-but-overall-opinions-remain-negative/.

Pew Research Center, "The Partisan Divide on Political Values Grows Even Wider," October 5, 2017, https://www.pewresearch.org/politics/2017/10/05/the-partisan-divide-on-political-values-grows-even-wider/.

Pew Research Center, "Partisan Antipathy: More Intense, More Personal," October 10, 2019, https://www.pewresearch.org/politics/2019/10/10/partisan-antipathy-more-intense-more-personal/.

Pew Research Center, "Trends in Income and Wealth Inequality," January 9, 2020, https://www.pewresearch.org/social-trends/2020/01/09/trends-in-income-and-wealth-inequality/.

Pew Research Center, "Americans Who Mainly Get Their News on Social Media Are Less Engaged, Less Knowledgeable," July 30, 2020, https://www.journalism.org/2020/07/30/americans-who-mainly-get-their-news-on-social-media-are-less-engaged-less-knowledgeable/.

Pew Research Center, "Many Americans Get News on YouTube, Where News Organizations and Independent Producers Thrive Side by Side," September 28, 2020, https://www.journalism.org/2020/09/28/many-americans-get-news-on-youtube-where-news-organizations-and-independent-producers-thrive-side-by-side/.

Pew Research Center, "Partisans in the U.S. Increasingly Divided on Whether Offensive Content Online is Taken Seriously Enough," October 8, 2020, https://www.pewresearch.org/fact-tank/2020/10/08/partisans-in-the-u-s-increasingly-divided-on-whether-offensive-content-online-is-taken-seriously-enough/.

Porter, Rick, "TV Long View: How Much Network TV Depends on Cop Shows," *Hollywood Reporter*, June 20, 2020, https://www.hollywoodreporter.com/tv/tv-news/heres-how-network-tv-depends-cop-shows-1299504/.

Program for Public Consultation, "A Not So Divided America: Is the Public as Polarized as Congress, or Are Red and Blue Districts Pretty Much the Same?" Center on Policy Attitudes and School of Public Policy at the University of Maryland, July 2, 2014, https://publicconsultation.org/wp-content/uploads/reports/Red_Blue_Report_Jul2014.pdf.

Putnam, Robert, *Making Democracy Work: Civic Traditions in Modern Italy* (Princeton: Princeton University Press, 1993).

Putnam, Robert, *Bowling Alone: The Collapse and Revival of American Community* (New York: Simon & Schuster, 2000).

Putnam, Robert, "The Prosperous Community: Social Capital and Public Life,"

American Prospect, December 19, 2001, https://prospect.org/infrastructure/prosperous-community-social-capital-public-life/.

Putnam, Robert, and Shaylyn Garrett, *The Upswing: How America Came Together a Century Ago and How We Can Do it Again* (New York: Simon & Schuster, 2020).

Ranalli, Brent, James D'Angelo, and David King, "The 1970s Sunshine Reforms and the Transformation of Congressional Lobbying," Congressional Research Institute, December 2018.

Ranney, Austin, and Willmoore Kendall, *Democracy and the American Party System* (San Diego: Harcourt Brace, 1956).

Republican Party, "Republican Party Platform of 1952," *American Presidency Project,* July 7, 1952, https://www.presidency.ucsb.edu/documents/republican-party-platform-1952.

Republican Party, "Republican Party Platform of 1956," *American Presidency Project,* July 7, 1956, https://www.presidency.ucsb.edu/documents/republican-party-platform-1956.

Roos, Robert, "CDC Sharply Raises H1N1 Case Estimates; Kids Hit Hard," Center for Infectious Disease Research and Policy, December 10, 2009, https://www.cidrap.umn.edu/news-perspective/2009/12/cdc-sharply-raises-h1n1-case-estimates-kids-hit-hard.

Rosenfeld, Sam, *The Polarizers: Postwar Architects of Our Partisan Era* (Chicago: University of Chicago Press, 2018).

Rosier, Sara, "Changes in Net Worth of U.S. Senators and Representatives," *Ballotpedia,* July 24, 2014, https://ballotpedia.org/Changes_in_Net_Worth_of_U.S._Senators_and_Representatives_(Personal_Gain_Index).

Rossiter, Clinton, *Parties and Politics in America* (Ithaca: Cornell University Press, 1960).

Rothfus, Keith, "How to Fix the House of Representatives," *National Affairs* 48 (2021), https://nationalaffairs.com/publications/detail/how-to-fix-the-house-of-representatives.

Ruckelshaus, Jay, "A Way to Tamp Down the Toxic Politics of National Identity," *Governing,* March 10, 2021, https://www.governing.com/now/a-way-to-tamp-down-the-toxic-politics-of-national-identity.html.

Rush, Taylor, "Heated Debate Over Swine Flu Vaccine Efforts Divides Some on Capitol Hill," *The Hill,* October 18, 2009, https://thehill.com/homenews/senate/63605-swine-flu-vaccine-debate-divides-some-on-capitol-hill.

Saad, Lydia, "What Percentage of Americans Own Guns?" *Gallup,* August 14, 2019, https://news.gallup.com/poll/264932/percentage-americans-own-guns.aspx.

Sasse, Ben, "Opening Statement: Brett Kavanaugh SCOTUS Hearing," September 4, 2018, https://www.youtube.com/watch?v=BwMgJzs5Q9A.

Schoenbrod, David, *Power Without Responsibility: How Congress Abuses the People Through Delegation* (New Haven: Yale University Press, 1993).

Schoenbrod, David, *DC Confidential: Inside the Five Tricks of Washington* (New York: Encounter, 2017).

Shafer, Byron, "Anti-Party Politics," *Public Interest*, Spring (1981): 95-111.

Shafer, Byron, *Quiet Revolution: The Struggle for the Democratic Party and the Shaping of Post-Reform Politics* (New York: Russell Sage Foundation, 1983).

Shafer, Byron, and Regina Wagner, *The Long War over Party Structure: Democratic Representation and Policy Responsiveness in American Politics* (New York: Cambridge University Press, 2019).

Shafer, Byron, and Regina Wagner, "The Trump Presidency and the Structure of Modern American Politics," *Perspectives on Politics* 17 (2019): 340–357.

Shah, Adam, Jocelyn Fong, and Zachary Pleat, "Beck, Limbaugh Fomenting Fear About H1N1 Vaccine," *Media Matters for America*, October 7, 2009, https://www.mediamatters.org/rush-limbaugh/beck-limbaugh-fomenting-fear-about-h1n1-vaccine.

Shakespeare, William, *A Midsummer Night's Dream*, 1600, Ed: Wolfgang Clemen, (New York: New American Library, 1998).

Sherif, Muzafer, O.J. Harvey, B. Jack White, William Hood, and Carolyn Sherif, *Intergroup Conflict and Cooperation: The Robbers Cave Experiment* (Norman: University Book Exchange, 1954).

Sheingate, Adam, "The Political Consultant Racket," *New York Times*, December 30, 2015.

Sheingate, Adam, *Building a Business of Politics: The Rise of Political Consulting and the Transformation of American Democracy* (New York: Oxford University Press, 2016).

Silver, Nate, "There Really Was a Liberal Media Bubble," *FiveThirtyEight*, March 10, 2017, https://fivethirtyeight.com/features/there-really-was-a-liberal-media-bubble/.

Skocpol, Theda, "How Americans Became Civic," in *Civic Engagement in American Democracy*, Eds: Theda Skocpol and Morris Fiorina (Washington, DC: Brookings Institution Press, and New York: Russell Sage Foundation, 1999).

Skocpol, Theda, and Morris Fiorina, eds. *Civic Engagement in American Democracy* (Washington, DC: Brookings Institution Press, and New York: Russell Sage Foundation, 1999).

Smarick, Andy, "Amy Coney Barrett and the Virtue of Self-Government," *The Dispatch*, October 26, 2020, https://thedispatch.com/p/amy-coney-barrett-and-the-virtue.

Smith, Adam, "Where is Our Freedom to Exercise Sympathy?" *Front Porch Republic*, October 30, 2020, https://www.frontporchrepublic.com/2020/10/where-is-our-freedom-to-exercise-sympathy/.

Stauffer, Anne, Justin Theal, and Brakeyshia Samms, "Federal Funds Hover at a Third of State Revenue," Pew Charitable Trusts, October 8, 2019, https://www.pewtrusts.org/en/research-and-analysis/articles/2019/10/08/federal-funds-hover-at-a-third-of-state-revenue.

Stevens, Thaddeus, "Speech of Hon. T. Stevens, of Pennsylvania, On the Bill (H.R. No. 20) Relative to the Damages to Loyal Men, and for Other Purposes," March 19, 1867, https://teachingamericanhistory.org/library/document/damages-to-loyal-men/.

Stolle, Dietlind, and Marc Hooghe, "Inaccurate, Exceptional, One-Sided, or Irrelevant? The Debate About the Alleged Decline of Social Capital and Civic Engagement in Western Societies," *British Journal of Political Science* 35, no. 1 (2005): 149–67.

Strazzella, James, *The Federalization of Criminal Law*, American Bar Association Task Force on the Federalization of Criminal Law, 1998, https://www.americanbar.org/content/dam/aba/directories/policy/1999_am_113a.authcheckdam.pdf.

Stroud, Natalie, *Niche News: The Politics of News Choice* (New York: Oxford University Press, 2011).

Sundquist, James, *The Dynamics of the Party System: Alignment and Realignment of Political Parties in the United States* (Washington, DC: Brookings Institution Press, 1973).

Sunstein, Cass, *Going to Extremes: How Like Minds Unite and Divide* (New York: Oxford University Press, 2009).

Swedish, Kristen, Gina Conenello, and Stephanie Factor, "First Season of 2009 H1N1 Influenza," *Mount Sinai Journal of Medicine* 77 (2010): 103–113.

Swift, Art, "Six in 10 in U.S. See Partisan Bias in News Media," *Gallup: Politics*, April 5, 2017, https://news.gallup.com/poll/207794/six-partisan-bias-news-media.aspx.

Tech Environmental, Inc., "Progress in Reducing National Air Pollutant Emissions, 1970–2015." Report prepared for the Foundation for Clean Air Progress, June 1999.

Thomas, Shawna, "Obama: I Won't 'Wait for Congress' on Economic Fixes" *NBC News*, January 15, 2014, https://www.nbcnews.com/news/world/obama-i-wont-wait-congress-economic-fixes-flna2D11930011.

Tocqueville, Alexis de, *Democracy in America*, 1835–40, Ed: J.P. Mayer (New York: Anchor Books, 1969).

Tolkien, J.R.R., *The Fellowship of the Ring* (London: Allen & Unwin, 1954).

Tversky, Amos, and Daniel Kahneman, "Availability: A Heuristic for Judging Frequency and Probability," *Cognitive Psychology* 5 (1973): 207–232.

Twain, Mark, *A Connecticut Yankee in King Arthur's Court*, 1889. (New York: Washington Square Press, 1971).

Twain, Mark, *The Complete Works of Mark Twain: Mark Twain's Notebook* (New York: Harper, 1935).

US Centers for Disease Control and Prevention, *H1N1 Vaccine Safety*, January 4, 2010, https://www.cdc.gov/h1n1flu/vaccination/vaccine_safety.htm.

US Department of Justice, "Federal Law Enforcement Officers, 2016," https://www.bjs.gov/content/pub/pdf/fleo16st.pdf.

US Environmental Protection Agency, *National Air Pollutant Emission Trends, 1900–1994*. October 1995, https://nepis.epa.gov/Exe/ZyPURL.cgi?Dockey=2000EAPE.txt.

US Federal Bureau of Investigation, "Hate Crime Statistics, 1996," https://ucr.fbi.gov/hate-crime/1996/hatecrime96.pdf.

US Federal Bureau of Investigation, "Crime in the United States, 2019," https://ucr. fbi.gov/crime-in-the-u.s/2019/crime-in-the-u.s.-2019.

US Federal Bureau of Investigation, "Hate Crime Statistics, 2019," https://ucr.fbi. gov/hate-crime/2019.

US Federal Bureau of Investigation, "NICS Firearm Checks: Month/Year," https:// www.fbi.gov/file-repository/nics_firearm_checks_-_month_year.pdf/view.

US Fish and Wildlife Service, National Wildlife Refuge System Mission and Goals, https://www.USFW.gov/refuges/policiesandbudget/HR1420_missionGoals. html.

US Forest Service, "National Forest System Land and Resources Management Planning," 36 CFR Part 219, *Federal Register* 44 (181) September 17, 1979.

US Forest Service, "Special Areas; Roadless Area Conservation," 36 CFR Part 294, *Federal Register* 66 (9) January 12, 2001.

US General Accounting Office, "Forest Service Roadless Areas: Potential Impact of Proposed Regulations on Ecological Sustainability," November 2000.

Valentino, Nicholas, Ted Brader, Eric Groenendyk, Krysha Gregorowicz, and Vincent Hutchings, "Election Night's Alright for Fighting: The Role of Emotions in Political Participation," *Journal of Politics* 73, no. 1 (2011): 156–70.

Vallier, Kevin, "Why Are Americans So Distrustful of Each Other?" *Wall Street Journal*, December 17, 2020.

Vesoulis, Abby, "'He's Saying One Thing and Then He's Doing Another,' Rep. Madison Cawthorn Peddles a Different Kind of Trumpism in a Post-Trump World," *Time*, January 21, 2021, https://time.com/5931815/madison-cawthorn-post-trump/.

Vinciguerra, Thomas, "The Truce of Christmas, 1914," *New York Times*, December 25, 2005.

Wakefield, Dan, "William F. Buckley, Jr.: Portrait of a Complainer," *Esquire*, January 1961.

Wallach, Philip, "How Congress Fell Behind the Executive Branch," in *Congress Overwhelmed: The Decline in Congressional Capacity and Prospects for Reform*, Eds: Timothy LaPira, Lee Drutman, and Kevin Kosar (Chicago: University of Chicago Press, 2020).

Watson, Bradley, *Progressivism: The Strange History of a Radical Idea* (Notre Dame: University of Notre Dame Press, 2020).

Wax-Thibodeaux, Emily, "After Arkansas Passes its Trans Ban, Parents and Teens Wonder: Should We Stay?" *Washington Post*, April 24, 2021.

Weintraub, Stanley, *Silent Night: The Story of the World War I Christmas Truce* (New York: Simon & Schuster, 2001).

White, Adam, "A Republic, If We Can Keep It," *The Atlantic*, February 4, 2020, https://www.theatlantic.com/ideas/archive/2020/02/a-republic-if-we-can-keep-it/605887/.

Wolak, Jennifer, *Compromise in an Age of Party Polarization* (New York: Oxford University Press, 2020).

Wolfe, Alan, *One Nation, After All: What Middle-Class Americans Really Think About* (New York: Penguin Books, 1998).

Wolfensberger, Donald, *Congress and the People: Deliberative Democracy on Trial* (Washington, DC: Woodrow Wilson Center Press with Johns Hopkins University Press, 2001).

Wuthnow, Robert, *Loose Connections: Joining Together in America's Fragmented Communities* (Cambridge: Harvard University Press, 1998).

Wuthnow, Robert, "Mobilizing Civic Engagement: The Changing Impact of Religious Involvement," in *Civic Engagement in American Democracy*, Eds: Theda Skocpol and Morris Fiorina (Washington, DC: Brookings Institution Press, and New York: Russell Sage Foundation, 1999).

Xu, Yanqi, "Explaining the Numbers Behind the Rise in Reported Hate Crimes," *PolitiFact*, April 3, 2019, https://www.politifact.com/article/2019/apr/03/hate-crimes-are-increasingly-reported-us/.

Yankelovich, Daniel, *New Rules: Searching for Self-Fulfillment in a World Turned Upside Down* (New York: Random House, 1981).

Zaller, John, *The Nature and Origins of Mass Opinion* (Cambridge: Cambridge University Press, 1992).

Zaller, John, "What *Nature and Origins* Leaves Out," *Critical Review* 24, no. 4 (2012): 569–642.

Zywicki, Todd, and Ilya Somin, "Federalism and Separation of Powers: Ramifications of Repealing the 17th Amendment," *Engage, The Journal of the Federalist Society Practice Groups* 12, no. 2 (2012): 88–93.

INDEX